W9-BGZ-354

SMOKE, MIRRORS, AND MURDER

SMOKE, MIRRORS, AND MURDER

AND OTHER TRUE CASES
ANN RULE'S CRIME FILES: VOL. 12

ANN RULE

LARGE PRINT PRESS
An imprint of Thomson Gale, a part of The Thomson Corporation

THOMSON

GALE

Detroit • New York • San Francisco • New Haven, Conn. • Waterville, Maine • London

THOMSON
™
GALE

LIBRARY OF CONGRESS CATALOGING-IN-PUBLICATION DATA

Rule, Ann.
   Smoke, mirrors, and murder / by Ann Rule.
     p. cm. — (Ann Rule's crime files ; bk. 12) (Wheeler Publishing large print hardcover)
    ISBN-13: 978-1-59722-661-5 (hardcover : alk. paper)
    ISBN-10: 1-59722-661-0 (hardcover : alk. paper)
    ISBN-13: 978-1-59413-263-6 (softcover : alk. paper)
    ISBN-10: 1-59413-263-1 (softcover : alk. paper)
    1. Murder — United States — Case studies. I. Title.
  HV6529.R846 2008
  364.152′30973—dc22

                                    2007041563

Published in 2007 by arrangement with Pocket Books,
a division of Simon & Schuster, Inc.

Printed in the United States of America on permanent paper
10 9 8 7 6 5 4 3 2 1

I am dedicating this book to two people who took a chance on me — a virtually unknown writer — many years ago: Joan and Joe Foley of the Foley Agency, New York City. Some authors change literary agents as often as they buy new cars, but I am sticking with the Foleys! They have long since become friends who are as close to me as family. I appreciate their pep talks, support, constructive criticism, experience, knowledge, and the fact that they always have my back. We have shared both ebullient good times and tragedies over the years, as all good friends do.

Thanks, Foleys!

ACKNOWLEDGMENTS

There are many cases in this book, all of them carefully investigated and researched, and all but two successfully prosecuted. I count on the survivors, witnesses, patrolmen, detectives, medical examiners, prosecutors, and judges as my resources as I seek the truth about what really happened. And I was, indeed, lucky to have found such cooperation from those who brought truth and justice out of mystery and tragedy in the cases featured in *Smoke, Mirrors, and Murder.*

I wish to thank Sue Jensen, Jenny Jensen, and Scott Jensen; Detectives Cloyd Steiger and Sharon Stevens, Seattle Police Department; Cheryl Snow and Marilyn Brenneman, Senior Deputy King County Prosecuting Attorneys; Val Epperson and Superior Court Judge Richard Jones.

To Captain Herb Swindler and Assistant Chief Noreen Skagen, Seattle Police Department, and Ila Birkland, the most efficient secretary the Homicide Unit, Seattle Police Department, ever had.

To Inspectors Bill Hoppe, Jim Reed, and Jack Hickam of the Seattle Fire Department.

To Detectives Jim Byrnes and Jan Cummings, Marion County, Oregon, Sheriff's Department; and Robert Hamilton, Oregon State Attorney General's Office.

To Detectives Sgt. Ivan Beeson and Sgt. Don Cameron, and Detectives Dick Reed, Dick Sanford, Billy Baughman, George Marberg, Joyce Johnson, and Al Gerdes, Seattle Police Department.

To my first — and only — research assistant, Tennessee Division: Beverly Morrison, in Henderson. And to McNairy County, Tennessee, Circuit Court Clerk Ronnie Brooks and Clerk Jackie Cox, Russell Ingle of the *Independent-Appeal,* Selmer, Tennessee; Tonya Smith-King of the *Jackson Sun,* Jackson, Tennessee, and Malley J. Byrd, Memphis, Tennessee.

As always, many, many thanks to my editorial team at Pocket Books: to my publisher, Louise Burke, whose enthusiasm is contagious; to my editor, Mitchell Ivers, whose voice on the phone or name on my e-mail is almost always cause for a smile. He still gives me more compliments and back pats than complaints; to his editorial assistant, Erika Burns, who put this book together — photo section and all — in perfect order on a tight deadline. And to the rest of the team, who worked efficiently and promptly, using more effort than readers — and sometimes authors — ever realize. I do appreciate you. Thanks also to Carly Sommerstein, Sally Franklin, and Lisa Litwack. And a special thank-you to Chuck Antony, the copy editor who sent back such a sweet-smelling manuscript. Thank you all!

CONTENTS

FOREWORD

Murder is a crime shot through with deception, subterfuge, wicked preparation, and cruel intent. By its very definition it involves trickery and lies; killers almost always seek to hide behind real or imaginary smoke screens, attempting to convince others of their innocence. They are, in a sense, "magicians of malice," intent on covering up the truth. Some are far more clever than others and their intricate plots often come frighteningly close to allowing them to walk away with few or no consequences. And there are always some who *do* escape punishment. Unfortunately, there *is* such a thing as the perfect murder.

The cases that follow cover the gamut of every genus of murderer; some were brilliant, while others were cloddish. One case may not have been a homicide but only a tragic circumstance that was virtually unexplainable. No one knows for sure. There is even a homicide case that may have had as its "watershed point" an Internet con game.

Each case is especially memorable to me, whether it happened as recently as 2007 or took me back to the seventies and eighties, when I first began writing for the fact-detective magazines. In those days, I was known as "Andy Stack" — because the editors of *True Detective* said their readers would not believe a woman knew anything about police investigations. It took me years, but I proved them wrong.

In this, my twelfth book in the *Crime Files* series, I include seven engrossing cases, winnowed out from the hundreds I have researched over the years: "The Deputy's Wife" (the book-length feature), "The Antiques Dealer's Wife," "The Truck Driver's Wife," "The Convict's Wife," "The Chemist's Wife," "The Painter's Wife," and, finally, "The Minister's Wife." Murder interrupted all their marriages.

Each of these bizarre stories had hidden aspects that surprised me when I first encountered them, even though I sometimes think that nothing can catch me unaware after so many years of writing true-crime cases.

But something always does. These cases did, and I hope they will keep you in suspense too. Whether in fiction or in real life, mystery intrigues us all. Every story I include in this collection explores the relationship between men and women, which in these cases proved to be an incendiary mix. In some, the male is the dangerous persona, in some the female — and there are a few in which you, the reader, will have to decide which one was the guilty party. The cases all involved deception, large and small lies that led inevitably to disaster.

Ann Rule

■ ■ ■ ■

THE
DEPUTY'S WIFE

■ ■ ■ ■

When I type the last page of a book, I am always struck by the same thought: how terribly *stupid* the convicted felon was! This killer had so much to be thankful for, and yet this macabre murder plot is so full of evil that it makes me shiver. The gleeful killer-to-be was "tickled pink" at a scenario designed to make multiple homicides look like an accident. The greedy plotter threw a good life away to end up with nothing — less than nothing.

This case is about a tragedy on its way to happening, and the cast of characters is as diverse and extraordinary as any I have come across. It is a recent case, its strange events playing out in the last few years.

Tragically, this case is reminiscent of the hundreds of e-mails and letters I receive from desperate husbands and wives — mostly wives. I always wish I could do more to help, but perhaps shedding light on one family's disintegration may encourage readers to face their own domestic problems and deal with them before it is too late.

I don't think anyone who looks at life through barred windows ever really expected to be behind them. And yet a prisoner's world becomes, for a time — or for life — one of spartan cells, walls with billows of razor wire atop them, bland food heavy on carbohydrates, and the same daily routine with orders issued by corrections officers. Worst of all, prisoners lose their freedom to come and go as they please. Even though I have been only a visitor in jails and prisons, I dread the sound of a steel door clanging shut behind me — along with the smell of Pine-Sol, cigarettes (although they are now forbidden in most prisons), urine, sweat — and the contagious sense of hopelessness.

A most unlikely prisoner is the antihero in this story, and I have no doubt at all that this individual's ending up in that role was shocking to everyone involved. This person started life with numerous disadvantages, but eventually found love, family, children, respect, and what seemed to be the good life.

And then this murderous plotter threw it all away.

More than ever before, tabloids and the

Internet are rife with divorce and custodial battles as America moves into the twenty-first century. Celebrities like Britney Spears and Kevin Federline, Kim Basinger and Alec Baldwin, and a dozen other famous couples seem more intent on *winning* than concerned about their children's security, thus mirroring the divorce wars of everyday people. Once marital vows shatter, couples on every level of society begin to struggle over who will get the children, who will get the money, the house, the vehicles.

Perhaps the events in this case would have happened even without divorce and property division struggles, but with the enmity that surfaced in what was anything but a simple divorce, an icy hatred began to grow, making the end of a marriage a horror story.

Could one half of a once-loving partnership be insatiable enough when it came to wealth that the lives of those who got in the way meant less than zero?

I think so.

Looking back with the clarity of hindsight, it is easy to spot signs of danger. They were as brief as a jagged sword of lightning stabbing down to a dark beach or a flicker of fire before a woods is engulfed in flames. But the signs were there, just as they are for many trusting partners. A flash of insight, buried quickly in denial.

We think we know someone as well as we know ourselves.

But we don't.

ONE
HAPPY EVER AFTER?

Sue Harris and her sister, Carol,* who was seven years older, grew up in an upper-middle-class home in Lake Hills, the most popular subdivision in Bellevue, an eastern suburb of Seattle, in the 1950s. Bellevue was like Levittown or a thousand other towns that sprang up after World War II, fulfilling the demand for new homes for young families. Initially it seemed a long way from Seattle, but it really wasn't, and when the first floating bridge across Lake Washington was built, Bellevue seemed only a hop, skip, and a jump away for the dads who continued to work every day. The moms mostly stayed home, waxed their floors once a week, and cooked meals from scratch, and if they had a career, it was probably selling Avon or Mary Kay products part-time.

*Some names have been changed. The first time they appear, they are marked with an asterisk.

In many ways the 1950s were an easier time, or maybe it just seemed that way. Couples got married intending to stay together, and the divorce epidemic that lay ahead was only a distant threat.

Along with most of the other fathers in the neighborhood, Sue and Carol's father, Hermann, was an engineer for the Boeing Airplane Company. Sue was born in December 1955, and despite the difference in their ages, she and her sister were uncommonly close as children, and that would continue as they grew to adulthood. If they expected life to be happy ever after, so did other little girls in Bellevue. It was the era of Barbie and Ken and playing dolls while mothers lingered over coffee in somebody's kitchen.

In Lake Hills, the fifties were a halcyon time. In the early sixties, though, couples with young children came close to panic when the Cuban missile crisis loomed. World War II had been fought far away, across oceans, but the Cuban crisis threatened to bring war to America itself. With that menace and the simultaneous anxiety it provoked, a small army of salesmen swarmed over Bellevue offering bomb shelters on the installment plan.

A model home in Lake Hills offered the latest upgrade in housing: a bomb shelter in the basement. And Rod Serling's *Twilight Zone* featured a memorable episode about neighbors fighting one another to crowd into such a shelter. It was the end of a time when everyone felt safe. Most home owners opted to move forward without shelters, realizing that their consciences wouldn't allow them to survive happily when most of their neighbors had perished.

And then John F. Kennedy was assassinated on November 22, 1963, and America changed forever.

Hermann Harris had clipped articles on bomb shelters, but his daughters weren't aware of that until after he died — much too young, at fifty-two — of a sudden heart attack. Their mother, Lorraine, was only forty-two when she was left to raise her two daughters: Sue was ten and Carol was eighteen. Fortunately, Hermann Harris had been wise in his investments and he left his family well provided for, and there were veteran's benefits from his service in World War II that would pay for his two girls to go to college.

Sue and Carol had seen a happy marriage, and although they missed their father a lot, their mother stepped up to take the reins of responsibility. She was a loving and brave woman and her girls adored her.

When Sue was in the third grade, her parents had bought a house in Newport Hills, a new community where houses and streets blossomed up the hill above the 405 Freeway. It was more expensive than Lake Hills and there was more chance there for individuality and architect-designed homes. Home values in Newport Hills grew exponentially over the decades ahead. They shot up even faster than the giant sequoia sapling that Hermann had planted in the Harrises' front yard when they first moved in.

Just below Newport Hills, adventurous contractors came up with a plan to build another, even more posh community by filling in the shoreline on the eastern edge of Lake Washington. It was called Newport Shores, and Sue's dad had scoffed at the idea, saying, "Who would ever want to live down in that swamp?" For once, he'd been wrong. Although the houses on the hills grew steadily in value, those on the shore tripled and re-tripled continually in listing prices over the next four decades.

Sue watched her mother evolve from a stay-at-home housewife to a competent head of her household, and Sue admired her more all the time. Lorraine Harris vowed that her daughters would go to college. Carol chose the University of Washington in Seattle, but

Sue picked Washington State University in Pullman, Washington, on the eastern side of the state. There, more than three hundred miles away from the Seattle area, the hills of the Palouse roll on endlessly, the soil and weather perfect for fields of golden, undulating wheat. The summers were blazing hot, while the winters brought frigid temperatures and deep snowdrifts. It was another world, and Sue Harris loved it.

Sue was a smart and pretty young woman who majored in business administration. Although she expected to marry one day and raise a family, she was looking forward to having a career first and she wasn't in any hurry to settle down. She had a great deal of confidence then and didn't plan to settle down until she was in her mid-twenties at least.

But that was before she met Bill Jensen. Sandy-haired Bill was six feet four inches tall, with an athlete's muscular build, not an inch of fat on him. Sue was a sophomore when she went to a meeting of the scuba diving club on campus. That's where she met Bill.

She was awed by the way Bill Jensen took over a room. "He was a great talker," she recalled, "and he seemed well informed on so many subjects. He wasn't somebody you could ignore. He really impressed me. He weighed less than two hundred pounds then, and he was in good shape."

Sue was almost twenty, and she assumed Bill was older than she was. She was surprised to learn that he was actually eighteen months younger. She found him quite handsome and she hoped to see him again. It seemed to be fate when she ran into him again when one of her girlfriend's dates had a party in his dorm.

When Sue arrived, she discovered that Bill also lived in that dorm and he was at the party. She was happy when he asked to walk her back to her dorm after the party, and delighted when he asked for her phone number.

"It would have been at the end of October 1975 when we met," Sue said. "I remember because my friends and I went to Spokane the next day — Saturday — and when I got back to my room, there was a note from Bill on my door reminding me to set my clock back because daylight saving time was ending. He added his phone number and said there was a chilled bottle of wine waiting, and asked me to call him when I got home."

Bill Jensen launched into a whirlwind courtship, and Sue still thinks of that fall at Washington State University as being a very happy time. Bill struck her as very mature and extremely confident, someone she could depend on. The first time he called her at her home in Newport Hills, her mother handed her the phone, saying, "It's for you. It sounds like one of your professors."

But it was Bill, and his voice *did* have that air of authority. He seemed such a solid and dependable guy, and Sue respected his determination to finish college even though he didn't have much money. Like Sue, he worked in the dorm dining room to help pay expenses. He also worked for Safeway in their beverage plant as a warehouseman, and later as a store detective. Bill managed to earn good grades — particularly in any course required for a degree in criminal justice, his major. In those classes, he got As and Bs.

He wrote two outstanding term papers in 1977 and 1978: "Jail Security" and the more ambitious "Socio-Psychological Profile of Becoming a Corrupt Police Officer."

When Sue brought him home to Newport Hills for Thanksgiving, her family welcomed him. And by her birthday, December 8, Bill had asked her to marry him.

To her own surprise, she found herself saying yes.

Bill Jensen's background was very different

from Sue's. Born in May 1957, he'd grown up in the area around Bremerton, Washington, and the huge naval station there. There was precious little stability in his early years. From the time he was little, he was bounced from one home to another, moving through a series of relatives' homes and sometimes even foster homes.

Bill's father was fifty-seven when he was born, and he had fathered several daughters by different women. He wasn't around much when Bill was small because he was in the navy and out to sea a lot. He was a mythic, heroic figure to Bill, who bragged that his father's ship had been under siege at Pearl Harbor.

Bill's mother was much younger, but she was an alcoholic, and her parenting skills were sketchy at best. When Bill was five his father died, and his mother wasn't in any shape to take care of him. State social workers stepped in to decide where he should go. He went first to his maternal grandparents, but then was placed in a foster home from the age of seven to eleven.

After that, he lived in California with his mother and stepfather for just two months after his eighteen-year-old sister spirited him away from a foster home and drove him to his mother's house.

"Bill had three full sisters and one half sister," Sue said. "His sisters were a lot older than he was and married young, so they were on their own."

Bill didn't meet his half sister, Wanda,* until he was thirty-three. Before that, he didn't even know what her last name was. Because his sisters were much older than he, he lived with his oldest sister, Iris,* when he was in junior high school. He suspected that he was taken in as a live-in babysitter rather than because his sister cared about him.

Being poor was a constant worry for Bill; most of the foster parents he lived with subsisted on a bare-minimum standard of living. He would remember one foster home where meals often consisted of catsup sandwiches.

Although he seldom talked about it to Sue, Bill occasionally mentioned that he had suffered both physical and emotional abuse when he was a child, and it's likely that is true. As soon as he was old enough, Bill went to work. He washed dishes and bused tables at local restaurants to earn a little spending money.

Bill's name wasn't Jensen then; he used his father's surname: Pate. Still, he never really felt that he belonged to his birth family. By the time he was sixteen, he was living with distant relatives. His third cousin was the mayor of Poulsbo, where most of the citizens were Scandinavian.

Bill became very active in the Lutheran church in Poulsbo, where he was a camp counselor and Lutheran youth president.

While the mayor's home was meticulously clean and there was plenty to eat, Bill wasn't happy because the rules were very strict. Once more, he was convinced that he had been accepted out of duty, and not because the mayor and his wife had any particular affection for him. And he chafed at the rules that seemed to have no reasons behind them other than to mete out discipline.

After he'd lived with the mayor and his wife for a year, Bill formed a powerful bond with a complete stranger: he was shooting at targets on a rifle range when he met a man of about fifty, who told Bill that he had just retired from the navy as a lieutenant commander. The two had a long conversation, and the retired navy man was quite taken with Bill.

Despite his rough childhood — or perhaps because of it — Bill had developed a charismatic façade, and he made an excellent, very likable first impression. His intelligence impressed his new friend. Bill joked as he complained about his suffocating home life, but the older man, whose name was Chuck

Jensen, felt kind of sorry for him. Jensen's background was something of a mystery, but he apparently had no family he was close to. He was on his own when Bill met him. Bill and Chuck Jensen became friends.

After they had known each other for a few weeks, Jensen realized how miserable Bill was in the regimented home of the mayor, and he offered the teenager a home — no strings attached. Bill accepted quickly.

Chuck Jensen set about teaching Bill manners, bought him some nice clothes, and acted as his surrogate father. Like young Bill, Chuck was something of a loner. He lived in a mobile home surrounded by acres of land. Jensen encouraged Bill in his lifelong ambition to be a cop.

One day, Bill would tell Sue Harris that he couldn't even remember when he hadn't been drawn to police work. At sixteen, he planned to go to college to get his degree in criminal justice, join a police department, and eventually become a special agent in the FBI.

Bill had to budget carefully to pay for college; Washington State University was known for its superior criminal justice curriculum and, indeed, was the *only* college that offered a four-year program at the time he graduated from high school. He had some veteran's benefits from his father's wartime service in the navy. Chuck Jensen also helped him, and he obtained some student loans. Besides his part-time jobs in Pullman, he worked summers for the Mason County Sheriff's Office on the Olympic Peninsula in an intern program offered there. He wasn't old enough to be a deputy, but he worked as a dispatcher in the mostly rural county.

Although Bill wanted to get married soon after he and Sue became engaged, she didn't want to give up the veteran's benefits that paid for her tuition, which she would lose if she married. She pointed out the wisdom in that to Bill. They both needed their fathers' legacies to finish college.

Reluctantly, Bill agreed that her argument made sense. There were times when they considered getting married before they finished school, but they always concluded they should wait; they were secure in the fact that they loved each other, and neither was jealous or insecure about the stability of their relationship.

Sue graduated before Bill did — in the summer of 1978, while Bill still had one more semester. She didn't want to move back to Seattle without him, so she continued on at Washington State and earned a second degree — this time in psychology.

Although she loved Bill, Sue was surprised when she realized that Bill Jensen was not the popular, outgoing guy she first thought he was. He was actually a loner. Despite the way she had viewed him at their first meeting at the scuba club, he really didn't have close friends. When they got together with a group, the others tended to be *her* friends, not his. She understood why he might not trust people enough to get close to them. After his pillar-to-post childhood, when he never really felt that he belonged anywhere, she reasoned, why shouldn't he take a wait-and-see attitude about people?

Sue saw that Bill could not keep a room-mate, that they moved in and out rapidly, but she didn't think much of it. There was very little about him that concerned her; when they were alone, they got along fine, and she didn't find his tendency to dominate conversations a deterrent to their relationship. He might be kind of bossy and even arrogant sometimes, but to her, he was interesting, and he knew so much about many things. She certainly didn't see him then as boorish and oblivious to other people's reactions.

Sue felt sorry for Bill when his mother humiliated him in front of other students in his dorm. "She would get drunk and call him from California, where she was living then,"

Sue recalled. "It bothered him so much he got ulcers from the stress. I remember once how angry he was when his mother couldn't get him on the phone and she called the resident adviser in his dorm. He was so embarrassed to think of how she must have sounded, knowing that she only called when she had been drinking."

Bill Jensen was struggling to make a better life for himself, one in which he could leave his birth family behind. He felt no particular allegiance to his mother; he had no reason to. She hadn't fought to keep him when he was five and the state's social workers moved in and took him away to a foster home. And she hadn't been very nice to him when Bill lived with her and a stepfather in California when he was in junior high. Beyond his adopted father, Chuck, Bill had never had any stable roots that would make him feel grounded in the world. Sue understood that, and tried to reassure him that he was a special person, successful and smart, and that he had a great future ahead of him. She loved him and vowed to be the kind of wife who would help him find a happy life.

The only disturbing experience Sue had with Bill in college was at his nineteenth birthday party. They had gone out with some friends, and both of them had a little too much to drink. Although she couldn't even remember what they argued about, it was serious enough for him to put his hands on her in anger, and she was left with black and purple marks where he'd grabbed her arms.

The fracas at Bill's birthday celebration had escalated to a point where somebody called the police, and they quickly broke up the party.

Sue would remember a long time later that the grad student who was the resident adviser in her dorm had looked closely at her bruised arms and warned her to be careful, saying, "This may be your first time — but it won't be the last time he hurts you."

Sue listened to her adviser, but it didn't sink in and she didn't believe it. She loved Bill, and she was anxious to make up with him. "I heard what he was saying — but I knew he couldn't be talking about Bill. He didn't know him the way I did."

Bill was a young man in a hurry, and he earned his bachelor's degree at Washington State University in three and a half years. When he did, he and Sue moved home to Bellevue.

They set their wedding date for May 5, 1979, right before Bill's twenty-third birthday. Even though Bill was now an adult,

Chuck Jensen had legally adopted him in February. From then on, Bill's legal name was Bill Jensen.

Sue knew that his relationship with his family was nothing like her own, and her mother and sister did, too, so they made sure he felt welcome in their family. If only being accepted into a warm and loving clan when one is an adult could make up for emotional abuse and deprivation in childhood, Bill Jensen might well have been a happy and successful man.

Still, it's almost impossible to build self-esteem atop a shaky foundation. Bill Jensen's life during the vital years between one and six, when a child is forming his own view of the world, was one of abuse and abandonment. As gruff and dominating as he appeared, he wasn't a man who felt confident inside.

He hid it well. He often told Sue, "I'm a survivor." Whenever they had problems, he added, "*We'll* get through this."

In the beginning, Sue found his "survivor" declarations endearing. And she always thought he said, "We'll get through this," although there were times when she wondered if he'd actually meant, "*I'll* get through this."

Bill had already survived a lot, and there

were events that kept reminding him of the turmoil he had come from. His mother died in the summer of 1977, and Sue remembered a bizarre experience when she accompanied Bill to the funeral in California. She was about to meet his family for the first time.

During the wake, the mourners imbibed heavily, and most were intoxicated as the day ended. Bill had rented a car and he and Sue offered to give two of his sisters a ride after the wake. Almost from the moment his sisters got into the backseat of his car, they began to fight about which of them had loved their mother more. Their verbal abuse quickly escalated to a physical fight.

"I couldn't believe it," Sue said. "They were actually scratching each other and pulling hair. I looked at Bill and the veins in his neck were just bulging because he was so angry. These were grown women who were almost a decade older than he was."

And then Bill Jensen suddenly whipped his car into a gas station, opened the back doors, and tossed his screaming sisters out. He left them there. How they would get home was anyone's guess, but he didn't care, and Sue couldn't really blame him for feeling that way.

Sue wasn't all that surprised when Bill told her he didn't want her inviting his sisters to their wedding, although she asked him if he was sure he wanted to leave them out.

"They'll just ruin it," he explained. "You saw how they behaved at my mother's funeral."

Indeed she had, and she didn't want their wedding to end up in a free-for-all. Bill's oldest sister was almost as tall as he was, an inch or so over six feet in her stocking feet, and there were some people around Bremerton who nicknamed her "Wild Iris" for her short fuse.

In the end, Bill convinced Sue not to send wedding invitations to any of his birth family.

Sue and Bill's wedding in the Mercer Island Covenant Church was a lovely event, albeit without the presence of his relatives — except for Chuck Jensen, and Sue thought of him as her new father-in-law. Bill had two friends he'd made in high school, and he asked one of them to be his best man. The rest of the wedding party was made up of Sue's family and friends.

Their marriage started out well. Sue and Bill had a great honeymoon. Bill and Chuck converted an old but sturdy Chevy van into a self-contained camper, and the newlyweds traveled around the United States in it for six weeks. Gas was relatively cheap then, and they cooked on the road and slept in the van. They had both worked hard in college, and their honeymoon was a relaxing and bonding time for them.

"Bill applied at some police departments before we left," Sue said. "He had an outstanding résumé, and while we were on the road, he got a message that his interview at the King County Sheriff's Office had gone so well that they were going to hire him."

But the King County personnel office told Bill he could finish his honeymoon — he didn't have to come right back to Seattle: he could join the fall class of basic police school in September of 1979.

He was due to graduate in December, and they would start the new decade with Bill's ambition to be a cop realized.

They found an apartment in Lake Hills where the rent was cheap; at least it seemed that way in the summertime. Bill and Sue moved in, but when the weather turned cold they discovered that the heating bill made the low rent seem something less than a bargain.

Still, the young couple were both earning good salaries — Bill as a deputy with the sheriff's office and Sue in a rather unusual job for a woman. During the summers while she was in college, she worked for Sears in the automotive department as a "tire buster." She got thirty-five cents more per hour than regular clerks. She didn't mind putting on new tires or installing batteries, and she made as much money as any of the male employees.

In her early twenties, Sue Harris Jensen was a confident young woman, happy in her marriage, and solidly behind her husband's goals.

As the Jensens settled in, she took a job with Automotive Wholesalers as a sales representative. She knew what she was talking about as she sold their products to auto parts, hardware, variety, and grocery stores.

"I always liked cars," she said, "and as a commission-only sales rep it wasn't long before I was making more money than Bill was."

Bill didn't seem to mind. He had grown up without money, and he didn't care who made the higher salary; he was glad that Sue was pitching in to build their bank account. In most things, Sue was amenable to doing things Bill's way, although she wasn't a subservient wife. She knew Bill admired her ability to talk to perfect strangers, and to find common interests with them.

Bill and Sue Jensen agreed that they wanted to have children one day, but they decided to wait four or five years. They were young, and they were both happy in their jobs. Bill had reached the first steps of his ambitions as a police officer, and Sue liked her job, too. She ended up working for Automotive Wholesalers for six years. With Sue focusing most of her attention on her husband, their relationship worked. They got along well during the first five years of their marriage.

Sue didn't become pregnant until mid-1984. She was delighted, although their good news was somewhat bittersweet. Lorraine Harris had been diagnosed with terminal breast cancer, and her family all knew that she probably wouldn't be around to enjoy her grandchild for long. Still, Sue's mother was upbeat and optimistic about Sue's pregnancy, and both Sue and Carol tried to spend as much time with their mother as they could.

Bill too seemed pleased that they were going to have a baby. But they began to have serious arguments. In one awful fight, Bill kicked Sue in the abdomen, and she was terrified that he had hurt the baby. She didn't report that to the police; it would have endangered his job. In time, she managed to push the memory of that violence to the back of her mind, making up excuses for him.

When Jennifer was born in March 1985,

Bill was very proud of his beautiful blond baby daughter. Sue had worked selling auto parts right up until Jenny was born, and she was happy to retire to be a stay-at-home mom.

In the fall of 1985, Lorraine Harris's doctors told her daughters that she probably didn't have much longer to live, and Sue spent every moment she could with her mother, watching Lorraine with baby Jenny. She was grateful for every day her mother had to enjoy her granddaughter, as brief as their time together was.

Working as a deputy sheriff can be a very stressful occupation, and there were times when Bill seemed tense and anxious. When he struck out at Sue, he blamed it on his job. Even so, Sue was shocked when, as her mother was dying, Bill announced that he needed a vacation. He wanted her to go to Hawaii with him. He appeared to have no perception at all that his mother-in-law was dying, and that she should come first. Instead, he was irritated that Sue thought his need for a vacation wasn't the most important problem they had. Rather than stand by her and her sister as Lorraine slipped away, Bill went to Hawaii with a high school friend instead.

Lorraine Harris passed away on November 18, 1985.

Sue remembered this insensitivity of Bill's, but they were both so happy with their new baby that, once more, she put it out of her mind. She tried to see things from her husband's point of view and thought that he must have been under more stress than she had known. But admittedly, she was less patient with his moods and his pouting now that she had an infant to care for.

Lorraine Harris's will left her assets to her two daughters, and because she had managed her money wisely, both Sue and Carol inherited a surprisingly large sum: hundreds of thousands of dollars. Lorraine left the house to her girls, and Bill, Sue, and Jenny moved into the house in Newport Hills where Sue had grown up. They put the proceeds from the sale of their house into an interest-bearing account — a joint account. Uncharacteristically, Sue deposited the money from her inheritance into a separate bank account, one in her name only. She did, however, write checks to deposit into their joint account whenever Bill asked her to do so.

Sue deferred to Bill in handling money, and he paid the bills and kept their books. She didn't check on how or where he spent their money. She didn't see any need to.

Bill handled their investments, and he took some dicey gambles in buying technology and computer stocks. Through a combination of luck and clever buying, the Jensens' fortunes rose. Bill bought Microsoft and Intel in the days when those stocks soared, making millionaires overnight. He didn't make that much money, but his buying on the margin appeared to be heading them in that direction.

Because Bill's job kept him on duty for long hours, and sometimes he slept during the day, Sue did all the yard work and painted their house inside and out; as the years went by she would be the Girl Scout leader, room mother, and volunteer for the myriad parent participation projects that needed workers at Jenny's elementary school.

Bill took a real interest in Jenny's involvement in sports. He was pleased when she turned out to be a natural athlete, and he coached her basketball and baseball teams. He took great pleasure in his role as a coach, and Jenny was proud that her friends liked her father so much.

There were some parents at the ball games who found Bill Jensen too critical, too loud, and too competitive for someone who coached youngsters. They thought he took a lot of the fun out of games that were meant for small children.

"Bill Jensen would yell and belittle other coaches and umpires," the mother of one of the girls he coached said. "He would use his size and intimidate anyone who disagreed with him — to the point that it would embarrass and humiliate the children and the parents."

Bill's size was a factor in the way he was sometimes perceived as an arrogant, almost bullying, man. Sue had liked the way he towered over her when she first met him, but by the seventh year of their marriage, it was no longer much of an attribute. Now he used his height and weight to bully her. He weighed over 250 pounds, and the scale continued to climb. He was given to temper tantrums, and although she usually tried to calm him down, Sue sometimes got mad, too. Shortly after her mother died, Bill had deliberately thrown a cherished figurine that Lorraine had given to Sue and it shattered into a dozen pieces.

"I was so angry," Sue confessed, "that I flung a picture frame at him. I called the King County Police. We lived in the same district where Bill had once worked, and the deputies who came out were the guys Bill had worked with."

Sue was the one who got a citation. Their

fights were more frequent, but Sue still hesitated to call the department where Bill worked. Making a domestic violence complaint against a deputy sheriff would jeopardize his career, and being a cop was all Bill Jensen had ever wanted to do. She didn't want to harm Bill's dream job, and so Sue backed off. If she hadn't been so angry that he'd deliberately broken something precious that her mother had given her, she would never have called the police on him that one time.

Unlike most police officers, who have a sense of camaraderie with their fellow cops, Bill Jensen had few friends in the King County Sheriff's Office, and no close buddies at all. He was frequently moved from one unit to another. He had a reputation as a braggart and certainly not as a team player. Winning was his foremost goal in whatever activity he participated in. In law enforcement, it is essential for officers to use teamwork in many situations, but that was one aspect of his job where Bill Jensen failed. That was probably why he was transferred often.

He sometimes patrolled on a motorcycle, and he really enjoyed that. He and Sue both had motorcycles.

Jenny was three and a half years old when

the Jensens' son, Scott, was born seven weeks prematurely on September 9, 1988. Scott was very frail and doctors warned Sue and Bill that he might develop cerebral palsy or other problems. At first he seemed to be delicate because of his premature birth, but neonatal specialists tested him for other possible causes. When he was allowed to come home, Scott had to have a heart monitor and both Sue and Bill worried terribly about him, checking on him often to be sure he was still breathing. Scott was ultimately diagnosed with Noonan's syndrome, a disorder that had only been isolated in 1963. It can compromise a number of body systems.

No one was certain that Scott's heart would be affected, and both his parents did their best to give their fragile baby boy the best care possible.

Sue suffered the post-baby blues more than she had with Jenny, but that was to be expected; she was so concerned about Scott. Bill tried to tease her out of what was undoubtedly postpartum depression by threatening to call "people in little white uniforms" to come and take her away. He warned her, teasing her sadistically, that she wouldn't be able to see her kids.

Scott did have some cardiac problems and a few other, relatively minor side effects of

Noonan's. He was in and out of Children's Orthopedic Hospital in Seattle, and he developed pneumonia. Sue rarely slept, and she recognized the wisdom of signing herself into Overlake Hospital for a week for help with her depression.

"I just felt as though I couldn't deal with another loss," Sue remembered, "so soon after losing my mother."

For months, it was touch and go whether Scott would survive, but he was a fighter and he made it. He was an adorable little boy, and both his parents devoted themselves to him. Bill couldn't have been a better father for him. If there were things Scott couldn't do, Bill was determined to find activities he *could* do.

He helped Scott with his manual dexterity with special toys, rode him around on his back, and took both his children to ride the merry-go-round at a shopping mall in Bellevue. Both Jenny and Scott adored their father, and from an early age did their best to please him. As he grew, Scott idolized his father — this tall, husky man in the police uniform.

This was especially true when Scott watched Bill on his motorcycle, and he and Scott shared a love of the big bikes. As soon as Scott could ride, Bill got him a small motorbike, and he was thrilled. Bill loved his small son and showed him more tenderness than he demonstrated even with his daughter or his wife. Jenny was feisty like her mother, and that sometimes irritated Bill, although he was very proud of her, too, and always enjoyed her company.

As Jenny grew, she was the very epitome of a beautiful, blond girl. And Bill Jensen bragged about his perfect daughter.

Bill Jensen's two children might have been the best thing that ever happened to him. They admired him, loved him without question, and clung to all the good memories they had of their early years with their father. In their eyes, he could do no wrong.

Still, for all positive images the Jensens' marriage exhibited, there were darker events, things that Sue tried to hide. Usually she was able to do that, fearing that if she told anyone outside the walls of their home it would be breaking her commitment to Bill.

But on December 9, 1988, Sue called her sister, Carol, and she was crying. Embarrassed to tell anyone else, Sue confessed to Carol that Bill had pulled hard on her shoulder and twisted her arm behind her back. She had bruises on both hands where he had held on to her, and she had bald spots where he had yanked out some of her hair. Carol insisted on taking Sue to her doctor.

While Sue was being treated, a King County Police car pulled up outside the Jensens' Newport Hills home. Bill had reported Sue as the instigator of their fight, and insisted that she had to be committed to be treated as a mentally ill patient. When Carol explained what had actually happened, the deputies pulled back and drove away.

The next day, Sue discovered that Bill had withdrawn $25,000 from their house-sale account. He hadn't mentioned it to her, and she was troubled that he had taken so much money out without their agreeing to it.

"But Bill always took care of the bills, and our investments," Sue recalled. "If I asked about any financial move he'd made or wondered about our accounts, he told me if I didn't like the way he was handling things, I could take over if I wanted to — and I always backed down. I knew he was better at it than I could be. That time in December 1988, Scott was only two months old, he was still on the heart monitor, and Bill and I were both nervous. And I wanted so much to have a happy family. I thought we could work it out."

As the nineties approached, Bill was part of a close family. Besides Sue, Jenny, and

Scott, he was always welcome at Carol's home. They all got together at Thanksgiving and Christmas. His wife loved him, his children adored him, and his sister-in-law and her fiancé were happy to see him coming.

Sue's main ambition in life was to be the best mother she could be, and she loved being home with Jenny and Scott. She continued to volunteer for any activity they were in where a mother was needed — from room mother to Scouts.

Bill got Jenny started with basketball in kindergarten and coached her teams all the way to sixth grade. They began baseball when Jenny was in the second grade. Bill was the coach for both sports, and she was proud to have her dad out there coaching. Jenny would remember their winning record, and that her girlfriends really liked her father. "He was a great coach, and it was fun!"

Sometimes, though, the Jensens' marriage was less fun.

In 1986, Sue and Bill had gone to counseling, a requirement after the domestic violence report when Bill had smashed the figurine. That early report said that it was "likely" that Sue was suffering from Battered Woman's syndrome, but Bill's stance in the few sessions he attended was that it was Sue who needed "fixing." Their psychologist felt that she and Bill did need marriage counseling, but it was hollow advice because both of them needed to participate fully if they hoped to save an increasingly combative marriage. But no amount of coaxing from Sue could get Bill to open up in front of a marriage counselor.

Sue and Bill continued to argue, but they always made up. Inevitably, Sue blamed herself, wishing that she hadn't said the wrong thing and annoyed him, or that she hadn't been so quick to argue with him. She was anything but a mousy wife; she was an active combatant. Still, there were a lot of good times between the difficult spaces. The Jensens took family vacations, camped out, and they all enjoyed the kids' sports.

Yet the incidents of physical abuse continued. Each time, after he'd hurt her, Bill told Sue it was her fault. She had made him angry enough to use force on her. Her perception of the world began to change; she looked at happy marriages around her and wondered what she was doing wrong. She began to blame herself for all the problems she and Bill faced.

Being married to a cop is never easy for a wife. There is always the fear that when they leave to go out on a shift, they may not come back. Some officers share what happens on the job with their wives, but most tend to keep it to themselves, trying hard to separate their home life from those things they see out on the streets.

Knowing that their husbands are often the objects of flirtation from other women who are attracted to the uniform, a lot of wives are either jealous or filled with anxiety. Socially, cops are treated differently by "civilians," who approach them at parties to try to get tickets fixed or complain about some injustice they feel they've suffered at the hands of the police. That's the reason cops tend to stick together, socializing with one another in venues where they don't feel as though they're under a microscope.

But Bill Jensen still didn't socialize with his fellow officers. Although there is almost always solidarity in police agencies and cops officially have one another's backs on the job, Bill didn't have any more close friends in the sheriff's office than he had had in college.

There was something about him that turned other deputies off — perhaps his tendency toward braggadocio, his know-it-all attitude, or his quick temper.

Bill continued to be transferred laterally within the department. After he graduated from the police academy in December 1979, he was assigned to the Burien Precinct near Sea-Tac Airport, where he worked a patrol car for about eight months. Next, he drove a "highway car," where he was on call in a thirty-block area.

"Basically, you're in charge," he explained later in his usual self-aggrandizing manner. "The reason they selected me for that was because I had a very calming effect in situations. I didn't let them get out of hand. As soon as I showed up, I was able to settle things down.

"They wanted people to calm situations down," he said, "not to exasperate people."

Bill usually worked Third Watch (11 P.M.–7 A.M.) or Second Watch (3 P.M.–11 P.M.). After a year in the highway car, Bill was transferred to the Kent Precinct in the southeast portion of King County, and he worked patrol there in a one-man car for four years. In an effort to penetrate a burglary ring, Bill did some undercover detective work, which he enjoyed. Although he had once hoped to move into a detective unit, that didn't happen, and Bill was transferred next to the North Precinct, where he once again drove a patrol car. He was on call for a number of lightly populated, unincorporated areas in King County.

Beginning in 1992, Bill had an additional

assignment with the King County Sheriff's Office: he was an emergency vehicle operations instructor. It was a natural for him, and one that fulfilled his need to be in a position of authority.

"What my duties were was the training via my fellow peers, sergeants, and whoever. I took them out and they learned how to do pursuit driving and defensive driving," he said proudly. "I really enjoyed that. It was a lot of fun, and I was really fairly decorated for that because I did a good job. It was a very intensive course. I think I can honestly say it was one of the most intensive courses I had ever taken, including college. I was kind of surprised how hard it was. Not everybody passed it."

Bill had a kind of blindness about how he came across to others. He was quick to brag and slow to compliment anyone else. He was the center of his own universe, focused only on himself. Even his children were a distant second, and his wife got even less affirmation.

In the first seventeen years on the job, Bill Jensen was never elevated to detective — or even sergeant. He stayed in his one-man car on patrol. Over those years, Bill gradually but consistently put on weight, so that the lanky youth who graduated from Washington State University disappeared behind added pounds. He weighed more than three hundred pounds now.

In 1997, Bill said he wanted a change of pace, and asked to be assigned as a court security officer in the Issaquah District Court. He had worked that area on patrol for years and wanted to get off the road. Issaquah is a mountain foothills town in the shadow of Snoqualmie Pass, located more than fifteen miles from the King County Sheriff's Headquarters in downtown Seattle. It was an easy commute, however, from the Jensens' home in Newport Hills.

"I thought court duty would be kind of fun," he commented. "I tried to stay on day shift as I got older — as a matter of it being easier with the family and sleep and everything."

His new assignment began on January 1, 1997. Jenny was almost twelve, and Scott was nearly eight. With their father working a day shift, they hoped to see more of him. Sue, too, wondered if Bill's new assignment could somehow change the dynamics in their home in a positive way. At last they would all be living on the same basic schedule; she and the kids wouldn't have to be alone during nighttime hours, and he could coach on weekends.

The King County Journal, the east side's newspaper, chose Bill Jensen as their "Hometown Hero" about this point in his career. Bill had met an injured ex-cop in Australia ten years earlier when the Jensen family was vacationing there. Bill and Graeme Dovaston became long-distance friends after that, and kept in touch with each other. Ironically (in light of what lay ahead for Bill Jensen), Graeme Dovaston had been struck by a car when he was a working officer, and his leg was broken in seven places. That was in 1973. Infection set in, and after a fifteen-year struggle, his leg had to be amputated. When Bill Jensen learned that a prosthetic leg had failed Dovaston and that his long-awaited trip to America had become a nightmare as he tried to maneuver on a wooden foot fastened with straps that etched wounds into his hips, Bill took action.

Bill lobbied two Washington State firms to donate parts for a prosthetic leg that worked, and then organized a fund drive to raise the rest of the $19,000 needed for the remarkable artificial limb. After twenty years of pain and disappointment, Graeme Dovaston was able to lay down his crutches and walk once more, thanks to Bill Jensen.

Bill, in his King County Police uniform, smiled broadly from the pages of his local paper as he held a picture that showed his Australian friend walking with ease. Once more, Jenny and Scott Jensen were very proud of their dad.

Still, the Jensens' children worried about the conflict in their home. They loved both their parents, and when Bill and Sue Jensen fell into arguments, Jenny and Scott tried to mediate, too young to understand their basic differences and the disappointments each of their parents felt in a marriage that sometimes seemed doomed to failure. Sue, the bubbly optimist, kept trying to bring Bill into a relationship in which they shared responsibility, while Bill, the sullen, self-focused pessimist, resisted — pulling further away. Sadly, it wasn't a particularly unusual situation in many American marriages.

Sue wasn't afraid of Bill, not at all. She had long since pushed her dorm adviser's warning back into her subconscious mind. She had almost forgotten her injuries at Bill's hands when Scott was a newborn, as well as those that came later.

She knew her children loved their father devotedly, and that Jenny and Scott wanted their parents' marriage to succeed. Bill was still coaching Jenny's teams, and he joined Scott in father/son Indian Guide activities.

He and Scott still rode their motorcycles together, Bill on the big "hog" and Scott on one geared to his size.

Every time Sue thought about leaving the man she'd been married to for eighteen years, she felt she couldn't do it — it would break Jenny and Scott's hearts. There had to be a way to get Bill to join her in serious counseling.

Sue no longer had the self-confidence she once had as a young bride and in the early years of her marriage. Bill told her repeatedly that she was the reason they had problems. By now, Sue believed him. Her parents had been happily married, her sister was in a long-term positive relationship with a fine man, and most of her friends enjoyed solid marriages. Maybe Bill was right — maybe it was something *she* was doing wrong.

Sue had always believed Bill and found him intelligent and a man who made sound financial decisions. She was no longer working at a job outside their home, happy to be able to stay home with her children, but in a way, that made her more vulnerable to Bill's steady chipping away at her self-image. She often resented Bill, with his anger and his vacillating moods, but she still respected his opinions, although certainly not as she had done in their college days.

Even though she had a degree in psychology, Sue wasn't sure what factors were involved in the way Bill jumped from one obsession to another. For a while, he focused on showing champion-class dogs — Great Danes, to be exact. They had a Great Dane as a beloved pet, but when the dog developed problems with irritable bowel syndrome, Bill ordered that it be put down. Sue begged to have another dog, but Bill agreed only if she promised that *he* would decide when the next dog would either be given away or euthanized.

Whatever irritated Bill had to go.

No matter how mercurial he could be, few would quarrel with the notion that Bill Jensen was a whiz at finances. And making money was the most pervasive obsession he would embrace. He was one of the first to jump on the future prospects of computer stocks. He became a day trader long before most people had ever heard the term. He was out of bed every weekday at 6 A.M. and began to check the stock market, evaluating, buying, and selling until 1 P.M. Now he bought even more stocks on margin, but as long as the market stayed up, that wasn't a problem.

One day, when it dipped dramatically just before the millennium, Bill was caught short with margin calls, and he lost a lot of money. But for most of the nineties, he held 350,000 shares of prime computer stock.

Bill Jensen continued to be a man who obsessed over one moneymaking scheme or avocation after another. In 1989, for example, during the Washington State Centennial, he found a way to make a lot of money very quickly. Through one of Sue's former bosses, he snagged the franchise on official State Centennial gold-plated guns. He took time off from his sheriff's duties to sell them at various venues — including the Washington State Fair. They sold for about $1,700, and $750 of that was pure profit.

Next he set about building the best computer possible, and spent close to $100,000 on computer ware.

He began to buy "collectible currency" on eBay and attempted to sell it at considerable profit. He attended conventions with others who were fascinated by coins and bills that were either history-laden or the result of mint mistakes that had slipped through before production stopped.

One currency convention in Tennessee led to his next preoccupation: genealogy. Bill developed an intense interest in his family's genealogy, searching out the Pate family (that was his birth surname). He traced that name back to Tennessee and a man named John O. Pate, who was thought to be Bill's great-grandfather. In the late 1890s, locals described John Pate as "mean looking, with a handle-bar mustache." Although he had a wife, he was involved with a woman whose last name was Crowder. When his mistress was unfaithful to him, John O. Pate was enraged.

The Crowder woman fled his wrath, only to meet up with Pate on the trail across Tennessee's Big Bald Mountain. In what historians called "a brutal murder and mutilation," Pate killed her. John O. Pate was about fifty at the time. He hid out in a cave on the northwest slope of Big Bald Mountain, and Margaret, his forgiving wife, brought him food. When lawmen caught up with him, he refused to come out until they threatened to toss dynamite into the cave. He was convicted on murder charges and served either nine or twenty years in a Tennessee prison, depending on which genealogy you read. Thereafter, he stayed clear of the law.

Riley Pate, who may also have been related to Bill Jensen, was sentenced to death in 1896 for the shooting of a fifteen-year-old youth who had thrown a rock at him when he was drunk. Mat Hensley, the victim, died of wounds to the "lungs and liver."

Although Bill Jensen had never considered himself a Pate, he was intrigued by his possible connections to the Tennessee Pates.

As Bill Jensen immersed himself in one near obsession after another, Bill and Sue grew further apart. She had come to a place where she simply quit trying to get him to do chores around their home and just did them herself. As far as their children knew, they were still a close family. Some days, Sue vowed to try harder; on others, she tried to cope with the desolate feeling that comes with an increasingly empty relationship. She concentrated on Jenny and Scott.

Bill continued to coach Jenny's teams. Sue worked hard to retain family traditions for her children's sake.

The Jensens hosted their traditional Halloween parties, where Bill invariably dressed up as a homicidal maniac, his skin and clothes stained with fake blood.

And everyone laughed.

Bill's gun safe held at least seventeen weapons, a few of them the gold-plated Centennial guns, but most were firearms he'd bought or traded.

If the delicate balance in the marriage could just stay suspended where it was, there was always the chance that the Jensens could stay together in some kind of détente.

And then, on July 23, 1997, their lives changed dramatically and there was no going back. Ever.

Two
Secrets and Lies

It was full, hot summer in Washington State in July 1997, and Bill Jensen continued to work as a court security officer in Issaquah, in the shadows of Snoqualmie Pass. It seemed to be a much safer assignment than patrolling at night in a one-man sheriff's patrol car.

But it wasn't.

Court was under way when a fugitive from the law who was armed and intoxicated entered the Issaquah courthouse through an unauthorized entrance. Bill ordered him to stop, and at first, he did. He gave his name as William Martin. Bill led him back to the desk area where he was stationed.

He ran Martin's name through the WASIC police computers and found that there were warrants out for Martin's arrest. Realizing that he'd been found out, Martin fled down two flights of stairs and was outside the courthouse and in his car when Bill caught up with him. Bill grabbed Martin through the window and held on tight, but the escapee managed to get his car started. He threw his vehicle into reverse, dragging Bill with him until Bill was forced to release his grip and fell heavily.

"He put a big dent in my knee," Bill said later. He recalled that he ached all over the following day, but expected he would heal within several days.

But he didn't. Unfortunately, Bill Jensen's right knee had been seriously damaged, more than anyone realized at the time. His back was injured, and his right ring finger had also been damaged. In most professions, that injury wouldn't have been particularly significant — unless it happened to a concert violinist or a police officer. Bill was right-handed, and he could no longer trust his aim when firing a gun.

Several times when he was driving after the incident, he was unable to move his foot from the accelerator to the brake. Again, law enforcement officers need to be capable of pursuit driving at high speeds and to have lightning-quick responses. Bill had been expert at that, but he wasn't any longer.

Bill had two surgeries on his right knee, and his physician reportedly told him he was too young to have a third, for fear he might end up in a wheelchair at an early age. When he walked, Bill's patella (kneecap) clicked. A complete knee replacement would last only ten to twelve years, and his doctor wasn't sure another replacement when Bill was only fifty would be advisable.

Bill Jensen could not help but remember how his Australian friend's police career had ended, or how much pain he had suffered after his leg was broken — and then amputated. Now, something similar had happened to him.

For all intents and purposes, Bill Jensen's dream of becoming an FBI special agent was now impossible. He had always planned to be a cop; he'd made it, and just before the age of forty his career might be ending. He didn't have enough years in to get his full retirement.

It was at this point in Bill Jensen's life that tremendous changes washed like acid over the Jensen family. Bill's newest obsession was about his health, his disablement, and his pain. He thought of nothing else.

In slow increments, Bill had changed so much that the man Sue had fallen in love with in 1975 was unrecognizable. The slender young man had long since vanished. Even before he was injured, Bill had put on more than a hundred pounds, much of it around his waist. His weight problems now became a vicious circle. Because it hurt to walk, he moved as little as possible, rarely exercising. He no longer coached Jenny's basketball and baseball teams but sat, instead, in the stands. When he moved, it was with an exaggerated limp.

And the less Bill Jensen exercised, the more weight he gained. He had reached 350 pounds, and was now headed toward four hundred. Sue had put on about twenty pounds, but she looked essentially as she had when they were first married. It wasn't Bill's appearance, though, that made her wonder where their marriage was going; it was his moodiness and his complete self-absorption, which put a pall over the whole family.

Bill had always been a man who held grudges, keeping track of those who he felt had wronged him. Now, since he believed he was almost totally disabled by his knee injury, he made plans to sue his insurance company for $1.7 million. The King County Sheriff's Office respected his almost twenty years as a deputy and offered him "light duty" at the sheriff's office for a few days a week. It was essentially desk work; it wasn't really being a cop — not to Bill Jensen.

He retired from the King County Sheriff's

Office in September 1999.

Bill grew more bitter as the months passed, and he blamed everyone around him for his personal knee-injury disaster. He spent most of his days and nights sitting in a recliner chair watching television, angry at the fugitive who had maimed him, angry at his wife, angry at his children, angry at his fellow cops, angry at the whole world.

Impatient, he scoffed at exercises that might have helped in his physical rehabilitation. He wore a heavy brace on his knee and walked with an exaggerated limp. His doctor referred him to the University of Washington Pain Clinic, but he walked in one door and out the other, denying the possibility that he could get along without pain pills. "It's just not going to work."

Sue sensed that things weren't right. Bill was starting to take too many of the painkillers that had been prescribed for him, although, initially, he didn't appear to be negatively affected. The pills weren't helping. He still complained of pain continually.

"It got to the point," Sue recalled, "that if he didn't take the pain pills, you'd wish he would have."

As Bill moved ahead with his suit against the insurance company, Sue agreed, at his insistence, to participate in a video presentation that allegedly showed how Bill and his family's lives had changed since his injury. Images of Bill coaching Jenny's sports teams and carrying his children on his back as he crawled on their carpet, and of him laughing with them, appeared on the screen.

Scott and Jenny spoke to the camera, explaining how much fun their father had been, but was no longer. The video showed Jenny mowing the lawn, although Bill had only rarely mowed the lawn even when he was able-bodied. At Bill's urging, Sue spoke of how his injuries had robbed her of his companionship as a loving husband. Bill's physicians described how his accident had left him incapacitated.

Much of what was said about Bill's knee and back pain was an exaggeration. It was certainly true that he was in pain, and early on he had worked hard with a physical therapist to alleviate some of that pain, but he no longer believed it would help. He was eating far more calories than he needed, and piling on pounds that put more stress on his knee and back.

Oddly, when Bill spoke to the camera about his childhood, he described it as if it had been right out of *Leave It to Beaver*. He characterized his early years as happy and normal, recalling that the Lone Ranger was one of his heroes. He told the camera that he'd liked cowboys and Indians and that he'd been an average kid, who grew up to be a loving husband and father and a brave police officer. He failed to mention his years in foster homes or the childhood abuse he had endured. He presented a life — but it wasn't his life at all.

When Sue looked at the final product to be used in Bill's lawsuit against the insurance company, it was almost heartbreaking. She was viewing her marriage and her family through the looking glass — the way she always hoped it would be, and never was.

Years later, when the suit was finally settled, Bill Jensen was disappointed. He didn't get the $1.7 million he had sought; he received $80,000, Sue was awarded $20,000, and Jenny and Scott each received $10,000.

Sue wasn't concerned; they had adequate savings and investments. They had bought out her sister's share of their home, remodeled it with money from Sue's inheritance account, and had a manageable mortgage. Bill would have his retirement money and his disability insurance payments, and he wasn't totally disabled. He could work at another career, and if need be she could get a job, too.

Sue still didn't consider leaving him, despite his grouchy demeanor. But she didn't know the secrets that her husband had kept from her.

One of the things Sue didn't know was that Bill had already applied to vest his police pension. Under the Washington State Law Enforcement Retirement Plan — LEOFF II — Bill had $154,746 coming to him. He chose to cash it out entirely. As his spouse, Sue was legally required to sign the application along with Bill, so that he could receive this money. She found out later that Bill had either forged her name or found some way around this requirement. He accepted the sheriff's pension money and put it in his own private bank account without telling her. Most of it went to buy collectible currency.

But hope for their future was looking up a little. When he realized that he had no choice but to resign from the sheriff's office on disability, Bill grudgingly agreed to be retrained for a new career. It seemed the perfect alternative for a man who was physically compromised. Bill had always been fascinated by computers, buying himself the very best and most advanced computer technology available. The Jensens lived in the shadow of the sprawling Microsoft campus, and Bill Gates himself, while not exactly a neighbor, lived only a few miles away. It was the computer industry boom, and Bill had the knowledge and the skills to take advantage of it.

He attended Bellevue Community College, where he became remarkably proficient in all things Microsoft. Bill Jensen was brilliant with computers, perhaps more suited to this career than to a deputy's. In March 1999, when he completed his courses, he was hired by City University at a salary of $100 an hour. He taught between ten and twenty hours a week. And that meant he was grossing $1,000 to $2,000 each week. Even though he complained that his knee bothered him tremendously, he was capable of bringing home between $52,000 and $104,000 a year for a part-time job.

With his retirement fund, the insurance settlement, the equities and investments he and Sue shared, and his teaching salary, life was far from over for Bill Jensen at the age of forty-one.

While it was true that teaching computer science might not have been as exciting or even as personally rewarding as being a cop, Bill had his family, a very comfortable home, and any number of options for the future.

He taught at City University until June 2002. But from 1997 to 2001, Bill spent the rest of his time watching TV, sleeping, or off someplace participating in activities that Sue Jensen knew nothing about.

In October 2000, a year after Bill retired from the sheriff's office, Sue poured out her feelings in her journal, hoping that Bill might see what they would both lose, what their children would lose, if he didn't make an attempt to resume their family life.

"Bill," she wrote, "today I attended my daughter's basketball game — alone. I thought how sad it is, you have no idea. Will you wake up one day and just have no idea of what you have missed?"

Another entry read: "I came home to find that you had finally gotten up at 12:30, unshaven and unbathed, to find you were not 'up to' attending Ryan's wedding.

"Sitting there alone in church made me realize how desperately I miss [your] companionship. I looked over at [a couple] holding hands and felt so very hurt."

Only special friends had been invited to the $100-a-plate reception after the close friend's wedding, but Bill refused to accompany her. "I look back at the time with the Johnsons — which was probably the best [time] there has been in our marriage. We behaved as a couple and actually enjoyed each other's company."

After working so hard for a year and a

half, twelve-year-old Scott had triumphantly passed a karate test to move up to the next belt, but his father wasn't there to see him glow with pride.

"Again," Sue wrote, "I thought how sad — for you to miss the hard work and drive he has fought for all of his life — a simple reward but so meaningful. I was so proud I cried. You chose to miss that moment in life."

"I always believed what Bill told me," Sue later recalled with some exasperation. "It never occurred to me that he might be lying to me or be unfaithful. We had our problems — but I always trusted him."

Bill no longer participated in his children's' activities. He said he couldn't coach Jenny anymore, or ride motorcycles with Scott. And that was probably true, but there were other ways he could have spent time with them. He occasionally went to Jenny's ball games, limping in from his car and sitting on the bleachers. But that didn't last long; if he couldn't be the coach, he didn't want to be there at all.

Sue, Jenny, and Scott tiptoed around Bill, trying not to do or say anything that would set him off into a screaming tantrum. Scott's tutor noticed how anxious and afraid Scott seemed, and he whispered to her that they couldn't talk very loud because it would make his father angry.

Even though Sue understood that Bill was depressed, he didn't seem to be doing anything to lift himself out of his situation, and his dark moods and outbursts of anger were making their whole family anxious and depressed too. His bad knee and constant pain were all that mattered to him, and he obviously had no interest in his marriage or his children. Sue wrote in her journal, trying to understand, "Bill, I know you are in pain, and it is not easy. But at some point you will have to accept that which you cannot change. It is up to you to determine your destiny."

They weren't really a family any longer.

Bill stayed up all night and slept through the day. During the few meals they shared, Bill lost his temper and sent Scott to sit in a corner for punishment for some small annoyance. Eventually, Bill no longer ate with Sue and their children.

Bill blamed Sue, insisting it was her fault that things were going wrong. He told her repeatedly that she needed counseling, and she agreed to go. Sue had begun to doubt what her husband told her. One night in December 2000, after the family had gone to bed, she was shocked to find him counting out large bags full of lottery tickets and peel-off pull tabs. She eventually learned he had spent $69,000 on them — most of them were from machines on the bar of a little tavern close to their home.

When she asked Bill about the lottery tickets and pull tabs, he had an easy answer. He explained he was saving them as a favor for a guy to use as a "tax write-off."

Later, Sue realized that her husband was using his computer for online gambling. While he had always taken chances in the stock market, she had never really thought of him as the kind of gambler who bought lottery tickets or spent much in Las Vegas. Her own limit was $300 for a weekend trip to Nevada, and while Bill wagered a little more, it hadn't been a problem. He always told her his gambling was "totally under control" and that he knew his limits.

He had kept his huge gambling losses hidden by changing the address on their bank statements to a post office box.

Sue realized that Bill was lying to her — had probably lied to her for many years. Every few months brought more secrets she had never known about. In May 2001, he told her that he had won a $10,000 cruise just for testing some new software. It was to be a wonderful trip for their entire family. It never happened.

She finally acknowledged to herself that every time something was really important to her or to Jenny or Scott, Bill would go out of his way to smash their joy. His birthday was coming up on Memorial Day weekend, and they made plans to take a family trip to Cannon Beach, Oregon. They went, but Bill was surly and critical of everyone, and nobody had any fun.

Around June 16, 2001, she learned that Bill had just spent $28,000 on collectible coins he'd purchased on the Internet. Their marriage had spun like a colorful top for twenty-two years, the lines and patterns blurred by Bill's glib excuses. Now, as it wound down slower and slower, Sue could see the pattern of lies.

It was all too much. Sue had finally hit a wall, and she told Bill she wanted a divorce. He begged her to stay. She said she would if he would join her in counseling.

Bill attended four sessions, but blew up when the counselor pointed out to him that *he* was responsible for the domestic violence incidents in his home. Bill refused to go back.

He chose what mattered most to him. It wasn't Sue — or even their children. Their marriage had become untenable. There was nothing left to save, and no way in the world to make it work.

They reached a watershed point on Friday, June 22, 2001 — the first full day of summer. Sue had made plans to drive Jenny and the girls on her basketball team to Spokane for the annual "Hoop-Fest" that drew teams from all over Washington State. They needed to take the Jensens' Sequoia SUV, the only vehicle big enough to hold seven passengers.

But Bill would not allow it. He forbade Sue to take it, and Jenny and the team had to scare up a ride with another parent.

"It was more than his selfishness," Sue remembered. "The team parents and the girls were my friends and Jenny's friends. This was my social life — all that I had — and I was embarrassed, and Jenny was, too — and disappointed. Bill and I had a big fight that day, and I realized I'd totally, finally, come to the end."

A battle comparable to the War of the Roses began that day. The house they lived in had been owned by Sue's family since she was in grade school. It seemed reasonable that Bill should be the one to leave and move into an apartment. Uprooting their children from the only home they had ever known and taking them out of their schools would be cruel. They were already devastated that their parents were divorcing.

Bill agreed to leave that Friday, June 22, but it wasn't an easy transition. He and Sue were both angry, and maybe he expected her to back down, but she didn't. Jenny had left for Spokane to play in the basketball tournament, but Scott was home when Sue called her sister and asked her anxiously to come right over. "I've called the police," Sue said.

When Carol pulled up to the house in Newport Hills, she saw several Bellevue Police cars parked outside. Scott was in the front yard, safe — but obviously humiliated to have all the neighbor kids watching. There should have been a way for Bill to move out without causing a scene, but that wasn't going to happen.

Officers Raskow and Boyd had responded to Sue's 911 call for help. They found her crying and upset, but saw that Bill was upset too. It was a common reaction to a domestic dispute, and neither of them appeared to be out of control.

Bill was mostly concerned over a box of documents, files of some of his financial dealings that Sue knew nothing about. Their argument was at an impasse but not flaring dangerously, and Bill left the house. The two patrolmen were preparing to leave when Bill drove back — just as Carol was trying to lock the box of files in the trunk of her car.

Bill grabbed it out. Kurt Raskow, the patrol officer, told Carol to put the box back into her car and instructed Bill to leave it there.

At that point, Bill Jensen erupted and went "ballistic." Even the Bellevue officers were surprised at his sudden mood swing as he went from being pleasantly cooperative to being angry.

"But we were dealing with a domestic," Raskow said, "and I've seen it before."

And then Bill's rage ballooned suddenly to a point where the Bellevue officer found him "way overboard from what I normally see. I thought it was going to be a big fight right there in the street."

Bill stomped over to the Toyota Sequoia SUV and ripped a wire out from under the hood. He threw his arms into the air as he headed back to confront Raskow, who was trying to comfort Scott. Bill went into the house, and Scott trailed after him.

Sue was crying and upset. She had called 911 for help, but the patrolmen explained that there had been no assault and that they could not deal with civil matters. Cars, files, and paperwork caught in a tug-of-war didn't constitute an assault.

The patrolmen could see Scott inside, peering out a picture window, and he looked safe enough; Sue didn't worry that Bill would hurt him. Bill loved Scott. But the two policeman were concerned when they heard pounding as if Bill was blockading the front door. They called their supervisor, saying that they were afraid the child might be being held against his will. Then Scott came out and spoke to his mother. He insisted that he wanted to stay with his father.

Advised by the Bellevue police to obtain a no-contact/protection order, Sue and Carol drove to the District Court and obtained one, but the officers wanted them to stay away until police served the order. Sue was worried sick about Scott, so Raskow and Boyd brought him along when they met Sue and Carol a few miles from Newport Hills and escorted them back to the Jensens' home. The police were concerned about another confrontation. Scott was okay, but torn, his loyalty to both his parents obvious.

It was something no twelve-year-old boy should have to go through.

Bill was inside the house, apparently still barricaded. Aware now that they were dealing with a former deputy sheriff who had a safe full of guns in the house, the Bellevue

Police chose a cautionary approach, and stationed eight officers around the perimeter of the property. A negotiator called the phone inside, but Bill wouldn't pick it up. They left messages on the answering machine, hoping that he was listening.

It was a very bad night. Sue and Carol waited outside. Sue wasn't sure what Bill might do — but she was still certain he would never hurt Scott.

For two and a half hours, they were at a standoff. And finally Bill walked out. Bill was served with the no-contact order, and allowed to go.

When Sue checked the master bedroom closet, she found that Bill's service revolver was gone. As for the seventeen guns in his safe, Bill told Officer Kurt Raskow that he had forgotten the combination to his own safe. After midnight, and just to reassure themselves that Jensen didn't have access to it, the Bellevue police arranged to bring their van to pick up the safe full of guns and remove it from the house. It was subsequently locked in the department's property room. That was probably a wise move; Bill had committed the combination to memory. He was in and out of it a few times each day, although Sue wasn't allowed to see what he kept in there.

Any police officer — Bill Jensen included — knows that the two most dangerous calls he can respond to are mental cases and domestic violence disputes. Bellevue officer Kurt Raskow admitted that he had feared for his own safety when the huge ex-cop went in an instant from being reasonable to towering rage.

All in all, the conclusion to that long June evening had been lucky. Nobody was hurt. Nobody was killed. Everyone involved — the Harris sisters, Sue and Carol; the Jensen children; the Bellevue police officers; and quite probably Bill Jensen too — was relieved.

Sue Jensen hired Janet Brooks* to represent her in her divorce proceedings. Sue had never had a will, assuming as most young wives do that she and Bill would be each other's heirs if one of them should die. She had never checked on the bank account she shared with Bill. They had begun it with $10,000; she had eventually contributed $208,000 with checks she had written from her inheritance account. Bill never put so much as a dime into the account, and for fifteen years he didn't take anything out without Sue's okay.

Bill had always figured their income tax

and did the filing.

It only made sense now for Sue to evaluate their assets as they would soon be negotiating the division of the property and funds they had accumulated in twenty-two years of marriage. She assumed that they were headed for nasty battles and that Bill would attempt to wear her down until she was "broke mentally or broke financially — or both."

Money meant everything to Bill Jensen, but it wasn't what was foremost in Sue's mind.

Sue made lists of what mattered most to her. Any woman caught in a litigious divorce would probably recognize and empathize with her final document:

1. My children
2. My sister
3. My health
4. My sense of peace
5. My future
6. My friends and the happiness friendships bring
7. My happiness
8. A sense of self-integrity
9. My sense of purpose, lifetime accomplishments
10. Financial security

All things being equal, it was a modest list.

In Washington State, if parties agree, it takes only three months for a divorce to become final. Sue had no illusions that Bill was hurting emotionally because he still loved her. It was just that he — like a number of husbands (and wives) — had always wanted to be the one to walk away, and he'd been ill prepared when Sue filed for divorce.

Janet Brooks worked with Sue in an attempt to determine which assets belonging to her and Bill were intact and which were somewhat diminished. They needed to find out what was community property and what was separate. It was standard procedure in any divorce. On some occasions, it is necessary to discover if there has been any "dissipation of assets" — that is, has either party disposed of money, stocks, vehicles, jewelry, or other valuable belongings that were shared by both the husband and the wife?

Novels, movies, and television dramas often depict one spouse or the other charging up to the limits of credit cards, sneaking money out of bank accounts, or cleverly hiding assets. Depending on the slant of scripts, spending an about-to-be-ex's assets can seem either hilarious or outrageous.

On her divorce attorney's advice, Sue attempted to freeze the accounts and investments she shared with Bill. But when she inquired about their joint bank account, she had a shock. The money was all gone. She had put almost a quarter of a million dollars from her parents' legacy to her into their joint account, and it was missing.

First, she cried. "I fell apart," Sue admitted. "But I had my sister and four good girlfriends who were there for me. My sister took me by the shoulders and there was no nonsense about her. She told me, 'This is exactly what Bill wants. He expects you to cave in. You have two kids. You've got to pull yourself together.' And I did."

And then, with Janet Brooks's help, she began to close out joint credit cards and freeze any other accounts that had been opened in both her name and Bill's.

Sue didn't know where Bill lived; he had disappeared, along with their Sequoia SUV. She had even become her own private detective, determined to find the missing Sequoia. In her old Mustang or Jenny's Impala she drove through parking lots looking for it. And then she deduced that wherever Bill was, he had probably flown there; he'd complained often enough that driving bothered his back and his knee. One day she went to the parking garage of the Sea-Tac Airport and drove up the winding ramps that led to each of the many levels there, looking especially in the handicapped spaces. And there it was. Bill had probably assumed it was safely hidden among the hundreds of vehicles left by travelers.

Sue used the key she had, backed the Sequoia out, and left the Impala that Chuck Jensen had given to Jenny — with no key. They could come back to get that later. She had to pay $300 in parking charges to leave the airport garage, but she had her SUV back.

She knew Bill would be very angry that she had found it. It was an expensive vehicle; they'd paid $48,000 for it the year before. To forestall Bill's taking it again, Sue hid the SUV in a friend's garage.

In the first court hearing after Bill was served with divorce papers in July, the judge had awarded the Sequoia to Sue. She would be the one driving their children to school, sports events, doctors, and dentists, and taking the pets to the veterinarians. That didn't sit well with Bill.

Sue chose to believe that Bill hadn't held Scott hostage on the day he moved out. Scott loved and trusted the father who had vowed the little boy would live, despite all odds, the father who sheltered him against the problems of the world. Even though Sue and Bill could no longer pretend that their marriage wasn't over, that didn't mean that Bill's participation in his children's lives would end.

And yet beginning in the summer of 2001, Bill rarely attempted to see his children. He clearly wasn't in the Seattle area. If his children heard from him once a month, they considered themselves fortunate. Once the divorce was final, surely they would be able to spend time with their father on a regular basis.

Even so, no one could have had any idea of the tortuous and precarious road the Jensens would take as they headed for divorce — or the shocking ending that lay ahead.

The breakup of any marriage that once began with high hopes is sad. That is hard enough; total, paralyzing terror is more than either the husband or wife should have to endure.

Sue expected that Bill would make her life difficult, but she still wasn't afraid of him.

At first, Sue Jensen and her children felt mostly relief that they no longer had to live with Bill Jensen's mercurial moods and his glowering presence. The no-contact/protection order was in place, but he made no effort to see Sue and contacted his children only sporadically. Those meetings and calls usually ended in tears.

Sue's attorney attempted to contact Bill's lawyer to ask that they cooperate on putting together an inventory of the couple's holdings. Once that was done, Sue could locate those assets and determine what had been used up or displaced, and negotiate repayment to the Jensens' community property.

Sue wasn't greedy, but she wanted a fair accounting. Most of all, she wanted to be sure that there would be adequate provision for any medical care Scott might need in the future. He was doing very well, but Noonan's syndrome made him vulnerable to a number of physical ailments, and Sue wanted to be sure he had the best care. Although Bill was supposed to continue their medical insurance, Sue was worried he would allow it to lapse — and he did. She kept up their medical insurance payments — even for Bill, because he reported all kinds of illnesses, from heart attacks to cancer.

Jenny would soon be going to the University of Washington, and her mother wanted to be sure there was enough money to pay for her tuition, books, and lodging.

Sue had never worried about taking care of their two children before; she had been secure in the knowledge that money had been set aside for them. But she was finding out that Bill had spent great chunks of that money. She had never been acquisitive or curious about the family budget, but now she vowed to find out where hundreds of thousands of dollars had gone, and to see that Bill paid back their community property.

That would not be easy. The entire summer of 2001 passed and they were no closer to arranging a meeting where she and Bill and their attorneys could discuss a financial settlement in the Jensens' divorce so they could move ahead to their decree.

At some point over the long summer of 2001, Sue Jensen had started to fight back and take over the reins of her life.

It was November 13 when the Jensens finally sat down in Janet Brooks's office in an awkward and tense meeting. Sue sat diagonally across from Bill as Janet Brooks began a deposition from him by asking him innocuous questions about his date of birth, his education, his current address. He gave an address in Bellevue, saying he had moved in only four days earlier.

He had no objection as she asked him about medications he currently took, listing almost a dozen mood elevators, heavy-duty pain pills, and over-the-counter pain medications. He acknowledged that he took those meds. Again and again, Bill Jensen referred to his chronic, intractable pain. He also explained that he had had a heart attack sometime in the prior five months, although he couldn't recall just when that was, the results of any tests he had had, or a diagnosis. He said he wasn't taking any prescription medication for his heart attack.

As Janet Brooks bore in on questions, Jensen's answers were either "I don't know," "I don't recall," or "No" — except when he was asked to describe the incident when he was injured. He remembered that and the aftermath precisely.

Bill Jensen said he had lived with his oldest sister in Bremerton for a while, and in scores of hotels and motels in the Seattle area and in Las Vegas over the five months since he'd moved out of the Newport Hills home. When pressed, he recalled that he had vacationed in the Bahamas in September. He insisted he didn't know how much rent he paid on apartments or exactly where he had stayed. He did remember that he was in Las Vegas on September 11 when the World Trade Center was destroyed.

It was apparent where some of the marital assets had gone: Janet Brooks finally managed to drag out the information that Bill had spent around $100 a night for lodging over the prior 150 days.

"Insolent" would be the word to describe Bill Jensen's attitude toward Sue Jensen's attorney. He admitted reluctantly to many visits to the top Las Vegas hotels, where gambling was the main attraction, but offered that he wasn't "allowed to gamble" there any longer. There was a good reason for that, and Janet Brooks would get to that later.

Bill hadn't been alone on some of his trips. He admitted that he had met a woman in her twenties at the Aladdin Hotel and taken her to the Bahamas, California, and back to Seattle with him. He knew her first name: Kristi. He said he didn't know her last name. "She had several names."

He denied paying Kristi for her company, but allowed that he probably had given her some money. He said he had also met people in the Aladdin and accompanied them to Ketchikan, Alaska, to a lodge for a fishing trip.

Bill smirked and laughed on occasion as he answered Janet Brooks's questions. His transfers of money and checks were almost incomprehensible. He had obtained power of attorney over his adoptive father's bank account, and had written himself several checks on that account — approximately $63,000 worth. He had paid "bills" from the joint account he'd had with Susan. Those totaled over $200,000 and were dated on the weekend after he vacated their home. He had gambling winnings of $27,000, and he'd sold Intel stock for $265,000, and he had borrowed $37,000 from his father. He had his $154,000 retirement fund. He had removed $202,000 from a Schwab stock investment account he shared with his wife.

The total money he had spent in less than six months was astronomical.

And Bill Jensen never admitted that he had taken the Sequoia van that had gone to Sue in an early settlement. He did say he'd been furious when she was given that vehicle because it was purchased for him when he was injured. He didn't mention another reason; they had bought it to replace a van that was totaled in an accident — and they needed something big enough to accommodate a 170-pound Great Dane.

Bill said it was his, and he had sold it. To assure that Sue wouldn't get it back, he explained, he had sold it to a woman he knew only as "Dee," whom he'd met in Las Vegas.

"What did you sell it for?" Sue's lawyer asked.

"Nothing," he said. "I sold it to her for nothing. She was going to come up to Seattle and drive it back."

He had been surprised that Sue found it at the airport, and angry that she was still driving it. Sue had tormented him, he said, and taken advantage of him. Bill Jensen insisted that he was the victim in all of the financial matters.

"Thanks to my wife, my credit is ruined," he said. "She has sent all of this court paperwork to all the credit card companies that I have. And every time I get a card opened back up, she sends another one and they close it. And I keep going back and forth — and back and forth."

Bill's ploy in selling the van didn't work; at a court hearing, the judge told him to get "Dee" on the phone and cancel the sale. Once again, Sue was awarded the Sequoia, but it would continue to rankle Bill.

Janet Brooks and the court reporter who was taking down the dialogue of this November 2001 meeting felt a chill as they glanced up and saw Bill Jensen face Sue and make a slashing motion with his finger as he drew it across his neck. It was a gesture that symbolized a throat being cut. At that moment, he looked at Sue and mouthed, "You're dead . . ."

None of the three women doubted that he meant it.

Sue's attorney remarked that she was noting his gesture in the record.

"You're a liar," Jensen growled.

The reporter marked the tape at the spot where the threat was made and they continued on. But later, Bill Jensen drew himself up to his full height and leaned across the table, staring at Janet Brooks.

"He looked at me, and told me to be very careful, and watch out for myself and what I was doing . . ."

Bill Jensen was a master at intimidation. Two months later, Sue's attorney withdrew from representing her in her divorce. Maybe he'd only been acting, but his threat had been too ominous for her to continue. She was frank with Sue as she said, "I'm sorry you have to deal with this kind of harassment, Sue, but I don't, and I'm withdrawing from your case. I've had enough. I'm done."

Sue couldn't really blame her. Bill could be very scary.

"Janet was a strong, tough woman," Sue said. "But she didn't want to deal with Bill."

Both Janet Brooks and Sue Jensen had called the police to report Bill's threats. The responding detective asked Sue if she thought Bill was going to act on his threat, and she replied that she really didn't know. He had always been full of bluster and threats. He had been physically abusive at times, but more often she was the victim of emotional abuse. She was still embarrassed to admit that Bill had hurt her physically two or three times a year in the two decades they'd been married. She'd never told anyone about that, only her sister.

At this point Sue was far more worried about Bill's driving her attorney away than she was that he might hurt her. He had threatened her so many times; she thought it was probably just more of his intimidation.

But she admitted that sometimes she was very frightened of Bill, afraid of his "exploding."

Bill had numerous problems that might well push him to the point of losing control. Beyond the credit card charges that Bill Jensen had run up for motels and hotels, restaurants, plane tickets, and the other things he had purchased since June 2001, his gambling debts were huge. While he had been a savvy gambler in playing the stock market during his marriage, he appeared to have no talent at all at the various gaming tables in Las Vegas.

In the same month that he derided and threatened Sue Jensen and her attorney, he was charged criminally by the District Attorney's Office in Las Vegas. It was not at all unusual for the prosecutor in a city where gambling was the top industry, to send out bad-check notices to those who had wagered more than they could afford. The office had a standard form printed just for that. But Bill hadn't responded to the "Notice of Bad Checks" letters, and DA Stewart L. Bell followed up with several "Warning of Criminal Charges" letters.

On July 13, 2001, Jensen had written an NSF check to the Paris/Bally's Hotel & Casino for $20,000, which brought with it $2,065 in penalties. Between July 12 and July 28, 2001, the Aladdin Resort and Casino took more bad checks, which, with penalties, totaled $26,545. After negotiations, Jensen agreed to repay the $48,610 in monthly payments of $200 for six months, and a final lump sum payoff on November 15, 2002.

Initially, Bill had been welcomed to a number of hotels in Las Vegas and given club cards offered to high rollers. But he was an abysmally inept gambler. Estimated accountings sent out to club members to use when they paid the IRS indicated Bill's losses.

Aladdin:	2001	$122,898
MGM Grand:	2001	$8,906 *from slot machines*
		$1,100 *from gaming tables*
King of Clubs:	2001	$3,233.95 *from slot machines*
Club Bellagio:	2001	$3,540 *from slot machines*
Paris/Bally's:	2001	$17,753

These losses alone from five casinos — more than $157,000 — would have wiped out Bill Jensen's retirement benefits from the sheriff's office. Some accountings showed only his losses; others indicated the amount he had put into slot machines.

Bill seemed to be teetering on the edge of self-destruction. Although he had ignored Sue's attempts to make their marriage better, he was now absolutely crazed because she had had the nerve to leave him and ask for a fair division of their property. He appeared to be determined to spend every cent he could get his hands on, on hedonistic ventures and other women. Sue was kept busy trying to plug holes in the dike that had once been her stable financial assets. She was able to retrieve some of the assets Bill had either spent or stolen.

The following year, 2002, Bill was living in an apartment only a few miles from Newport Hills, and his children visited him a few times. But he wasn't living alone, and Jenny's and Scott's visits were nightmarish. They both still hoped there could be a way that he could come home, and that they could go back to the early days with a father who had seemed to care about them, but Bill appeared to have no conception of the pain they were in. He told Jenny on one visit, in February 2002, that her mother and aunt "deserved to die" for what they had done to him. When she asked him about the girl he was living with, he said he did have a new girlfriend, but that it was none of her business. And then he called his teenage daughter a "selfish piece of shit" before he pushed her out the door of his apartment.

Jenny was devastated.

Bill warned Scott, still only twelve, that he should be prepared for both his parents to die because it was likely that they would.

Sue did her best to bind up the emotional wounds Bill continually inflicted on their children.

As 2002 began, she had a new attorney. John Compatore was an ex-cop himself, a kind but tough man who was not easily intimidated. Compatore had the order of protection against Bill Jensen reinstated on July 26, 2002, but the Jensens' divorce was no closer to being finalized in 2002 than it had been a year earlier.

Sue counted on her sister, Carol, and her friends to find some sort of peace in her life — but as 2002 drifted toward autumn, she found herself moving from frustration to fear. She knew Bill, and she knew that he always got even with anyone he thought had wronged him.

And now, *she* was the enemy.

I have a large file drawer full of e-mails and letters from scores of desperate exes who have long since given up on love; they hope only to live their lives without having to look over their shoulders to catch someone following them, not waking in the dead of night at the slightest sound and lying in the dark, scarcely breathing, wondering if someone has crept into their homes.

Sue Jensen had become one of those people.

In September, Sue walked out to get her morning paper and realized that there was a big vacant spot in her driveway. She saw that the Sequoia SUV was gone again. She knew who had taken it. That SUV was a major bone of contention with Bill. He had wanted it from the very beginning. They were still together, of course, when they'd bought it, but Sue had discovered that Bill had deleted her name from the title. Now she understood why. He had apparently bided his time until she felt safe enough to park it in her own driveway, and then taken it back.

"You'll never find it now," a friend told her. "It's gone for good."

Because she had been given the Sequoia in their first divorce hearing, Sue — who made the insurance payments on it and all their other possessions — should have been in line for the insurance payment on a stolen vehicle. It could have been stolen by someone other than her estranged husband, but Sue doubted that.

She got on the Internet and began a search for someone who might be trying to sell a Sequoia. She found nothing in the state of Washington. She kept trying, and at the end of October 2002, Sue located a Sequoia SUV that had been sold to a dealership in Beaverton, Oregon. The color, model, and description were right. When she checked on the VIN (vehicle identification number), she knew she had found the SUV stolen from her.

Told that she probably couldn't get it back because her name wasn't on the title, and that she would likely be forfeiting the insurance payment, too, she shook her head impatiently. "I don't care — it's the right thing to do."

She never saw the Sequoia again, but she eventually was recompensed by her insurance company.

Christmas 2002 was bleak. The old traditions seemed to mock Sue, Jenny, and Scott. The year ahead seemed to hold danger instead of promise.

Sue Jensen now firmly believed that she was going to "end up dead" when Bill finally reached his boiling point. That would be his "final word," the revenge he always sought. She hadn't spoken to him in months, but she discovered on New Year's Eve that Bill had canceled their medical insurance. Sue couldn't apply under her own name until she was legally divorced, and it could be catastrophic for them to risk going without it. When Scott called Bill the first week in January 2003, she picked up the phone.

"I told him all he had to do was e-mail the insurance company and we would be reinstated."

With Scott's continuing medical expenses, they desperately needed to have medical coverage. They argued. And Sue made a terrible mistake; she told Bill that he would go to jail if he didn't stop acting in contempt of court orders.

His voice grew steely.

"If I go to jail, you're going to your grave."

Bill also threatened John Compatore's life. By making those death threats, he had violated the order of protection.

On January 21, 2003, Bill Jensen's harassment reached such a peak that Sue filed felony–domestic–violence charges against him. He was arrested, but he bailed out within a day. His adopted father, Chuck Jensen, put up his bail. Bill showed up for his court date on those charges, but Sue had been warned by a domestic violence victim's advocate not to subject herself to that.

Bill turned her absence into a win for himself; he obtained an order of protection against her.

And all the while, Sue's fear that Bill would do something violent toward her — and even toward their children — grew. The more he lost control of his own life, the more furious he became. His physical strength was gone, diminished when he failed to take advantage of physical therapy. Whether he really suffered from cardiac problems or leukemia — which he now claimed to have — Sue didn't know.

His financial empire had collapsed, and his career in law enforcement was over. Always before he had been able to blame Sue for what went wrong in his life. Of course, he still did, but any reprisals against her had to be done from a distance.

Bill had an apartment where he could look down on a strip mall, a shopping area Sue had always frequented. One night, she and Scott had gone to Blockbuster to rent a video, and he apparently spotted her car. Close to midnight, she got a phone call from the Newcastle Police Department, in whose jurisdiction Bill's apartment was located.

"We understand you are harassing your husband," an officer began. "You were stalking him at his apartment."

Sue put Scott on the phone. He volunteered that he and his mother had picked up a movie and then gone straight home, and they hadn't gone to his father's apartment. That seemed to satisfy the police.

Bill next claimed that Sue had phoned him and threatened to kill him on at least two occasions. It was a ridiculous accusation. Sue was doing her best to maintain some kind of stable home for her children, although she knew it was a futile endeavor. They were full of teenage rage, missing the father they had once admired and loved, sometimes blaming her for the breakup of her marriage. Even when they sent him letters blaming him for deserting them, she knew they still loved him.

Sue's neighbors and friends had rallied around her when they witnessed the debacle of Bill's departure from their home after the long standoff with police. Many of them gave statements and depositions about what they had observed in the Jensens' volatile marriage. When he showed up at Scott's or Jenny's games, people turned away from him. Some of them were afraid of him; some were disgusted by his vendetta against his estranged wife.

But almost everyone was concerned about what he might do. John Compatore stood beside Sue, and so did her sister, Carol. But basically she felt alone, stalked by a man who wouldn't let her go, who told anyone who would listen that Sue had ruined his life. "She's almost forced me to become a street person."

It didn't matter that it was Bill who had thrown money away with abandon, most of it Sue's. He wasn't on the street, but he no longer had hundreds of thousands of dollars at his disposal.

On Wednesday night, February 26, 2003,

five days after the late-night phone call from police, Sue was cooking supper at 6:30. She heard a knock on their front door, and she opened it to find several Newcastle Police officers standing there. Thinking that they were responding to her complaint about Bill's violation of the protective order, she invited them in and asked them if they would like a cup of coffee.

"I was walking toward the kitchen," she said, "when they told me to turn around and put my hands behind my back. They had come to arrest me!"

Stunned, with Scott watching, Sue allowed herself to be handcuffed as the officers told her that Bill had reported that she had barged into his apartment, shouting, "I'm going to kill you, you bastard!"

Had this been true, she would have violated the protection order he had obtained against her! The eighteen-year-old girl who was living with him had backed up Bill's accusations, repeating what he told the police as if she had memorized it. Even though the girl had a record of arrests for shoplifting, forgery, and identity theft, her word was good enough to have Sue arrested.

The nightmare was growing more bizarre.

Scott would be alone until Jenny came

home, and Sue was desperately upset at having to leave him, in shock to find herself being put into the backseat of a patrol car. She had gone on some errands at the strip mall near Bill's apartment, but spying on him was the last thing she had any desire to do. She knew she could account for every place she had been that afternoon, but the police told her she would have to go to jail first, and provide that information in the morning.

"Luckily," she said, "we passed Jenny coming home, and they stopped and let me talk to her. She was more upset than I was, but she said she would call my sister and another friend, and see that someone would be at the house all night with them."

It seemed impossible; Sue had feared being killed, but she had never imagined that she would go to jail. But there she was, fingerprinted, mugged, strip-searched, and placed into a cell with other women in the King County Jail.

She didn't sleep all night. In the morning, the prosecutor's office called down to the jail and said, "Get her out of there — now!"

As it happened, Sue could indeed account for every minute of the afternoon of February 26. She had picked Scott up from middle school about 3:20, visited with his tutor until 3:45, purchased a prescription at the Coal Creek Shopping Center at 3:51, and gone to the Safeway supermarket; she had receipts with the times and date stamped on them. She had even run into several friends who remembered talking with her. When she returned home, she'd sent several e-mails, and they, of course, had the time and date on them.

She never had to go to court on the alleged violation of Bill's order of protection against her. But being right and having proof weren't nearly enough to erase the fear that had begun to walk with Sue Jensen everywhere she went. She couldn't sleep, and she broke out in hives.

"Even the dog got hives," she told a friend. "My hands shake so badly that I drop things all the time."

The dog — Sue's beloved Great Dane — was one line of protection for her, about the only thing that allowed Sue to have a few hours of sleep at night.

Sue felt that if she could go forward with her felony–domestic–violence charges against Bill, she might be able to find a modicum of safety. A year earlier she wouldn't have had the nerve. Now she felt as if she had nothing to lose, and she wrote to Norm Maleng, the King County prosecutor, and to the King

County Sheriff's Office asking for help in bringing those charges against Bill.

She contacted Diane Wetendorf, whose national organization helps domestic partners of the small percentage of police officers and firefighters who abuse the power that their careers give them.

Wetendorf's site (www.abuseofpower.info/Wetendorf.htm) has helped many victims who have hidden the domestic abuse they suffer, covering up their stories. Diane Wetendorf's Web site declares its purpose:

Our need to be heard and to be visible
is beginning to overcome
Our fear.
We are breaking our silence.
We are no longer invisible.
We are not alone.

And Sue did feel less alone, but she was no less frightened. Bill had not beaten her down as she knew he'd expected to do. She was on the offensive and that was infinitely dangerous. She didn't want anything more than she had wanted in the beginning — only to be free, and to have enough of their family's assets so she could take care of Scott and Jenny. But she knew instinctively that she couldn't back down. Bill wouldn't go away.

He would bide his time, and then he would kill her.

He had made that dread promise to her when he drew his finger across his neck, and when he told her she would go to her grave.

Sue was getting pledges of support from the prosecutor, the sheriff, the county executive — but none of them seemed aware of the urgency she felt. She feared she might well be dead before those assurances were put into play.

And then tragedy struck — a city away, a county away — to another woman who had tried in vain to divorce her policeman husband. The scenario was so familiar to Sue Jensen, it might well have been *her* story.

Crystal Brame was thirty-five, the lovely young wife of David Brame, the chief of police in Tacoma, Washington. The Brames had a son and a daughter, and in television coverage of Chief Brame's activities, Crystal always appeared to be gazing at her husband with pride and love. But in truth, she had been living a life of desperate captivity, adhering to a positive public image under her husband's orders, but held hostage in a marriage where she had no freedom at all. David Brame kept track of every single move Crystal made. He even made her weigh herself in front of him, warning her she must not get fat. She wasn't even allowed to talk with her neighbors.

Brame was so obsessed with controlling his wife that Crystal had reached a point where she could no longer stand to remain in her marriage.

When she asked for a divorce, she had written her own death warrant. She had been warned, but with the help of a counselor and her family, she was trying to break free. When Crystal Brame wanted to leave, David Brame had followed her, choked her, threatened her life. He had warned her that he hadn't even begun to punish her and that she hadn't seen anything yet.

On April 26, 2003, Crystal and the Brames' two young children were in a shopping mall parking lot in Gig Harbor, where they lived. Crystal had spotted the Tacoma Police vehicle following her, and recognized her estranged husband. She didn't have a chance. In front of horrified onlookers, David Brame shot his wife in the head with his department-issued handgun. And then he committed suicide, with a bullet to his own head.

Their children were witnesses to the tragedy. Crystal Brame clung to life for seven days, and then she, too, died. Her death shook Washington residents, and there were outcries demanding to know why someone hadn't foreseen David Brame's dangerousness and done something before it was too late. Eventually, heads rolled in Tacoma city government.

But Crystal Brame was still dead.

Sue Jensen grieved for Crystal Brame and truly understood what it was like to have walked in the same shoes. She felt ice in her veins as she believed she was glimpsing her own future. There should have been some way for Crystal to protect herself, but there wasn't. And there was no way for Sue to save herself.

Every wall she put up had collapsed. Restraining orders were, in the end, useless when she was alone. She couldn't be alert all the time. If Bill intended to kill her, she knew, he would find a way. What sleep she did find was permeated with horrible nightmares. Bill had told Jenny that her mother and her aunt Carol "deserved to die." He had warned Scott that he would probably have to grow up without either of his parents, hinting broadly that they would both be dead.

There was death all around her, and Sue could no longer see a way out.

Sue's attorney, John Compatore, was getting under Bill's skin, and so he too became a target. Bill threatened him with violent reprisal. Compatore lived in a quiet neighborhood, a low-crime area. Sometime in April 2003, the tires on his wife's car went flat after she'd driven only a block from their garage. On inspection, Compatore found nails had penetrated the side walls. He knew the garage floor was perfectly clean and there were no nails there. A month or so later, her tire went flat again. Again, there was a nail in it. Compatore detected signs shortly afterward that indicated someone had attempted to burglarize his home.

Compatore wrote to county authorities, echoing Sue's fears: "I am a retired police officer and I know that Bill Jensen is a dangerous man. I would trust implicitly what Susan Jensen can tell you about her husband."

After wading through a morass of delays, postponements, and roadblocks Bill Jensen had thrown up to stop Sue from getting a divorce, even Compatore began to wonder if Bill would ever be convicted for any of his acts of harassment.

Jensen had now threatened Sue and both of her attorneys. He had gone through five attorneys himself, scaring them away when they learned of his harassment and when he lied to them consistently. He had told at least two witnesses that he understood how someone could "go postal."

It was May 2003, and Sue feared that even her death might not be enough to satisfy Bill's rage. "Going postal" was a term that suggested an episode of mass murder. She wondered if it would take a bloodbath of major-headline proportions to satisfy Bill.

There was a warrant out for Bill's arrest for threatening John Compatore, but once again, no one could find Bill. He wasn't living in his apartment. He was supposed to appear in court on May 22, but he didn't show up. His father had put up his house for Bill's bail in his earlier arrest, and risked losing it now.

It was more frightening, somehow, not to know where Bill was. On her lawyer's advice, Sue left town for the weekend. If Bill should have to go to jail, he would be so angry. He was making more threats to any number of people, many of them perfect strangers. When a hospital pharmacist refused to refill one of Bill's pain medications, even he became the target for a veiled warning.

Sue froze as she saw a stranger lurking across the street from her house. "I was sure it was a hit man," she said. "And I knew that I couldn't make it into my house as he started toward me. My legs wouldn't move. I was actually relieved when he held out his hand, and it was only an order of protection that Bill had filed against me."

Sue waited for the other, probably fatal, shoe to drop.

Jenny was going to graduate from high school on June 18, 2003, and the ceremonies would be held in the Hec Edmondson Pavilion at the University of Washington. All the girls who had been on the teams Bill had coached since Jenny was five would be graduating too. They had become the focus of some of Bill's rage. Sue knew Bill felt betrayed by both the parents and the team members — none of whom were friendly to him any longer when he occasionally showed up at games.

It was true that Bill's bizarre behavior had stamped him as a pariah in his old neighborhood, and he had often complained how bitter he was about their lack of gratitude for all he had done for his teams. He had volunteered his time coaching them, but nobody appreciated him or gave him credit for all he had done, and he resented them mightily.

Jenny's approaching graduation ceremony frightened Sue more than anything. She knew that Bill planned to attend, and it seemed like a venue where he might, indeed, "go postal."

Something was going to happen, but Sue didn't know when or what it would be.

THREE
A DEADLY CONSPIRACY

With the help of Assistant District Attorney Kathryn Kim in the King County prosecutor's Domestic Violence Unit, Sue pursued her attempts to have Bill go to trial for felony harassment and for his violations of the no-contact order. Yet no one involved felt that charges against Bill would stick. Despite her police record, the young woman who lived with him was considered a credible witness. If Bill went to jail, as an ex–police officer he would be in great danger, another reason he might not be prosecuted as vigorously as an ordinary person on the street. Despite what had happened in the Brame case, Bill Jensen tended to come across as no more than an irritating, mean-spirited, and petulant man who was trying to make his wife miserable, which is not, technically, a crime.

The woods — and the divorce courts — were full of men like that. Even with all of the guns he had, he himself didn't seem capable of real violence. Except for the 2001 arbitration meeting with Sue and her attorney, Bill hadn't come near Sue. He had manipulated bank accounts, stocks, and vehicles, and had misused credit cards, but he hadn't hurt her physically since she'd asked him to leave.

Bill Jensen now weighed over four hundred pounds, and — according to him — he had a bad knee, a bad back, diabetes, chronic fatigue syndrome, depression, hypertension, cardiac problems, festering skin infections, and cancer. He was broke and had no means of support other than his disability payments. He cried to anyone who would listen that his wife was very wealthy.

On May 1, 2003, Jensen described his predicament. "She has used her wealth and 'strength' to put me out on the street and nearly caused me to become a 'street person.' Mrs. Jensen clearly decided she no longer wanted to live with a disabled man suffering from leukemia," he wrote in an attempt to have John Compatore censured by the Washington State Bar for unprofessional conduct.

"So she threw me out on the street in June 2001. . . . Ms. Jensen has so flagrantly lied, put on a charade and air[ed] — to everyone . . . her attorneys, judges, prosecutors, family, friends, and our children that I am some sort of drug addicted and violent man. This I am *not*."

How dangerous could he actually be? And where was he?

The general feeling was that Bill Jensen had gone underground in Las Vegas, hiding there to avoid arrest. It had been his habit to run to Nevada whenever he felt he was going to be in trouble with court orders.

But he could not hide forever. When he came back to the Bellevue area, Bill Jensen was arrested and booked into the King County Jail. It was May 29, 2003. As an ex-cop, he was housed in a maximum security section of the jail — administrative segregation — or as prisoners called it, "the Hole." It was a pod of cells earmarked for those who needed to be in protective custody or who might be a danger to others. In one of the C tanks on the eleventh floor, each man was housed in a single cell, and was allowed out into the dayroom area — alone — for only an hour a day.

This time, Bill Jensen didn't bail out; he had used up his own money, and his father, who was now in his eighties, no longer wanted to risk losing his home. Bill's latest attorney told him he would probably be in jail until the end of July, when his case would come to court.

At first, those who feared what Bill might do next heaved a sigh of relief. Sue didn't have to worry about something awful happening at Jenny's graduation ceremonies; her father wouldn't be able to attend. Their family and friends had a happy celebration, cheering as Jenny received her diploma.

It was only a short respite, but even that was welcome. And yet, with this slight cessation of anxiety, Sue began to question herself, wondering if she had tried hard enough to preserve her marriage. Was there something more she could have done to make it possible for Jenny and Scott to have a father? When she read the Bible, the words seemed to say that divorce was wrong. She had always been a woman who tried to do the right thing, and, although she never wanted to live with Bill Jensen again, she felt a little sorry for him, locked up in jail.

She was on the teeter-totter of emotions that so many battered women experience. Her attorney and her closest friends rushed to validate her bravery in following through with Bill's arrest. They would not allow her to slip back into the way she had always rationalized the bad times in her marriage — by shoving abuse, intimidation, and blame far back into her unconscious mind.

Women who have never been the object of

domestic violence roll their eyes when they hear that Sue had even a moment's doubt, but women who have been there understand her ambivalence.

She turned to Diane Wetendorf's site for help in dealing with this next escalation of her long, long divorce action. Bill would be out of jail soon enough, and she read that she had to be ready — to hide, to run, to testify against him, if necessary. Told that Scott and Jenny would probably have to be interviewed — and perhaps even testify — her heart sank. Sue had hoped they wouldn't be drawn into this tangle any more than they had been.

Sue's fear came back, blooming stronger than ever. She had a safety plan, but when she studied domestic violence cases, particularly cases involving police officers, she realized it was very rare for those convicted to receive more than token sentences.

"I am afraid," she said, "that without further assistance, short of having to disappear, I will most likely be targeted by my husband as soon as he is released. I know Bill well enough to know . . . that he would eventually find me."

The other prisoners in Bill Jensen's jail tank didn't know who he was, and he certainly didn't tell them he had been a cop for twenty years. Those in neighboring cells were mostly gang members, white supremacists, career criminals, and angry men who were known to start fights in jail. Bill could be very likable when he tried, and he got along with the men in other cells.

All jail inmates complain about something — their "old ladies," the food, cops, their attorneys. Bill waited until he understood the dynamics in his pod of cells, and then he confided that he'd been "screwed over" by a woman in his life.

It wasn't as if the pod inhabitants were all sitting around the tables in the dayroom; only one of them could be out at a time. But their cells were close enough together that they could carry on conversations, and the man who was out of his cell for his hour could stop by and visit all the other prisoners. They could trade candy bars, envelopes, items needed in their segregated world.

Part of the mystique of being in jail or prison is the challenge to put something over on corrections officers. Notes are smuggled, or whispers are passed from one cell to another until messages get to the intended recipient. Most of the men in Bill Jensen's pod were repeat offenders, and adept at evaluating new guys. They listened now to Jensen and saw that he was highly disturbed about situations he couldn't attend to while he was locked up.

The rumor in the tank was that Jensen had money — possibly big money — but he was playing things close to his vest.

Yancy Carrothers* was a "frequent flyer" in the King County Jail. Indeed, he felt as much at home in jail as he did anywhere else, and didn't really mind being arrested again and again. Yancy was proud to be known as a kind of career criminal, and often bragged that he'd been trained by his father to be an above-average practitioner of crime from the time he was a child. He took pride in the fact that he knew most of the guards in the jail as well as the inmate "regulars." Yancy knew which prisoners were important in their gangs, who was planning an escape, and what the messages circulating in the tank were about. He knew how to send "kites" (notes) to jail management in a discreet manner.

Yancy had a long, long rap sheet. He had numerous convictions for VUCSA (violation of uniformed controlled substance abuse — drugs), drunkenness, and assault. He liked to hint that he had been involved in far more violent felonies, although he stopped short of spelling out the details.

Yancy Carrothers was nearing middle age, and his craggy face was marked by the indulgences he'd chosen. He looked somewhat older than he really was. He was as rail-thin as Bill Jensen was overweight, about five feet ten, with dark, longish hair. A man full of nervous mannerisms, he was smart and streetwise, and he let it be known to his fellow prisoners that he would do almost anything for money — or for drugs.

Whenever Yancy Carrothers went to jail, he invariably ended up in the protective custody tank; he had a reputation for starting fights in jail, and the jail supervisors didn't bother putting him in with the general population, knowing that, inevitably, there would be a fight with Yancy in the middle of it.

He himself wasn't sure why he tended to hit other prisoners in jail, but there was something about the county jail that made him want to fight. He may have known the reason very well: whenever he came into jail it was fresh off an arrest for being drunk or high on drugs, and in that state he was quite combative. He claimed to be a "pussycat" by the time he got to prison after weeks or months in jail. He hadn't had a drink or drugs for some time, so he wasn't inclined to fight.

Despite his awesome number of arrests

and his tendency to act first and think later, Yancy had a sentimental side. He had lost the woman he loved, and even though they'd never married, he considered himself a widower.

On June 17, 2003, Yancy Carrothers found himself in the same protective custody tank as Bill Jensen: North 11, Lower B Housing Unit. There weren't many white prisoners there at the time, and he felt that drew them together initially.

Among his other talents, Yancy was an artist. He drew portraits and animals, and he was pretty good. Occasionally he decorated envelopes for other prisoners in exchange for favors, and sometimes he just passed the time in his cell by sketching.

Yancy was aware of the big man named Bill who waddled painfully around the dayroom, but he waited — as always — for the stranger to approach him. Bill was out in the day area for his hour of comparative freedom when he stopped outside Yancy's cell and began a conversation. They touched lightly on a number of subjects, feeling each other out.

Yancy considered himself something of an expert on the law, and they spoke a little about the justice system. He didn't know what Bill was in jail for, but the massive guy seemed to have some knowledge of different statutes, and he also talked as if he was pretty smart. Yancy could identify with that; he'd always known he was very intelligent, too, and capable of thinking way ahead of most people he dealt with.

Neither man gave away much information, waiting for the other to go beyond idle chatting. They danced around like two boxers waiting to get in the first jab. Yancy was savvy about evaluating people, and he was in his element. He knew all the ropes.

Bill had to be in "ad seg" for some reason, although Yancy wasn't sure what it was. He didn't look gay, one of the reasons prisoners ended up in this tank. Yancy had never run into Bill before, so he figured that the guy might be a protected witness from out of state, wanted by the Feds, or some kind of known troublemaker. That didn't seem likely; he was too fat to be any threat in a fight. Maybe that was why he was in protective custody; in the general population, any guy who weighed at least four hundred pounds would be a target of harassment and teasing by other prisoners.

The two prisoners got in the habit of stopping by each other's cells when their free hour came around. Bill told Yancy that he'd heard he was a "stand-up guy."

"Who told you that?" Yancy asked.

Bill jerked his head toward a cell where a prisoner dressed in the white uniform of an "ultra security" inmate — a gang leader — was housed.

Yancy nodded as Bill went back to his own cell.

There weren't that many secrets in their tank because the men there could hear one another's conversations, even though they couldn't always see who was talking. Yancy had heard Bill complaining about how much stress he was under, and all the problems he had. At first, he complained about his financial troubles, but then he said his wife was the one who had caused them. He wasn't that different from anyone else in the King County Jail; a lot of prisoners had worries about the women in their lives, and the majority of them blamed their incarceration on someone else. And for the moment, none of them could exert much control over anyone else, although the gang leaders had a certain cachet, even locked up in jail.

At the time Yancy Carrothers and Bill Jensen were locked up in the tank on the eleventh floor, there were, as Yancy referred to them, "a couple of other gentlemen — M.O.G. Gangsters: Crips, Bloods, B.G.'s."

One of them was awaiting trial for the

cold-blooded murder of a young police officer in a small King County town. When he was asked for his ID, the gang member had pulled out a gun instead. Fortunately for Bill Jensen, none of the gang members had the slightest idea he'd been a cop for twenty years.

Yancy himself told Bill that he had once been in the upper echelon of a lesser-known gang: the Kings.

"They all know me — all the guys in here," Yancy bragged to Bill as he polished his own image the next time they talked. "They'll vouch for me. Maybe I can help you with your problems if you told me what they are?"

Bill studied him for a moment or so, evaluating what he said.

"Well . . . let me think about it."

"If you need any more recommendations, you can ask more of the guys here."

Yancy sauntered off to take his shower. He wasn't averse to doing almost anything if the price was right. He'd be out on the street soon, in contact with his backup people, able to help the fat guy with whatever was bothering him. He didn't know if the guy really had any money. He didn't look like he did, but you never could tell — even though he was pissing and moaning about having money troubles. The guy didn't have any visitors, and didn't seem to be getting mail either.

Yancy was prepared to wait, and let the guy dangle. Experience had taught him not to be too eager to make a deal.

Sue Jensen and her sister, Carol Harris, were going to have to face Bill in court; every defendant has the right to face his accuser. The date of the first hearing after Bill's arrest was set: July 28, 2003. They both dreaded it, and more than that, they hoped devoutly that neither Jenny nor Scott would have to appear.

Bill was in jail, and it didn't appear that he would be bailing out before their court date. That gave Sue a little sense of security, but she still jumped at sounds in the night, and often stared into her rearview mirror to watch cars that had taken what seemed like too many of the same turns that she had. She had a burglar alarm, a gun, and her dog. She tried not to hover over her children and let them have as near a normal life as she could. They were very angry with her for sending their father to jail.

She understood that.

The fourth of July came and went, and Yancy Carrothers and Bill Jensen spent quite a bit of time talking to each other for the two hours each day one or the other was out of his cell. They appeared to be becoming good friends, although friendships forged in jail are by their very nature not destined to last. The choice of companionship is limited behind bars, and most prisoners go their own way when they get out.

Bill even purchased one of Yancy's artistic efforts to write to his children, an envelope with a beautiful long-stemmed red rose on the front.

Yancy was released on July 10, and he had prospects he didn't have before he met Bill Jensen. He was armed with a phone number that belonged to a woman who lived near Bremerton, Washington. Bill had given it to him; it belonged to Bill's older sister Iris.

Within an hour of his walking out of the King County Jail, Yancy Carrothers called Iris. She was expecting his call, but she waited until he gave her an agreed-upon password: "Flying Kings."

He and Bill came up with that, honoring the gang that Yancy had once belonged to.

"Oh, yes," she responded, "Bill told me you would be calling. I was wondering why you didn't call me last night."

"I didn't get a midnight release, like I thought I was going to. I just got out."

Iris Pate and Yancy Carrothers discussed when and where they would meet. She understood she was to give him some money — $2,500. Bill had told her that it was for his bail, and since she now held her brother's power of attorney, she was in a position to give the cash to the friend he had specified.

They decided that Iris would come across Puget Sound from Kitsap County on the ferry, an hour's ride, and Yancy would meet her at the ferry dock. He told her what he looked like, and she described herself.

Once Yancy had the money, he knew what he was supposed to do next. It had to be accomplished in less than two weeks. Bill had stressed that the timing was vital. He wanted his problems solved before July 28. And if things worked out as he had choreographed his plan, there would be more money for Yancy — a lot more money.

Yancy met Bill's sister at the ferry, counted the bills she gave him, bought her a Starbucks latte, and waved at her as she reboarded the ferry for its return run to Bremerton, completely unaware of what the cash was for.

On July 23, Sue and Scott Jensen were home alone shortly after 9 P.M. Summer evenings in Seattle yawn on endlessly, but it was almost fully dark now.

She jumped when the phone rang. The male voice on the other end of the line said he was a Seattle Police detective. He told her that it was a matter of urgency for him to talk with her, and asked directions to her house. Without thinking, she gave him the address and driving directions.

As soon as she hung up, Sue berated herself for being so gullible. How did she know it was really a detective who had called? It could be a setup, and she realized she had practically rolled out the red carpet for a stranger.

When she heard someone knocking on her door, she sent Scott out to the back door with a cell phone, telling him that if she shouted "Go!" he was to dial 911 and then run to their neighbors.

This was the way they lived now.

Sue peered nervously through her drapes; she could see an unmarked car in front of her house, and a big man dressed in street clothes standing outside her door. He identified himself, but she didn't trust him.

"Hold up your identification," she instructed. "I need to be sure who you are."

He held up his badge and his police identification, and she opened the door and let him in. She had never seen him before.

He explained that he was a Homicide detective, not from King County, but from the Seattle Police Department. Half expecting him to slap handcuffs on her for some further complaint of Bill's, she invited him to sit down.

"Mrs. Jensen," he began, "my name is Cloyd Steiger. I wanted to talk to you in person, and as soon as I could."

She waited, her heart thumping. Either Bill was dead or maybe something a lot worse had happened.

Steiger seemed to be a kind man as he questioned her about her marriage and her upcoming divorce. He told Sue he needed to validate information he'd received a few hours earlier. The source of this intelligence was a little suspect, but it had had the ring of truth to it.

Sue gave the detective a rundown of the chaos in her life over the past few years, and he nodded. He had heard enough to go ahead with what he needed to tell her.

"I want you to pack and get out of here as soon as you can. We think someone is going to try to kill you."

Strangely, or perhaps not so strangely, she wasn't even shocked. She had known that she was a target for almost two years, and it was almost a relief to have it finally happen.

"It was Bill, wasn't it?" she asked.

"We think so."

"I know he wants to kill me," Sue said slowly. "I knew he would do it. I even went to the *King County Journal* editor back in February and told him that if I ended up dead, Bill would be behind it."

Cloyd Steiger told Sue that the Seattle Homicide Unit had reason to believe that a plot was in place to accomplish her murder. But it wasn't just her death a contract called for.

"What do you mean?"

"Your sister is on the list, too," Steiger said quietly, waiting for that news to sink in before he went on.

"My sister?"

"Your sister . . . and your daughter, Jenny —"

"Not my daughter!"

Sue had been afraid that Bill might hurt her dog, and even that he might do something to her sister because he knew how much Carol meant to her.

"I knew he'd look for a way to get under my skin, and hurt me the most," Sue said, almost to herself. "And I realize he's angry enough to just do away with me — but I never *dreamed* that he would want the kids dead!"

"I want you to find your kids, tell them to pack what they need for a couple of days, and leave here," Steiger said. "Get a hotel — a motel. Stay with friends or relatives. But you have to get away from your house."

Sue was stunned. She still couldn't comprehend that Bill would hurt their children. She simply could not visualize that Bill would do anything to either Jenny or Scott. She wondered if Cloyd Steiger had gotten some kind of garbled message.

He shook his head. "All three of you," he repeated. "You can't tell anyone but your sister. Don't tell your children. Make up some excuse about why you have to get out of here, but we can't take a chance that your kids might tell someone."

Steiger told Sue that he was working with someone who had instigated an investigation into a murder-for-hire plot, but he couldn't tell her who it was. He had only found out himself hours before, and although they were working as fast as they could, his team didn't know all the facts yet. They knew of a couple of people who might be involved, but there was the possibility that the person who wanted her family dead had hired additional people.

As soon as the Seattle detective left her house, Sue called her daughter. Jenny was out with friends, and when Sue reached her and told her that it would be better if she didn't come home for a few days, that it would be a good idea if she stayed at her best friend's house, her daughter thought she had gone nuts.

"But it was safer for her to stay away from us," Sue said. "I let her think I was acting wacko; it would keep her from asking me questions I couldn't answer."

Scott didn't know what was wrong, but he quickly caught his mother's fear. He didn't resist when she told him they had to leave their house right away.

Both Scott and Jenny had been angry with Sue most of the summer, still halfway loyal to their father and sorry for him because he was in jail. Now she was once again interrupting their attempts to have fun. But she was adamant when she told Jenny not to come home and Scott to cancel his plans with his friends.

Sue, Scott, and their Great Dane, Goliath, were in their car in no time. She called John Compatore on her cell phone, and he told her to drive to someplace out in public like the nearby strip mall or a theater while he called to verify that Cloyd Steiger actually *was* a Homicide detective with the Seattle Police Department. Someone had been stalking both Sue and her attorney, and neither accepted strangers at face value. Sue's instincts told her to trust Steiger, but she no longer believed in her own perception.

In her car, Sue called her sister and told her with code words that they were all in danger, and needed to leave their homes. Scott was sitting next to Sue when she did that, and she couldn't come right out and tell Carol what was wrong. Luckily, the two sisters understood each other so well that Carol caught on right away.

They discussed getting on a plane. But where would they go? Maybe, they debated, they should go in different directions, to throw off anyone who might be following them. Sue's adrenaline was coursing through her veins and the darkness beyond the lights of the mall seemed to hide watching eyes.

Compatore called to say that Cloyd Steiger was who he said he was, and that was slight comfort. Only slight.

Sue called around to try to find rooms in a motel — and hoped she could take their dog, too. Sneaking a Great Dane into a motel or hotel wouldn't be nearly as easy as if they had a poodle or a Pomeranian. As it turned out, it didn't matter; there *were* no motel rooms available. Seattle's Seafair celebration had just begun, and thousands of tourists were in the city to enjoy it, filling hotels and motels located within a thirty-mile radius of Seattle.

It was after 1 A.M. Everyone was exhausted and it looked as though they had no choice but for Sue and Scott to move into Carol's house; that wasn't an ideal solution, but at least it was away from their house. From what Cloyd Steiger had told Sue, it sounded as though someone knew exactly where she, Jenny, and Scott lived, what cars they drove, almost everything about them.

Someone could be outside in the trees watching their house right now, waiting for Sue and Scott to come back home to take a bead on them with a high-powered rifle as they got out of their car. No, they couldn't go home.

Sue wished that she could tell Scott and Jenny what was going on. If she could, they wouldn't be giving her such a hard time. They probably believed she'd really gone crazy.

It might have been easier if she had.

Yancy Carrothers had enjoyed his freedom for a very short time. He had accomplished some of the items on his mental "to do" list, but he drank too much one night and found himself back in the King County Jail. Once there, he was gripped by anxiety, and he made a number of attempts to get a letter to Bill Jensen, and sent kites out to someone he had worked with before. Yancy also tried to place a number of collect phone calls — the only way jail prisoners can call out.

At last he had connected.

On July 24, Bill Jensen had an unexpected visitor. A very attractive young black woman named Lisa was waiting for him in the visiting area. She had a great body, and her hair was done in an intricate series of cornrows.

Jensen walked to Stall 4 and sat down; Lisa took a seat opposite him, and they each picked up a phone on their sides of the glass partition.

"Hi," she said, smiling. "I'm Lisa."

"Hi, I'm William. Nice to meet you."

Lisa explained that "Y" was in jail again because he'd been arrested for failing to check in with his probation officer.

"Oh," Bill Jensen said, looking somewhat relieved. "I thought I got scammed. Is he in here now?"

She quickly explained that he was, but that it wasn't because of any trouble about Bill's "business" transaction with him.

"Good. I didn't know what happened. I thought everything went sideways."

Lisa shook her head slightly and then discreetly removed a white envelope from her bra, opened it, and removed a sheet of yellow legal paper. She held the bottom quarter of it up to the glass partition so Bill could read it. It was a letter of introduction from Yancy. As he read, Lisa saw a corrections officer heading toward them, and she grabbed the note and hid it between her legs. She made small talk until the guard moved on, and then put the note up to the glass again.

Bill read swiftly, and then said, "Okay, I got it."

Lisa tore the note into small pieces, put it back in the envelope, and sealed it.

"Good, good," Bill said, satisfied that Yancy had sent her.

"You supposed to sign out a prescription and some pills from your property to me?" Lisa asked.

"Oh shit," he stammered. "I can't do it. I thought I got scammed, and my sister came and got all my property."

"What's the message for Y?" she asked.

"Okay. Let me think. Let me think. Okay, tell him it's a go."

Lisa told him she was concerned that the pain pills were gone. Y's brother wanted the pills to do his part of the plan. "Can't you get them from your sister?"

"No — there's not any way — not without raising suspicions. Just tell him it's a go."

Lisa explained that Y had a different visitor's day, and she wouldn't be seeing him today to tell him that Bill hadn't come through with his part of the deal.

"I can have the other half of the money by the fourteenth," he promised.

She told him that Yancy didn't go for people changing plans on him. She ticked off the instructions Bill had for Yancy on her fingertips, asking, "Anything else?"

"Yeah. Tell him it has to be done by the first because my trial starts the fourth or fifth of August."

Lisa seemed very concerned that she had all Bill's orders memorized, and she asked him to repeat them several times.

He nodded, and then added, "Just tell him that I don't have the money now because I thought I got scammed. I let my sister use the money to pay bills. He'll understand. I won't have the money as soon as he wants it, but it's guaranteed. [Tell him,] just go ahead and do it."

She seemed to have the message all straight, and Lisa explained that Y wanted her to come see him on Saturday, July 26, but she said that she probably wouldn't be able to come back to see Bill until Thursday, July 31.

That would be cutting it close for his timeline, but he nodded.

"Did you have to sign in to see me?" Bill asked, almost as an afterthought.

"Yes," she said. "But signing in wasn't a problem. I used my sister's name. Anything else you want me to tell Y?"

"Yeah, tell him good luck."

"How will you know it's done?" Lisa asked. "I have to come back and let you know when it's done?"

"Just tell him to do it — and I'll know. I'll get the message when it's done."

"Okay. 'Bye. See you later!"

"Thank you. Nice meeting you. 'Bye."

Lisa *was* able to come back in to see Bill Jensen on Saturday, July 26. He seemed far more at ease with her on her second visit. She told him she had received a letter from Yancy. He wasn't going to get out of jail until the fourth, and that would be too late to do the job Bill wanted.

"So everything that he wants us to do is just going to be me, and his brother."

That seemed to alarm Bill Jensen. He explained that his sister was getting suspicious because she'd called Yancy's phone and it was disconnected. She'd spent some of the money he owed Yancy. He thought it might be better if he paid Yancy the other half himself after he got out of jail. He didn't

145

even know how much money was left.

Lisa asked Bill where he was getting the money. Did Yancy know?

"Yeah, he knows."

Lisa asked him when "they" would be together. She meant Sue and her sister, but she didn't want to say it aloud. "The only time you think they will absolutely be together is Monday — before court?"

"Yeah."

Bill was nervous, and said he wondered if the jail phones were recording their conversation.

"Nah," Lisa said. "I've been in jail a bunch of times. They're old. They're not recording."

"They're not?"

"They don't — they hardly fucking work."

Bill seemed to relax when she reassured him. He repeated that the two women would be coming to the pretrial hearing together on July 28.

"Do you know where they're going to be?" she asked.

"Well, I know the one will be coming down from Kirkland, the sister-in-law."

"And will she go by and get your wife?"

"Probably."

"They going to have anybody with them?"

"They're just going to be the two of them, probably."

"Okay. Where is your daughter going to be?"

"She's probably going to be home."

"At your house?"

"Yeah."

"So if we catch them at the house, leaving, we can get your daughter too?"

"Probably. Now, the son will probably be in there, too."

Lisa sounded surprised. "Oh, I didn't know you had a son."

"Yeah."

"Wait a minute," she said, flustered. "I'm confused. Well, I ain't — nobody mentioned no son to me."

Bill hastened to explain that his son would be no problem for them. He was only fifteen.

"Is he big?" Lisa asked suspiciously.

Bill assured Lisa that Scott wasn't a huge teenage football player type, and wouldn't give them any trouble. It probably wouldn't be difficult for Lisa and Yancy's brother working together to overcome him.

Now Bill Jensen described his sister-in-law's blue Volkswagen, and Sue's 1988 Mustang convertible, but when Lisa asked how to get to his family's house, he looked worried. He had been in jail for two months, and he'd noticed that the address had been left off when he'd been served with the last protection order. He mused aloud that Sue might have sold the house and moved.

"Can she sell it without you?"

"Yeah — it's a long story but she's got full ownership right now."

"Can your sister find out if she's still living in it? Does your wife talk to your sister?"

"No. If she did move, she wouldn't want me to know about it, anyway. Like — *where*."

"What's your wife look like?"

Bill Jensen described Sue and then Carol, giving their height, weight, hair color, age. His voice was as calm as if he was telling a salesclerk about them as he bought a present of clothes.

Lisa repeated the car descriptions. And then she asked about Jenny. "Your baby got a car?"

"I don't think so."

She asked about his son. "You don't want nothing to happen to your son, right?"

"Not particularly — no, not particularly."

"All right, we can leave him then? If we can get them away, even if we have to, like, you know, tie him up, knock him out — something — but we can leave him there?"

"Yeah."

"What if something happens to him?" Lisa asked.

"Oh well."

"Oh *well?*" For a moment, Lisa's world-weary attitude faltered, and then she nodded. "All right."

She could tell that Bill Jensen was calmly prepared to see his whole family gone. Now he warned her that Sue wore an alarm button on a chain around her neck. If she activated it, it would call the Bellevue Police.

Lisa asked Bill to tell her both addresses, reminding him that she had to memorize them until she walked out of the building. She didn't want the jail guards to see her writing anything down. She repeated the addresses over and over.

Next, Bill described what the house in Newport Hills looked like, including the seventy-foot sequoia tree in the front yard.

Finally impatient, Bill reminded Lisa that Yancy had all that information already.

"I know," she said, "but he ain't out."

She was getting antsy, even though Yancy had reassured her it would be easy. "He keeps telling me on the phone, 'You can take care of this. You can do this. This ain't going to be hard. They ain't going to put up a fight — '"

"Yeah . . . yeah," Bill interrupted, eager to

calm her down. It looked like it was going to be Lisa and some guy — probably Yancy's brother — who would carry out his instructions.

"How old is your daughter? What's she look like?"

"She's eighteen."

"Jenny."

"Jenny, all right. Jenny. Sue. Carol.

"She's pretty," Bill said about his daughter. "Kind of light brown hair. About five seven, five eight. And she's in good shape. Athlete . . . Basketball, softball — she's a good athlete."

Lisa asked Bill if he wanted her to take his family away from the house.

"Yeah. I was hoping that — well, he [Yancy] was going to try to make it look like it was an accident, but —"

"All right, that's cool. So we ain't trying to make it look like they just packed up and left, and you gotta wait. They ain't nobody heard from them?"

"Right."

Bill admitted he was nervous getting so many people involved, knowing what was going to happen. Lisa reminded him there were only three — Yancy, herself, and Yancy's brother. As far as she was concerned, she was going back east with her kids, using fake

ID, and would be long gone. She wouldn't be talking to anyone.

Bill assured her that there would be "big, big dollars," although Yancy knew that they would have to wait on that. "It's all going to come through, you know, the estate process. You know what I'm saying?"

They had talked for a long time, speaking through the glass with phones held to their ears. Whenever Lisa mentioned money — $2,500 that Bill was apparently supposed to give to Yancy before August 4 — Bill returned to how chagrined he was that ten days had gone by after Yancy bailed out before Lisa showed up. He had felt like a patsy, like someone had duped him. Although that seemed to have little to do with the money Yancy wanted now, Bill Jensen kept repeating his grievances.

Lisa said she owed Yancy because he'd been cool with her when she was down on her luck. "He tells me, 'This is going to work,' and I'm cool with that. I ain't asking for no money. But I don't know you from Adam's house cat."

What was she supposed to tell Yancy? Was she supposed to say he had to wait for "the big money"?

"Right."

Bill told Lisa that his sister had had the

second payment all ready to give Yancy — $2,500 — that she'd been Johnny-on-the-spot, but Yancy hadn't shown up. So it was his own fault that he didn't have that money.

"I don't want any more suspicions from my sister," he cautioned.

"We need someplace to stay," Lisa argued. "I'm giving up my apartment. If we do this by the first, I don't want to be there."

Of course she and Yancy needed to have a car. There were other expenses to be paid.

Bill insisted that he didn't know how much money his sister still had after the bills he'd told her to pay. "She may have maybe only $500 or $700 left. I don't know."

"Are you going to be able to get more?" Lisa pressed. "'Cause when we do this, we gotta *go!* I can't see us staying around."

"No, I understand." Bill soothed her. "I explained to him that when this was done, there's a shitload of money in each estate that should roll my way, but I don't know how long it's going to take to get that out. It's all a legal process . . . but it's all there. You see what I'm saying?"

She did, but Lisa kept asking Bill Jensen questions. And he was apparently so anxious to have his wife, daughter, and sister-in-law dead within the next week that he was willing to explain in detail just how much money he would receive from their estates.

"The house is paid for — it's a $400,000 house with no debt on it."

She seemed to be impressed, and she wondered how he'd made that much money being a "computer geek."

"I did okay," he said succinctly.

Bill admitted that he was a little worried that his wife might have rewritten some documents that would make everything roll to his son.

"You want us to get him too?" she asked again.

"Well, it's a possibility. Yeah."

"Yancy doesn't do minors."

"I wouldn't *want* to hurt him, but —"

But there it was. Bill Jensen didn't want anyone between himself and what he estimated was Sue's and Carol's million-dollar fortune, and he realized now that his son would probably stand ahead of him in the money line.

Lisa assured him that Yancy would be "pissed" to hear that Scott was now part of the hit. He wouldn't want to kill a boy.

Bill had come to a decision. It had to be all four of his relatives. There wasn't anyone else who would prevail over him when the estates were probated. Even if Yancy didn't like it, he instructed Lisa: "Well, my suggestion then . . . is, *Clean house.*"

Although he spoke cryptically, she knew what he meant.

Bill had promised Yancy $100,000 and he was now willing to add a $50,000 bonus if everything went right.

Lisa countered with $50,000 per person, $200,000 for all four.

Bill disagreed, saying that he had heard the going rate for hits was $20,000 to $30,000 per person.

She wondered how he knew that, but she told him he would have to work it out with Yancy. That wasn't her department.

Bill was still worried that something might go wrong, and if it did, he told Lisa, she and Yancy and the other man had to promise to keep their mouths shut.

"I'm gone," Lisa said. "You don't know me. My real name ain't on nothing I been using. Everybody's on their own. That's the kind of people we are."

"Just make it look like an accident," Bill Jensen said, "if you can."

"All right. Got it."

"Okay."

And she had, indeed, "got it." Lisa, AKA Seattle Police detective Sharon Stevens, walked back to the Homicide Unit with a crystal-clear recording of her conversation with Bill Jensen.

Jensen himself returned to his cell, pleased that he had managed to carry out such a clever plan to wreak vengeance on his estranged wife. Whether he truly believed that there was a huge fortune awaiting him when his wife, his sister-in-law, and his two children were dead, only he knew. He had whittled away at the bank accounts and stock portfolios he and Sue once had until they were much diminished. But he had bragged to "Lisa," who was really an extremely effective detective, as well as a brilliant actress, that there was "big money" ahead. If, indeed, there was, one would suspect that Bill Jensen might do his best to avoid sharing much of it with Yancy Carrothers and his partners in crime.

It may have been that revenge was even more important to Jensen than an inheritance. He had seethed for weeks when he found himself in jail. He'd always considered himself far smarter than his wife. He'd controlled her, lied to her, even terrorized her, and yet she was free and *he* was locked up.

He smiled a grim little smile as he entered his cell, confident that he would be out soon. How could he be convicted of felony–

domestic–violence if there were no witnesses against him?

And he was sure now that by his court date there would be no living witnesses left.

Yancy Carrothers wasn't exactly the hero type, but he had his ethics and his point of no return. As he had spent more time listening to what Bill Jensen wanted him to do, he'd been more and more revolted. The guy was perfectly willing to kill his own family! Yancy's "wife" had worked the streets, but he'd loved her, and he still grieved for her. She had been a murder victim. He figured if a man was lucky enough to have a wife and a couple of kids, he should be grateful. But Bill was eager to throw them away for money.

Yancy had helped police before — solved a few murders for them — and he was proud of that. He wasn't a "snitch" who went running to tell on someone for every little picky thing they did — but it made him feel important and worthwhile to know he'd saved some lives. Now, Yancy had become the person who stood between two terrified women and two teenagers and someone bent on destroying them. That was a very large responsibility for someone who spent his life tiptoeing between being a prisoner and being a regular citizen, always living on the edges of society and looking for a quick buck and an easy way to get forbidden drugs.

He had thought about ripping the man named Bill off, and he'd taken the money from his sister down at the ferry dock. He'd been willing to take the pain pills, and prescriptions for more, that Bill had in his property box, too, but Bill had outfoxed him there.

But would Yancy Carrothers really kill four innocent people to make $150,000? No. Would he step forward to save four people he didn't even know, even though it might cost him his own life?

That he wasn't so sure about, but in the end, he found himself worrying about the intended victims, afraid that Bill would simply find somebody else to do it if he wasn't stopped. Yancy realized he wasn't a killer, or someone who could order a hit on innocent victims.

Bill Jensen wouldn't find out all the details of how he'd been found out — not for months.

Still, wheels were turning. Bill had only a few days to congratulate himself on his clever plan before it ended in ashes.

FOUR
CLOSING IN

Cloyd Steiger had been a Seattle Police officer for a quarter of a century, a detective for thirteen years, and in Homicide for a decade. He was a big, rumpled-looking man who didn't look like a detective — and that afforded him an advantage as he investigated some of the more difficult cases that came across his desk. Steiger took pride in his work, and being a cop was important to him. He felt that a police officer owed it to the community to be honest and someone who could be trusted. Steiger had no patience at all for rogue cops who put a smudge on the whole profession's reputation.

Homicide detectives have to be open to information from all manner of sources. They usually talk to those closest to murder victims first — families, friends, coworkers — and look next for witnesses who may have just happened on vital information. Sometimes those who investigate homicides get information from more exotic tipsters. Most prisoners in jails and penitentiaries aren't violent. They might commit thefts and burglaries, sell illegal drugs, rob banks, or use fraudulent schemes to benefit themselves, but they look down on killers — particularly on those who hurt women and children. Child killers and rapists are at the bottom of the ladder in prison pecking order.

When someone who walks most of the time on the other side of the law contacts a Homicide detective with what may be vital information, the detective listens.

When Bill Jensen's attorney once asked Cloyd Steiger why he always accepted collect phone calls from prisoners, he explained succinctly, "If you're looking for information on crooks, you don't go to Boy Scouts. You go to the crooks. If they're willing to tell you something, you should listen. Whether it's good or not and you use it is one thing — but if you don't listen, you'll never know.

"Usually," Steiger continued to explain, "you'll get a phone call from someone who has information about something you're working on. I'd meet with them, see what they have to say, and see if it's a known case, listen to see if things they are telling me are consistent with what I already know about the case — and go from there."

Steiger also looked to see what the motivation behind the informant's coming to him was. He tried to keep an open mind, and he accepted collect phone calls from jail. You never knew.

As it happened, Cloyd Steiger knew Yancy Carrothers; he had followed up on what Yancy had told him on two murder cases, and found that it was the truth. Yancy had helped bring about convictions in both instances. He had also helped prevent a jail-break in which corrections officers could have been injured.

Steiger had received a collect phone call from the King County Jail on the afternoon of July 23, listened to what Yancy Carrothers had to say, and within an hour walked over to the jail and arranged to bring Yancy back to an interview room in the Homicide Unit. Before he did that, Steiger checked to see if there was a prisoner named William Jensen on the eleventh floor of the jail.

There was.

On the way back to Homicide, the detective and the prisoner stopped at the property room and removed something from Yancy's belongings — a piece of paper.

In the newly constructed Seattle Police Headquarters, every interview room was wired for sound and videotaping. Yancy neither asked for nor was offered any payment for what he was about to say. He knew he was on camera. He showed Cloyd Steiger the sheet of paper he'd kept in his property box. At first glance, it was only a list of names, physical descriptions, addresses, car makes, and license plates — but it made an unnerving kind of sense as Yancy explained what it was.

The three names were a hit list. And the victims-to-be could be found at those addresses or driving the cars listed on the page.

Steiger had begun a more thorough investigation into what almost surely was a murder-for-hire plot. There were only three names on the first list he saw: Sue Jensen, Carol Harris, and Jenny Jensen. That was why he had driven to Newport Hills and knocked on Sue's door late on a Wednesday night.

She validated everything that Yancy Carrothers had told him about her husband's vendetta against her. She just hadn't known that he had already hired someone to kill her.

Cloyd Steiger wasted no time. Early Thursday morning, July 24, he conferred with Senior Deputy Prosecuting Attorney Marilyn Brenneman. She had been the lead prosecutor in at least two King County cases where greedy and controlling husbands had murdered their trusting wives, and she had been responsible for both of their killers going to prison for life. It had been too late for those hapless women, but it wasn't too late for Sue Jensen. Marilyn Brenneman agreed with Steiger that they needed to move ahead rapidly to forestall any murder scenario that Bill Jensen might have put in motion when Yancy Carrothers hadn't delivered as quickly as he wanted.

Cheryl Snow, the senior deputy prosecuting attorney who was the new head of the King County prosecutor's Domestic Violence Unit, was also consulted. Her unit had been concerned about Bill Jensen for months and had been responsible for his arrest and his upcoming court hearings. They knew a lot more about Bill Jensen than Yancy Carrothers did. Yancy didn't know that Bill was an ex-deputy — but Marilyn Brenneman and Cheryl Snow did.

And so, with Steiger, Marilyn Brenneman had agreed that they had to send someone into jail to talk to Jensen, someone who would pretend to be an emissary from Yancy Carrothers, so that he would believe his original plot was going forward.

They could not do anything to entrap Bill

Jensen; he had to be the one who brought up his desire for three murders to go forward.

Sharon Stevens had listened to Cloyd Steiger's request for her help, and she volunteered at once to become "Lisa" — a woman Yancy had described to Bill Jensen as someone he trusted.

Sharon met with Yancy, but only to learn just enough about him and what he had told Bill Jensen so she wouldn't give herself away.

"I wanted her to go in there cold [about the murder plot]," Steiger said, "and see what she could get out of him, knowing just what she did."

Yancy had written the letter of introduction, and Lisa had been instructed to tear it up after Bill Jensen read it through the glass, and seal the fragments back up in the envelope.

Sharon went into the jail alone, made that first contact, and came back to the Homicide Unit, where she immediately typed out a report of what had transpired. After another meeting with Marilyn Brenneman, the investigators decided to move their probe up a notch. They had requested and received authorization for Lisa/Sharon to wear a wire when she visited Bill Jensen a second time.

It had been a technical challenge for Cloyd

Steiger and Marilyn Brenneman because it was difficult to tape on both sides of the glass partitions in the visiting area. They got help with that from Drug Enforcement Administration (DEA) agents, who arranged to be in the control room near the jail elevators, where they could view the visiting area.

DEA agent Terry Damon handed the tape of Sharon Stevens's entire conversation, with Bill Jensen captured on it, to Cloyd Steiger. While he played it back, he simultaneously made a copy of it, and then put the original in an evidence envelope marked with "Case No. 03–340145," his name, William Jensen's name, and "Digital micro-cassette, recorded during undercover operation."

One day, a jury would listen to it — all the instructions for murder, including Jensen's conscienceless phrase "Well, my suggestion . . . then is, *Clean house.*"

"Clean house" meant the murders of Sue, Carol, Jenny . . . and even Scott. Would Jensen's children ever recover from the awful knowledge that their own father wanted them dead?

Cloyd Steiger went to the eleventh floor of the King County Jail on July 29 and placed William Jensen under arrest for four counts of solicitation to commit murder.

During the trial to come, responding to

the defense attorney's questions about his scornful attitude during the arrest, Steiger refused to apologize for his inability to hide his disgust for a man who had once been a fellow officer of the law.

"I told him he was in an unusual predicament," Steiger acknowledged. "In fact, I said, 'Let me think of a word to describe it. Oh, yeah — you're *fucked*.' It angered me that he was a former police officer — because that's what everyone hears on the news. 'Former police officer tries to kill family.' *I* was insulted as a police officer."

Bill Jensen, who had considered himself a master at manipulating others to get what he wanted, was stunned to find that "Lisa" wasn't who he had believed her to be.

And he was even more astounded to learn that Yancy Carrothers, a man Jensen believed was no match for his superior intelligence, had broken his promise to keep a deadly secret.

On July 29, 2003, King County prosecutor Norm Maleng charged William Jensen with four counts of attempted murder for hire in the conspiracy to kill Sue, her sister, Carol, Jenny, and Scott.

That news was the lead story on all of Seattle's evening television broadcasts.

At last.

What had been roiling below the surface, the concentrated efforts to destroy Sue Jensen and everyone she loved, was finally exposed to the light of day.

It was a painful night for the Jensens and Carol Harris. They clung together, bolstering one another and joined by friends who loved them. It was very, very difficult to see their story play across television screens. Tabloid shows and newspapers were calling for interviews.

Dirty cops are fodder for the media. Maybe Bill Jensen had forgotten what he had written about in his "A" term paper at Washington State University a quarter century earlier, "Socio-Psychological Profile of Becoming a Corrupt Police Officer."

It would be a long time before Bill Jensen went to trial. Prosecutors Cheryl Snow and Marilyn Brenneman would be the ones to face him in court. The fact that they were female — highly intelligent and attractive women — probably wouldn't please him; he had habitually ranked women lower in his estimation than men. Given his resentment of his own mother, that probably was predictable.

In the fall of 2003, Marilyn Brenneman

suggested the possibility of a plea agreement, not for Bill Jensen's sake but for Sue and their children. A plea would mean no trial, and there would be no appeals or uncertainty. The Department of Corrections could transfer him out of state to a prison where he would have no contact with people with ties to Washington, and it would reduce media coverage of a trial in the Seattle area.

Even though a plea bargain would mean a shorter sentence for Bill Jensen, it was unlikely he would ever walk free. The possibility that he would live a long time in prison was slim. Marilyn Brenneman checked to see if he really did have chronic lymphocytic leukemia as he had claimed. When it came to his health, Jensen was like the boy who cried wolf. But in this instance he had been telling the truth.

Chronic lymphocytic leukemia (CLL) is a cancer of the white blood cells and bone marrow, characterized by uncontrolled growth of the blood cells. Many cases of CLL are detected in routine blood tests of people with no symptoms. CLL doesn't progress as rapidly as acute leukemia, but it was one more addition to the many physical disabilities Jensen already had.

Sue Jensen saw the positive side of a plea

agreement, agreeing that Bill would probably receive a long enough sentence that they wouldn't have to be afraid of him any longer.

But Bill Jensen wanted to go to trial, believing, apparently, that he would surely prevail and convince a jury of his innocence.

With delays, it was late May 2004 before his trial began. Ironically, he and Sue were still married; her divorce action was stalled in the morass of legal filings.

FIVE
TRIAL

Superior Court judge Richard Jones would oversee the Jensen trial. It was Judge Jones who had sentenced Gary Ridgway, the Green River Killer, to an almost endless series of life sentences for the murders of more than four dozen young women. Jones, the brother of famed musician Quincy Jones, was thoughtful and meticulous in his rulings. That was fortunate, because his wisdom would make any appeals difficult.

James Conroy represented the defense. More often than not, Bill Jensen would appear in the courtroom in a wheelchair.

They began on May 24, 2004. Conroy started his objections early; he was concerned about the whereabouts of Yancy Carrothers, who had not been located. He didn't want Cheryl Snow's opening statements to mention Yancy; in fact, since the material witness seemed to be unavailable, Conroy asked that the case against his client be dismissed in the eventuality that Yancy never appeared.

Cheryl Snow said that Detective Cloyd Steiger had always been able to locate Yancy Carrothers and she had faith that he would find him.

Judge Jones asked that the jury be brought in.

Cheryl Snow began. She spoke of the emotions that had driven the defendant — William Jensen — to a "truly evil deed." They were "fear, hatred, and greed.

"Fear by the defendant that he was being cut off from Sue Jensen's money. Fear by the defendant that he was facing imminent prosecution and that Sue Jensen would be a witness against him. Hate toward Sue Jensen for all that she had caused him. And finally, greed — his desire to inherit Sue Jensen's fortune, even if that meant getting rid of everyone who stood between him and the money. That," Snow pointed out, "was the defendant's motivation in committing the crimes against his wife, Sue Jensen, against Sue's sister, and against his own children."

The jury stared back at Cheryl Snow as she outlined twenty years of history between Bill and Sue Jensen, leading up to the almost unbelievable outrages she said Bill had committed against his family.

Cheryl Snow and Marilyn Brenneman would alternate questioning witnesses. They had prepared a remarkably tight case, and they would bring forth all the witnesses who had seen or heard the defendant's threats of violence and death against his wife — his comments that he understood "going postal."

Sue Jensen testified briefly, trying not to look into the eyes of the man she had lived with for almost a quarter century, still feeling somehow that this could not really be happening.

The gallery looked up expectantly when Yancy Carrothers's name was called. Yancy, a material witness, was being held in jail — to forestall the possibility that he might wander off. He didn't seem to mind. He entered the courtroom walking with a cane; he had been in an accident. He took the witness stand with some élan, though. He knew he was something of a star.

He explained the jail accommodations to the jurors, and he told them that after their first meeting, the defendant had asked him how he might be able to help him with his problems with his wife.

Cheryl Snow questioned him: "During your specific conversations [with Bill Jensen], was there ever a suggestion or an agreement in regards to your taking any action towards his wife?"

"Not until the next day. I approached his cell and said, 'Have you thought of what you wanted done and whatnot?' He said, 'Yes, I'd like her sniped' — which means with a sniper rifle from a distance."

The witness told the jurors that he had commented to Bill that that sounded "amateur," and he suggested that wasn't a "professional elimination."

Yancy said Bill had asked if he could come up with a better plan. "I said, 'Give me a day or two, and I'll let you know.'"

When Yancy told Jensen that he might have a better plan, he learned that Bill wanted more people killed, not just his wife.

"When you say he added family members," Cheryl Snow asked, "who specifically did he add that he wanted to be killed?"

"The first one was his sister-in-law, because then the money would go to his daughter and his son. I don't know how wealthy they are. He said they were wealthy to a point. And then, when I explained the way I would do it — *if* I was to do it — I said, 'Well, wouldn't your daughter get all the money instead of you, now that she's eighteen?' He went, 'Oh, yeah. Let me think about this for a little while.' So the next day, he said, 'I wouldn't mind if she goes with them.' I said okay. He asked me a price. I told him one price for all."

"What was the price?"

"A hundred and fifty thousand dollars."

"That was for killing how many people?"

"Three. I told him it wasn't enough, and if it was done right, there'd better be a bonus. He said he couldn't give me a bonus until after the job."

"Did he explain why?"

"Because he had to inherit the money."

Yancy told the jurors that he had asked for "up-front" money and also told Bill Jensen that he could make it look like an accident.

"How did the defendant respond to that?" Cheryl Snow asked.

"He loved the idea. He got tickled pink."

Snow asked the witness if there had been any more planning about how this should occur. Carrothers said that was when Jensen had started to give him descriptions and addresses of the specified targets.

Cheryl Snow introduced into evidence the sheet of paper that Cloyd Steiger had removed from Yancy's property box.

"Can you tell me whose writing that is, or who wrote that document?"

"He wrote the first one," Yancy answered. "And then I wrote this one because he didn't want his prints on it, or anyone to see it."

Yancy Carrothers was almost *too* good a witness, rushing forward with information before Cheryl Snow had a chance to ask the next question. She reminded him to answer one question at a time.

This scene in Judge Jones's courtroom was reminiscent of *The Sopranos* on television, only it was all too real.

"Who wrote the material on the document you're holding in your hand?"

"Mr. Jensen. I copied it."

"Who provided the information that is listed there?"

"Mr. Jensen."

"How did he convey that information to you?"

"He wrote it on a piece of paper just like this. He brought it to my 'room' [cell], slid it through the door, told me to copy it and rip up the one that he did. Then I told him, 'Oh, I don't have any paper. Have you got a piece of paper so I can copy this?' This paper came out of his notepad also. His prints are on it. I made sure of that."

Yancy was clearly aware of forensic evidence, and he smiled at the jury to be sure they caught the fact that he had tricked Bill Jensen.

Now, at Cheryl Snow's request, Yancy

read the words on the page aloud for the jury, beginning, "Wife, Sue Jensen, white female, 47 years old, five six, 155 pounds, dark brown hair . . . Big house on corner . . . Car, Ford Mustang convertible . . . blue and white . . . Sister, Carol Harris, white female, early 50s . . . Daughter, Jenny. She lives with mother —"

"I'm going to stop you right there," Cheryl Snow cut in. She wanted the jury to understand exactly what this piece of paper was. "And that information was provided to you by the defendant?"

"Yes ma'am."

"Prior to meeting the defendant on the eleventh floor of the King County Jail, had you ever met Bill Jensen before?"

"No."

"Had you ever met Sue Jensen?"

"No . . . I had never seen any of their family in my life."

The May afternoon grew late as Yancy Carrothers spelled out the details of a plot to kill three people. He testified that he had identified himself to Bill Jensen's sister by using the code word "Flying Kings" and received $2,500 "front money." Yancy stressed that he knew that the job was to be carried out before Bill went to trial on the felony–domestic–violence charges. Jensen wanted to be sure there were no witnesses against him.

Yancy Carrothers gave no indication in his testimony that he wasn't prepared to carry out the plan. He was voluble, accommodating, expressive, and he was akin to a creature from another planet to the jurors. None of them had ever seen a hit man in person.

Judge Jones dismissed them for the day and said they would convene again the next morning.

The face of Bill Jensen, wearing a black sports jacket and looking annoyed, flashed across television screens all over Seattle that night. He was an immense man whose face was dotted with several angry-looking eruptions. It was difficult to imagine him as he had once been — a tall, trim deputy in a perfectly pressed uniform.

As court began the next morning, Cheryl Snow began to defuse what she was sure would be brought out on cross-examination by defense attorney James Conroy. She would beat him to it.

"Mr. Carrothers, is it accurate to say that you have a lengthy criminal history?"

"Yes — it is, ma'am."

"Is it true that you have problems with alcohol?"

"Since I became a widower. Yes."

"Do you have problems with drugs?"

"At times. I *enjoy* them more than they're a problem."

"Is it accurate to say that, in some ways, you've spent most of your adult life behind bars?"

"Yes — I'd say about seventeen years."

"And how old are you currently?"

"I'm forty-two."

There was a rakish kind of handsomeness about Yancy. He resembled a carnival barker, fast-talking — but with a certain charisma. One expected him to wink at a female juror at any moment. He knew who he was, even though his image was hardly that of an upright citizen. As strange as it sounds, he was believable.

He explained that he was housed with the O.G.'s (original gangsters) when he went to jail, a badge of honor among jail inmates.

Bill Jensen's sister Iris had given him twenty-five $100 bills at the ferry landing, he testified, but there was to be more in the way of a payoff if he should choose to carry out Jensen's murder plot.

"We were to meet Monday for an additional $2,500 and a bottle of OxyContin [pills] that are worth probably another $2,000 on the street. It's a synthetic heroin and it's very well known on TV and whatnot and shootable. It kills people and people get addicted to it a lot."

Bill Jensen had been prescribed OxyContin for "severe pain," and he also had a prescription for more on his jail books.

"How did you know that?" Cheryl Snow asked Yancy.

"He had told me."

Iris Jensen was supposed to get the OxyContin and the prescription for more pills out of Bill's property. The pills were worth from $40 to $50 apiece on the street. Yancy acknowledged that he had much experience in "turning drugs" for money.

"Can you tell us what Mr. Jensen said to you as part of that agreement?"

"Part of it was for if the $5,000 didn't cover my research before the contract would have supposedly been fulfilled. It would have also been used to tranquilize the people as the accident that would have been set up occurred."

But the second meeting between the witness and Iris Jensen never took place, so she didn't deliver either the pills or the second $2,500.

Cheryl Snow asked Yancy what had happened to prevent their second rendezvous.

"I went to a friend's house and got intoxicated and got arrested in front of their apartment. They found me with a bottle of Absolut [vodka] in my hand, diamond rings, and a sweat suit. They thought I was a big drug dealer and they ran me in."

If this was a movie and not a conspiracy to commit murder trial, Joe Pesci would have played Yancy Carrothers. He was rueful, but also rather pleased to explain that he had also been holding a Gucci watch, and the sweat suit was a very high-end name brand.

"Did you have any drugs on your person?"

"No — but the apartment was a drug house."

And so Yancy had gone off to jail. He wasn't in any danger of a long sentence, and he could do jail time standing on his head, but he was now full of anxiety that something might *really* happen to Bill Jensen's family. Yancy had been confident that he could romance Jensen along, wangling money and drugs out of him, while at the same time he could avoid hurting anyone. But when he landed on the eleventh floor again, and Bill pretended he didn't even see him, he feared that Bill might have hired someone else.

"Who, if anyone, did you contact?"

"First of all, I wrote a letter to Mr. Jensen, and then I tried to call Mr. Steiger. I left messages — kites, they call them. Jail mail."

Yancy's letter warned Bill that nothing must happen to Sue or her sister or her daughter. He read it to the jury as the gallery leaned forward, straining to listen.

"I'm writing to you in regards to things we discussed — you've given a deposit on. I now wish for you to send the last $2,500 to [my] King County Jail booking account, as I have had a few setbacks. Consider this one of our last conversations unless you don't do as I have asked. You have four or five days for it to hit my account, or I'll have to go to the prosecutor and the Homicide unit and so on. I have more than enough to make you do a lot of years. I have the paperwork you gave me with all the info and your fingerprints, plus my statement.

"Also, you are to tell no one and no harm is to come to any one of these ladies or your ex, your sister [sic], or your daughter. You must not harm them, Bill. I will not contact you [until] after we both get out, and you may then get most of the evidence I have on you. Until then, you must do exactly what I have instructed you to do. P.S. I know you don't want your daughter or anyone else to know."

Yancy testified that he figured that would keep the Jensen women safe over the weekend, in case he couldn't get through to Cloyd Steiger.

"That wasn't your only purpose, was it?" Cheryl Snow asked.

"Well, sure. I wanted my other $2,500. I'm a businessman."

As it turned out, Bill Jensen never received that letter. Yancy *had* reached Steiger, and the homicide detective had jailers intercept it, confident that the intended victims were warned, protected, and that Bill Jensen would believe that Sharon Stevens was "Lisa," the hit woman.

There were plots within plots, but the most important thing for everyone concerned — from Yancy to Cloyd Steiger — was that Sue Jensen and her family would be safe.

Yancy settled in to explain all the intricacies of the plan to brief Sharon Stevens, whom he pointed out in the courtroom as "that nice lady over there in the green pretty outfit." She had to know certain things about the real Lisa before she approached Bill Jensen. But she was not to know about the murder plot itself.

Yancy Carrothers wasn't being paid for his cooperation — either in money or in time off a jail sentence. But for the moment, he seized his own payoff as he sat in the witness chair. He saw himself as a heroic king-of-the-mountain, and he regaled the courtroom with his grasp of criminal activity, police procedure, physical evidence, and con games. It was a small price to pay for his saving several lives. He boasted that he had promised Bill Jensen that a "pretty black lady" would be coming to see him. And that was exactly what had happened.

It worked. Jensen had bought the whole thing, and gone ahead confidently, it seemed, with his deadly games.

And they had certainly been deadly games. There was a bleak irony in Jensen's repeated offers of "big, big money" to Yancy. Maybe the ex-deputy believed that he was in line for a huge inheritance, but it just wasn't there. Neither Sue nor Carol Harris had inherited millions of dollars — not even 1 million. There was the house in Newport Hills, a residence Bill had shared for twenty years, and there had once been about $210,000 that Sue had put in their joint bank account. But Bill had spent that long ago. He had no information at all about what his sister-in-law might own.

Either he had woefully overestimated the "fortunes" his wife and sister-in-law had or he wanted revenge so much that he was willing to kill.

Bill Jensen was talking about $150,000 but

he didn't have even the $2,500 to pay Yancy the second half of his "research" money. Sue had to work for a living, and so did her sister. Scott and Jenny had part-time jobs to help out.

There was no fortune.

On cross-examination, James Conroy hammered at Yancy Carrothers about his criminal record, trying to impeach him as a witness, but his questions and Yancy's answers had little impact. Yancy came across as a wannabe rather than a heavy hitter, his answers laced with humor rather than evildoing. Court watchers stifled giggles when Yancy explained that the many gangs he was affiliated with had infiltrated the diaper-service industry, and hinted that he was an agent for many undercover groups — whose names he was not at liberty to divulge.

But he had somehow pulled off what seemed impossible; even though he exaggerated about his connections, his testimony and the backup physical evidence in the form of notes, letters, audiotapes, and fingerprints had been absolutely convincing.

No one knew what the jurors were thinking, but court watchers murmuring in the court-house corridors said they believed Yancy Carrothers. When he testified that Bill Jensen's favorite scenario for the multiple hits was to do something to his wife's car that would make it "fly over the edge of a hill or a mountain at certain times of the year," he was believable. Jensen had suggested that his wife, sister-in-law, and daughter often went shopping together, and if Yancy could find a way to slip OxyContin to Sue and tinker with her car, they could carry out the perfect murders.

"I didn't think his ideas were too bright," Yancy offered, "like taking out a high-powered rifle and shooting them."

It sounded like something the Three Stooges might come up with, but the witness said that Jensen had been coldly serious.

Conroy, for the defense, suggested that Bill Jensen had been deliberately stupid, that he had been setting Yancy Carrothers up.

"You didn't know he was a police officer? Correct?"

"No."

On redirect, Cheryl Snow asked Yancy if he had "forced" Bill Jensen into a murder plan.

"No ma'am."

"That piece of paper — that yellow piece of paper that you showed us where you had the details of Mr. Jensen's wife, his daughter, his sister-in-law — did you have to twist Bill

Jensen's arm to get all those details out of him?"

"No ma'am."

"Did you have to twist Bill Jensen's arm to get the location of his wife and sister-in-law's homes — their addresses?"

"No ma'am."

"Did you have to twist Bill Jensen's arm to get the description of his wife's home with the big tree in front . . . the description of her car . . . his sister-in-law's car . . . to [hear] that his wife had an inheritance, and that he would inherit that money if she was dead?"

"No ma'am."

"At the very end, it was going to go to his son, and then he wanted his son killed. Did you have to twist his arm to get that information out of him?"

"No ma'am."

"Mr. Carrothers, my last question. On the defense's suggestion to you that poor Bill Jensen got tricked by you into agreeing to this plan, do you think that's accurate?"

"No. I think Bill Jensen is an idiot."

"For what?"

"He is an ex-officer. He disgusts me. That's all I can say."

Yancy Carrothers had been on the witness stand for almost a full court day. Even with his checkered background, he had been an excellent witness for the prosecution. Jim Conroy wanted his testimony disregarded, which was understandable, and he especially wanted Detective Cloyd Steiger to avoid validating Yancy in any way when he took the witness stand. Cheryl Snow agreed to the latter.

Iris Jensen testified next, and Marilyn Brenneman questioned her about her meetings with Yancy Carrothers and about her statements to Brenneman when she had gone to Iris's home in Bremerton.

Iris had a very bad memory, or at least she seemed to recall only vague bits and pieces of what had happened.

Although she had been estranged from her brother in the past, she said they had been quite close over the last five years. She believed that she had given the man with the code word "Flying Kings" money for Bill's bail. Her testimony had little impact one way or the other.

Cloyd Steiger followed. He gave a clear, step-by-step overview of the police and prosecuting attorney's office probe into the murder plot that had been hatched by Bill Jensen. It had to be a swift strike, as they sent Detective Sharon Stevens into the jail twice. And on the second visit, she'd worn a wire and caught Jensen's voice on tape as he outlined his instructions.

Steiger was an old master at testifying. He could not be shaken by any ploy the defense might attempt. And Conroy didn't try for long to do that.

Sharon Stevens *was* a pretty black woman, but she wasn't the prostitute that Yancy had said "Lisa" was. She had been a detective with the Seattle Police Department for seven years, and she currently was assigned to the Sexual Assault and Child Abuse Unit. She had agreed immediately to help Cloyd Steiger find out exactly what Bill Jensen had on his mind on July 23, 2003.

Stevens answered Cheryl Snow's questions about her appearance when she walked over to the King County Jail the next day. She had given a false name even to the jail staff.

"What did you look like?" Snow asked.

"I was in a role. I actually had on blue jeans and a T-shirt. My hair was in individual braids — about midback length. I had removed all my jewelry. I had removed all my makeup — so I kind of looked plain."

"Do you think it's fair to say you're someone who maybe looks younger with makeup off?"

"Yes, I do."

Stevens identified photographs of the jail's

visiting area, pointing out the booths with single stools and speakerphones with which to communicate with the prisoner on the other side of the glass.

She testified that Bill Jensen had seemed relieved when he saw her. "He seemed like he had been expecting me. He was very comfortable. He spoke with me freely — wasn't hesitant to talk to me."

She explained that she wasn't familiar with this area of the jail and that the jail staff had no idea who she was. She'd been nervous when she held the note from Yancy Carrothers up to the glass so Jensen could read it. "I assumed that probably would have been against the rules."

Sharon Stevens told the jury that she had been careful to have Bill Jensen repeat his list of instructions several times. She wanted to be positive she had heard him correctly, and have it firmly in her mind when she reported back to Cloyd Steiger.

"Can you describe Mr. Jensen's mood or demeanor when he told you to tell him [Yancy] good luck?" Snow asked.

"I would characterize him as being very excited, more like giddy, in the way of having me there, knowing that his plans are still going through. He smiled at me while we were speaking . . . very, very comfortable with me. We were talking like old friends."

When Sharon Stevens returned for her second visit with Jensen, she couldn't go incognito. The DEA agents would have to be there to record this visit, and the corrections sergeant needed to know who Sharon was.

This time, Jensen wasn't surprised to see her. She held up another note from Yancy, and he read it quickly before she shredded it, put it back in its envelope, and tucked it into the waistband of her jeans.

At this point, Cheryl Snow delivered the coup de grâce of the state's case into evidence: each juror was given a transcript to follow as he or she listened to the defendant's voice ordering the murder of four people.

The courtroom was hushed as Bill Jensen's and Sharon Stevens's voices came over the sound system. What was said had been shocking even to the detectives and prosecutors, who were all too familiar with the depths that some conscienceless minds will sink to; and now the words and thoughts that played out on this afternoon struck both the gallery and the jurors like blows to the heart.

One juror wiped the tears that coursed down her face, and a fellow juror handed her a tissue. The defense would later ask to have her dismissed. Judge Richard Jones didn't acquiesce. Honest emotion is no reason to dismiss jurors. "The types of cases that we try in King County are difficult, trying cases," Judge Jones said. "If we were to try every single case in a vacuum without any juror having any degree of sensitivity, it would be a far cry from reality. That's not what we are experiencing today. The Court finds there is no basis to exclude the juror."

How on earth could Bill Jensen explain away this gruesome evidence? And it was gruesome — not in the sense that bloody clothing might be, but because it was a husband and a father willing to sacrifice his own family in the hope of gaining a fortune.

James Conroy wanted to bring Jenny and Scott Jensen into the courtroom to show that his client had been a good father. Marilyn Brenneman argued vehemently against that, knowing it would be an excruciating ordeal for them.

The defense also asserted that Bill Jensen had no reputation for inflicting excessive force during his two decades as a deputy. Brenneman pointed out that there was a vast difference between what happened on the job and what happened in the home.

Marilyn Brenneman was a tough opponent, always maintaining grace under pressure, probably because she knew the law backward and forward and she had a keen sense of humor that defused courtroom battles. She saw no humor at all, however, in cases where women or children were victimized.

She needed now to show that Yancy Carrothers was not known in the King County Jail as a snitch. Corrections officers testified that Yancy didn't wear a "snitch jacket." There are many complicated layers determining jail reputations. Yancy enjoyed, indeed, his position as a "stand-up guy," albeit sometimes given to fisticuffs when he came in intoxicated.

On June 2, 2004, over Marilyn Brenneman's and Cheryl Snow's fervent objections, James Conroy brought Jenny and Scott Jensen into the trial to testify. It was a fruitless and sad decision. Neither of them was on the stand for more than a few moments, and they had nothing to add that might help the defense. They identified the defendant as their father, their voices choked with tears.

Ten days after his trial began, Bill Jensen took the witness stand.

It was Wednesday morning, June 2. His attorney led him through a lengthy description of his years as a police officer, his service to the community, the years he coached softball and basketball, and moved on to his disabling injury, suffered when he chased a wanted man out of the courthouse in Issaquah.

He spoke with enthusiasm of his second career teaching computer science. Conroy interrupted him before he explained why he hadn't stayed with that job, leaving the impression that it had been a successful venture.

He asked Jensen about the deposition where he had made the "slashing motion" across his neck.

"Mr. Jensen, what were you trying to do when you did that?"

"I was trying to push my wife's buttons," he answered easily.

"She described it as a very stupid thing to do. How would you describe it?"

"A stupid thing to do. It was. She was laughing at me, you know, and it was a very immature, childish thing to do."

Jim Conroy asked Bill Jensen about another alleged threat to Sue: " 'I'll tell you the same thing I told my attorney — if I go to jail, you'll go to your grave.' Do you remember saying that?"

"I don't remember saying that at all. Quite

often, both of us would be talking at the same time. . . . I remember saying something about 'You're going to hell if you don't behave.'"

Bill Jensen appeared puzzled, unable to recall that particular argument. "Could she have misunderstood me? Gosh, if I was going to kill somebody, I sure wouldn't be telling my attorney first. It didn't make any sense."

And that "misunderstanding" was, Jensen said, what had caused him to end up in jail for "felony telephone harassment," a "silly, Class C felony."

The questioning moved swiftly to Bill Jensen's first meeting with Yancy Carrothers. He insisted that he'd been warned from the beginning that Yancy was a snitch, and not to be trusted. He knew this, he said, before Yancy even came to the tank where he was being held.

Slowly, the defense strategy was emerging. Jensen said that no one on the tier was aware that he had been a police officer for twenty years. And that he had not approached Yancy; it was the other way around.

"The first time he came up to me was with his artwork. He really wanted me to look at his artwork that he does in his cell. He made a big deal out of that, you know, and then he was really paying me a lot of attention."

"As time progressed, what did Mr. Carrothers do?"

"He offered to kill my wife for money."

"Why did he do that?"

Cheryl Snow objected repeatedly to questions that required the defendant to speculate about Yancy Carrothers's motivation, and Judge Jones sustained them.

Conroy moved on to suggest that Bill Jensen must have been angry and upset when he arrived on the tier.

"Oh, yes, I was. Definitely."

"And Mr. Carrothers volunteered to help you?"

"Yes, he did."

"How often would he come to you and volunteer to assist you with your problems?"

"Almost every day. And you know, it started with him apologizing to me about overhearing or eavesdropping on my conversations I had on the phone, which is within earshot of his cell."

Led by his counsel's questions, Bill Jensen testified that Yancy Carrothers had gone to great lengths to describe his abilities in certain areas, and repeated that he could "help him out." He had asked questions about the defendant's family.

"Did you believe that he was trying to kill

your family?"

"Yes, I believe that was what he was going to do."

Jensen's position was that he was locked up in jail, hounded by a stranger who was determined to kill his family, a stranger who started out asking for $30,000 for each person.

"What was your intention at that juncture insofar as this particular conversation?"

"My intentions?" Jensen sounded confused. Often, it took him a beat to pick up the gist of his lawyer's questions.

"Yes."

"My intention was to put Carrothers away for the rest of his life."

It seemed that the defense attorney was dragging information out of Bill Jensen. His answers were short and slow.

"Why is that?" Conroy asked.

"Because I could not even stand the man even suggesting what he was suggesting."

Jensen said he knew of Carrothers's reputation, had heard enough about his so-called abilities, and he was incensed.

"And then it became your intention to do what — a reverse sting?"

"Yeah."

"What did you do in an effort to accomplish this particular task?"

"There came a specific day around July 1 when I realized . . . that this man was serious about wanting to kill my family. I then started taking notes about everything that he said, and everything that was done."

"And what was your plan, then?"

"I wanted to build a good enough case against him so that I could go to the Seattle Police, report him, and also talk to the prosecutor about a trade on my current charges — if I brought him Mr. Carrothers."

This was Bill Jensen's defense.

He told the jurors how very difficult it had been for him to befriend someone like Yancy Carrothers. "It was extremely hard," he sighed, "but I did it."

Not only was Bill Jensen giving himself a unique defense — the reverse sting defense — but he was depicting himself as a hero, sickened by his daily contact with a man like Carrothers but soldiering on nevertheless.

"Toward that end," Conroy asked, "did you then give him details about your wife and your kids and where they lived?"

"Yes, I did."

While that bizarre answer sank into the minds of those observing, the defendant was excused and another witness took the stand. This man was also an alumnus of the eleventh floor ad seg tank. He swore that he had warned Bill Jensen that Yancy Carrothers was not to be trusted. That, of course, would bolster the defense position that Jensen had never intended to have his family destroyed. Far from it.

Marilyn Brenneman could not ask this prisoner about *his* past — the defense had won this one in a sidebar argument. Jensen's supporter had a record of sex offenses against a minor, but the jurors never heard that.

The witness supported Jensen's contention that he was doing his own undercover operation, fully aware that Yancy wore a snitch jacket.

But why had he taken such chances with the lives of the intended victims? Bill Jensen had given a man he believed to be a killer a virtual road map to his family.

Back on the stand, Jensen said he had taken voluminous notes on each day's conversation with Yancy as part of his reverse sting operation. In fact, he said, those notes were right there in the courtroom, on the defense table. This came as a surprise to his defense attorney — and to Cheryl Snow and Marilyn Brenneman. The notes had not been provided in discovery. Apparently no one was aware of Jensen's notes — except for Jensen himself.

The prosecutors were quite sure he had

written these notes *during* his trial, after listening to testimony, so that he would have them to substantiate his claim that he'd been only a detective trying to trap a potential killer. They had watched him scribbling frantically at the defense table.

As Jim Conroy questioned him, Bill Jensen disclosed more of the minute details he had provided to Yancy Carrothers — right down to cell phone numbers. Anyone armed with that intelligence could have located the four intended victims easily.

Why had he been so specific, and why had he given a man he believed to be a killer the real information? Couldn't he have given him fake addresses and vehicle descriptions? Conroy obviously saw a problem there, and questioned his client about it.

"Well," Jensen responded to his attorney's questions, "I was quite convinced that you could not arrest or charge somebody for [having] fictitious names and addresses. I started at one and kind of went up to three as I made the calculation, knowing I had to give this to him in case he . . . somehow verified it. Plus, I knew he wasn't going to be able to do the hit without all the down payment."

It was an almost confabulated answer.

Answering Conroy's questions, Bill Jensen

was saying exactly the same things that Yancy Carrothers had testified to — all the money discussed, all the possible MOs — only the defendant insisted this had all been part of his own efforts to get evidence against Yancy.

He plunged on in his testimony, leaping ahead of his lawyer's questions. Jensen boasted that he had even given Carrothers a way out. He had exaggerated the amount of his inheritance.

"In my own mind, I'm a person of fair play; give the person an opportunity to back out. I wanted many, many a back door to leave if he wasn't committed. So I gave it to him. That was a pretty serious doubt I thought I planted in his mind. It also helped me to gauge his greed. I was really after his greed — just like, in my opinion, a miner might think there's gold someplace, but not have a lot of evidence."

All the while, Jensen said he had needed a lot of evidence himself before he felt ready to go to the police and the prosecutor. He said now that he had been suspicious of "Lisa," finding her younger than he expected. "That was why I cut short my first meeting — conversation — with her. She was a whole lot more intelligent, brighter, pretty, young looking. What is she doing running around with Carrothers? It doesn't fit."

Conroy managed to get in a question. "Did you have a protracted conversation with her on the twenty-sixth? And why?"

Jensen nodded. "I wanted her to thoroughly believe that I wanted to go forward with this complete plan. I wanted to hook her."

"Did you purposely interject details so that you could recount those details?"

"Yeah." Jensen asked to see his notes. He was so transparent. It was obvious he had written the notes during Sharon Stevens's testimony — so that his own testimony would match hers, only with his own spin on it.

He repeated many times that he had simply been building a tight case to take to the police. He had deliberately tried to put Lisa at ease, Jensen said, once again adhering to Stevens's testimony.

Cheryl Snow objected; Bill Jensen was now literally *reading* his notes. He denied constructing the notes in the courtroom, and angrily shouted at Cheryl Snow when she suggested that, "You're a liar!"

But it wasn't easy to believe him. Several jurors looked at him with disbelief. The suspicious notes were on the same type of paper that had been in front of him all during the first ten days of testimony.

Judge Jones sustained Snow's objection, and Jim Conroy reminded his client that he must not read. He should be testifying only to what he remembered.

When he finally was confronted by Detective Cloyd Steiger at the time of his arrest, Jensen testified, he'd been "very, very taken aback" by Steiger's attitude.

"Did you ever have any intentions whatsoever of actually carrying through with some plot to kill your family?" Conroy asked.

"Never. I love my kids. I still kind of love my wife. She's the mother of my kids. There's no way that I was ever going to let anybody hurt them. But, boy, from where I was at, I wanted to put him away —"

"Mr. Carrothers?"

"Yeah. Mr. Carrothers. I wanted to put Mr. Carrothers away for life."

"No further questions."

Cheryl Snow rose to cross-examine Bill Jensen. "You stated that you didn't feel Detective Steiger was going to listen to anything you told him about all of this undercover work that you had been doing for the last month? Is that correct?"

"I did not feel that Detective Steiger would have listened to me at all," the defendant said stiffly.

"You had been waiting, you say — you tell us today while you're under oath to tell the truth, tell us that for two months you conducted what you call a 'reverse sting' operation? Correct?"

"Yeah, that's what I like to call it. He's trying to get me to pony up some money for a crime that I really don't think he's going to commit. So I reverse it."

Snow's tone was full of doubt. "You state that you just kept waiting because you kept thinking, 'I hope I get enough information so I can eventually go to the Seattle Police Department.' Correct?"

"That's correct."

"Yet when you meet Detective Steiger face-to-face . . . You meet *two* detectives on July 28 and there's your big moment to turn over all your information about this undercover operation you've been running, and you tell them *nothing?*"

"That's correct."

"Not a thing?"

"That's correct."

"And it wasn't until today that, for the first time, you pulled those notes out of Lord knows where — and offered them to this Court? Is that correct?"

Trickles of sweat had begun to drip down

Bill Jensen's face, but his voice remained steady. "That's totally correct."

He admitted that he had told his attorney that he had written down some things, but he hadn't asked anyone to bring it to the attention of the police or prosecutor's office. He wasn't yet ready to spring his trap.

Cheryl Snow moved a little closer. "You didn't write those notes until you sat in court here. Isn't that true?"

"What was your question again?"

"You sat in court and reconstructed those notes, didn't you, Mr. Jensen?"

"What was that?" He seemed to have been suddenly struck deaf.

She repeated the question.

"No, I did not."

"You looked the jury in the eye and talked about how much you loved your family, and you provided someone that you thought wanted to kill them with all of the information necessary to do so?"

"I did not really believe he was ever going to kill my family. I wasn't going to give him enough money to do so. It was difficult to determine his intent, but she [Lisa/Sharon] sure made it clear that he certainly wanted the down payment to go through with it —"

"And you gave him all this personal information about this family that you tell us today you loved so much?"

"I just said yes," the defendant said petulantly.

"You used your family as the bait to set these people up?"

"Now, I didn't have any choice because that's what he already knew I was in jail for. So I couldn't have used . . . nobody else could I have used."

Bill Jensen must have known that he had lost — that his ridiculous defense wasn't convincing anyone. But he stubbornly answered the questions Cheryl Snow posed, each one more devastating to his case. He was angry, but he continued to come up with excuses.

Now he offered another reason for dragging his finger across his throat in what might have appeared to have been a threat to his estranged wife. It hadn't been a death threat at all; he was only harking back to the days when he and Sue were scuba divers.

"It meant, I'm out of here — I'm out of air," he offered lamely.

Finally, Bill Jensen *was* out of air.

On Friday, June 4, 2004, after hearing closing arguments, the jury retired to deliberate about the fate of William Jensen. They returned in less than four hours.

The verdict was guilty of four counts of solicitation of first-degree murder.

Six months later, December 10, 2004, while Christmas decorations adorned the King County Courthouse, the principals gathered once more in Superior Court judge Richard Jones's courtroom.

Jennifer Jensen, now a beautiful young woman, asked to address the Court before Judge Jones pronounced the sentence. She read what she had written, and if the circumstances were any different, her father might have been proud of her brilliance.

"To this day, I simply cannot fathom what has happened to my precious family, that this man sitting before us conspired a plan to murder his wife, her sister, his own children. The depths of evil have taken over my father's mind and soul in such a way that I deemed utterly impossible.

"Not only will I forever live in fear and anxiety, but I will continue to fear for the life of my best friend and companion: my mother. She's the most valuable person in the world to me, and the thought of having her taken from me brings a prolonged heartache to my soul."

Jenny's voice broke, and Judge Jones told her to take her time, she was doing just fine.

"I simply cannot let myself imagine this horror. This fear will remain a constant for my entire family until my father is securely locked in a prison cell as far away from us as possible.

"What he's done to me cannot be expressed in words, for there are no words that can explain the pain, trauma, and humiliation I have gone through. And to even think of what could have happened. I simply cannot go there.

"The fact that such brutal and cruel thoughts flowed through my father's mind and were actually intended to be carried out proves that this man deserves the maximum punishment to the furthest extent of the law.

"My father once wore a badge of justice as an officer of the law. His punishment should serve in example for our society. He's a disgrace not only to me as his daughter or to my family, but to the King County Police force and to the truly honorable policemen and -women in our country."

Jenny wrote of her almost palpable fear of being murdered. "Whenever I walk from my car in the driveway — just to my front door — I scan the street and sometimes run, imagining the hit man popping up and shooting me. I'm also scared in my own house late at night, picturing someone behind a corner, waiting."

She asked the Court for a maximum sentence, and then turned toward her father. "You should be so incredibly ashamed of yourself."

Jenny spoke for several more minutes. Any normal man — father — *would* have been ashamed.

William Jensen didn't seem to be; he was going over *his* remarks in his head, and gathering a stack of documents he wanted to hand to the Court. He had a different tack to take with Judge Jones, and he was anxious to present it.

Sue Jensen could not bring herself to speak, but she handed what she had written to the judge. So did Carol Harris.

The man about to be sentenced had yet another attorney representing him. That lawyer presented a statement, using what ammunition he had — which wasn't much.

Cheryl Snow asked the Court to impose a sentence within the standard range for four such heinous crimes. She saw no mitigating factors at all.

Bill Jensen's moment had come. Leaning heavily on a cane, he assured Judge Jones that he would look directly into his eyes, and he would tell him the truth "before you sentence me to some place in hell."

He had come up with a new argument. "There are *two* Bill Jensens," he began.

In essence, Jensen said he blamed jailers and the jail medical staff for giving him the wrong pain medications, which had changed his thinking, blurred his perception. That wasn't his fault, of course. He went over the same story he had told during his trial, but blamed his response to Yancy Carrothers's trickery on his having ingested the wrong meds. His mind had been skewed by Oxy-Contin, ibuprofen, and other drugs — all in the wrong dosage.

Everything that had happened was some-one else's fault, and Bill Jensen was an inno-cent victim, catapulted from that "silly Class C felony" to where he was currently.

What had happened was all a mistake, misunderstandings, people plotting against him. The real Bill Jensen wouldn't hurt any-one.

"I want my family to totally understand that from Day One, they have been safe. Whether they believe it or not. I pray that the Lord will bring them there. But they are not in any danger from me, and never have been."

He offered the stack of papers to Judge Jones, who thanked him politely and said he would read them over the morning break.

When Judge Richard Jones returned, he commented that most of the documents Jensen had given him were grievances against the King County Jail or law enforcement officers or Jensen's attorneys. They were not to be considered in this venue. And almost all of the rest of the paperwork had already been before the Court, and a matter of court record already filed.

"These motions are dismissed and denied."

In the judge's view, the cases Jensen had cited after reading some law books were of "meager assistance" to his arguments.

Richard Jones is a soft-spoken judge, and during trials, participants only rarely have a sense of what he is thinking. He prefers it that way, determined to be as fair as possible to both sides. But now he prepared to sentence William Jensen.

And now, at last, his opinions came out for those in the courtroom to hear.

"Mr. Jensen," he began, "we find ourselves conducting this sentencing right in the middle of a season that should be geared around peace, hope, and sharing. We are right in the middle of a season when families are crossing miles across the planet to spend a few hours with family.

"Right now, as we speak, there are young men and women fighting for our country on the other side of the planet — and dying — with their last wish being the chance to spend a few precious moments with family.

"Mr. Jensen, there are those who will come into existence and spend their entire life chasing a dream of having a family. Mr. Jensen, you had a family. Regardless of the issues you had with your wife, you obviously had children who dearly loved you and cherished you.

"But, when given the choice, when given the choice of what was more important, instead of showing your children love and affection, you were giving physical descriptions to a hit man. And when asked about the involvement of your son as being a casualty of what was going to take place, your callous response was, 'Oh, well . . .'

"Your greed and hatred and fear of losing things and wealth to your wife are the real factors that clouded your judgment to the point of having four people executed in order to accomplish your goals.

"Greed has been defined as an excessive desire to acquire or possess more than one needs or deserves, especially with respect to material wealth. Mr. Jensen, when you boil it down to the pure essence of what you did, you placed money over family, you placed hatred over compassion, and malice over common sense. That is a dangerous and deadly combination, and that was your downfall.

"Mr. Jensen, you told me there were two Bill Jensens. But the reality is there really is just one Bill Jensen. And that one Bill Jensen and the actions of that Bill Jensen will cause you to spend the rest of your life in prison, and your family spending the balance of their lives wondering what they had done to deserve you in their life, a husband and father who had no concept of the value of family."

And with that, Judge Jones sentenced Bill Jensen to 180 months on Count I, which would run consecutive to 180 months on Count II, which would run consecutive to 180 months on Count III, which would run consecutive to 180 months on Count IV.

Sixty years in prison. Bill Jensen would be credited with 501 days for time served.

He would have no contact with the four potential victims he had sought to have killed.

Christmas was two weeks away, but the family who had once loved Bill Jensen would celebrate without him. Forever.

Sue Jensen was finally awarded a divorce in 2005, and she now uses her maiden name. She works to advise and support other women who are caught in terrifying domestic violence situations, particularly the wives or girlfriends of law enforcement officers or firefighters. She has been there, and she understands.

Scott and Jenny Jensen have blossomed and lead successful lives. Each has surpassed everything their mother had hoped for them.

There are still nightmares for Sue, Jenny, and Scott, bad dreams that creep up without warning. The shadows are still there, and it may take a lifetime for them to realize that they deserve to walk free and in the sunshine. Anyone who has lived under siege understands how difficult it is to trust again.

Sue Harris is grateful to an unlikely ally: Yancy Carrothers.

"I don't care what he may have done in the past, or what kind of life he leads," she told a friend. "He saved my life. He saved all of our lives. If he hadn't come forward and told the police what Bill was planning, I wouldn't be here talking to you now. So I thank Mr. Carrothers, and I always will."

Bill Jensen is currently incarcerated in an

isolation unit at the Washington State Penitentiary in Walla Walla, Washington. As a former cop and a would-be family killer, his life would be in danger in the prison's general population. He has filed an appeal and he visits the prison library to study law books there every Thursday.

Whether Bill Jensen listened to Judge Richard Jones's remarks about how precious a loving family is, no one knows. History suggests that he rarely listened to advice from anyone.

He had it all. He threw it all away.

Although Sue Harris and her children are safe, there are thousands of women and children who are not. They are somewhere along the inexorable progression from the promise of love to disappointment to isolation to emotional abuse to physical abuse to fear to loss of hope, and finally to either divorce or death.

It shouldn't be that way. People like Detectives Cloyd Steiger and Sharon Stevens, prosecutors Marilyn Brenneman and Cheryl Snow, and survivors like Sue Harris Jensen are trying to make life happier and safer for those who are still afraid of someone who should love and care for them.

Every domestic violence support group

in America needs our donations of money, clothing, furniture, toys, vehicles, shelter, and time. Go to www.domesticviolence.com to contact the groups near you.

THE DEPUTY'S WIFE

Billy Pate, age 7. He lived with relatives and in many foster homes, never quite belonging.

Bill Jensen was slim and handsome when Sue Harris met him in 1975. They married four years later in Seattle.

Sue Harris and Bill Jensen's wedding in May 1979. It was Bill's birthday, and they looked forward to a great future together. Their honeymoon was a tour of America.

Bill, Sue, and Jenny on vacation. The Jensens shared a lot of wonderful trips—around America and even to Australia.

Bill, Sue, Jenny, and Scott Jensen in 1988, a complete family at last.

Bill Jensen realized his dream of being a cop. A King County deputy sheriff, he loved his job. Both his son and the neighbor kids looked upon him as a hero. He and Scott did everything together.

Bill Jensen was proud of Jenny's athletic ability, and he coached her baseball team for several years. Her friends liked her dad, although some of the parents found him a little hotheaded over umpires' calls in what was, essentially, a children's game.

Jenny, #10, and her friends needed a basketball coach, too—and Bill stepped in. Her memories of the dad she knew in her happy childhood would never quite fade, despite the horror to come.

Bill shows young Scott how to take accurate aim with a rifle. Given what came after, this photo- graph is eerie. At the time, Scott was thrilled.

ABOVE LEFT: *The Jensens always threw big Halloween parties, and Bill invariably dressed up as a character right out of* Friday the 13th *or as Freddy Krueger, with his skin and clothes spattered with fake blood.*

ABOVE RIGHT: *Bill Jensen worked patrol in rural sections of King County, Washington, in a one-man car. He was never promoted to detective, although he occasionally worked in some undercover operations.*

After Bill Jensen received a knee injury as he chased a wanted felon, he put on a lot of weight. Still, he tried to continue dirt-biking with Jenny and Scott. But sides of himself he had kept hidden from his wife and family began to appear. Sue Jensen was shocked.

Bill Jensen in a role that was totally alien to him until 2003. Now he was on the other side of the law, charged with felony harassment and domestic violence.

King County Superior Court judge Richard Jones presided over Bill Jensen's trial. Highly respected, Jones would have the final word in this case.

ABOVE LEFT: *Senior Deputy Prosecuting Attorney Marilyn Brenneman had a very successful record for bringing justice to hapless women caught in dangerous relationships.*

ABOVE RIGHT: *Senior Deputy Prosecutor Cheryl Snow, successful in prosecuting DV cases, told a jury that Bill Jensen had plotted a "truly evil deed" as he awaited trial on other charges. Snow and Brenneman ripped away the self-serving façade of a defendant who believed he could convince a jury otherwise.*

Seattle Police Homicide detective Cloyd Steiger and Sex Crimes detective Sharon Stevens worked on a plan to prevent four murders and to get evidence against a would-be fatal manipulator. Sharon wore a wire and played the role of streetwise prostitute to perfection, and left the King County Jail with a tape that left no doubt about the suspect's intentions.

■ ■ ■ ■

THE
ANTIQUES
DEALER'S WIFE

■ ■ ■ ■

Literature is rife with stories of men who draw women to themselves the way some flowers attract butterflies. They are the Svengalis and the Bluebeards of fiction. They range from Rudolph Valentino to Frank Sinatra to Elvis Presley to the most current heart-throb on television. At cocktail parties or college lecture halls, these men are always surrounded by attractive women who ooh and ahh and nod their heads with exaggerated agreement about whatever opinion they voice. They brim with charisma, even when they may not be all that handsome. And if they *are* handsome, too, their feminine targets are that much easier to seduce.

Raoul Guy Rockwell was definitely a charmer, as dangerous as he was compelling. Wealthy Seattle matrons and single women hung on his every word, and many of them secretly — or not so secretly — thought seriously about having an affair with him.

Some of them ventured beyond the thought, captivated by his hypnotic stare and the sharp scent of his English lime cologne and the smell of the rich tobacco blend in his ever-present pipe.

Rockwell's story rose to the surface shortly before my own years as a police officer in the Seattle Police Department. The detective sergeant who tracked him was a man I had worked with on several sexual assault cases when he was a patrol officer and I was a very gullible and inexperienced investigator in the Women's Division (as we were known then).

I've never written this case before, but it has always been a big part of my memory of early days in the department. It is grotesque, baffling, fascinating, and frustrating. Later in my life, I had a writing studio in a houseboat on Lake Union, close by where the murder mystery happened. My neighbors had never heard of the mysterious Raoul Guy Rockwell and didn't know of the massive police operation that took place in the fall of 1960. It seemed impossible to me that such a headline story could evaporate like the early morning fog over the lake when the sun penetrated it.

And yet I'm sure there are many who will remember this story, and who have wondered for decades whatever became of the man who captivated his fans for a few years and then vanished, leaving hundreds of questions behind.

When this mystery began in the spring of 1960, John F. Kennedy had just announced his candidacy for president, America's first seven astronauts were learning to live in zero gravity, and "Itsy Bitsy Teenie Weenie Yellow Polka Dot Bikini" topped the music charts.

"The Twist" was the most popular dance in the country.

It was another time. Still, revisiting the saga of Raoul Guy Rockwell makes one wonder how anyone aware of his crimes could forget him.

Raoul Guy Rockwell, who was always referred to by all three of his names, suddenly appeared in the art and antiques world of Seattle in the late 1950s. No one was sure where he had come from, and later, even less sure of where he had gone. He wasn't yet forty-five, although he seemed more mature. He opened an antiques gallery in a ramshackle three-story house close to a houseboat community on Fairview Avenue East, a structure repaired willy-nilly over previous decades with whatever was handy, so that part of it had cedar shakes and other sections plain board siding. The windows didn't match, and some were covered with plastic sheeting instead of storm windows to keep out the rain. Rockwell decorated the entryway with stained-glass windows he had purchased when an old church was demolished, but he didn't pain the exterior.

Almost five decades later, the land he

bought is well-nigh priceless, but he purchased the creaky structure, which had once housed a rug cleaning business, with relatively few funds. Somehow, he had the touch that made the weathered gray building look quaint and "interesting," rather than junky.

Rockwell filled the first floor with all manner of collectibles — large pieces of furniture, paintings, objets d'art, rare coins, Northwest Indian icons, and his claimed special area of expertise, Ashanti weights. He traveled often to buy items for his inventory, most often to Canada, but also to Portugal and Ghana, in Africa, to buy the precious little carved bronze Ashanti weights once used by natives as counterbalances to weigh both gold dust and salt.

Rockwell often spoke of his amazing luck in being able to buy a collection of 152 such weights, more valuable each year as their number was limited. They had great religious and cultural significance to those who used them. Hundreds of the rare bronze icons were buried with those who owned them in life.

When Raoul Guy moved into the barnlike house, he brought his family with him. His second wife, Manzanita, was thirty-nine, an attractive and vivacious redhead who favored scarlet lipstick. Manzy, as she was called, had a much more ordinary job than her flamboyant husband: she worked at a bank in downtown Seattle. Although Raoul Guy and Manzy had no children together, she had a very pretty eighteen-year-old daughter from a former marriage. Dolores Mearns was a freshman at the University of Washington.

The family lived in an apartment on the second floor of the antiques gallery. How long Raoul and Manzanita had been married, no one knew. Although she seemed to understand that her husband had to have a certain persona to attract clients to his business, she often grew weary of the many women who had decided that shopping there was *the* thing to do. Driving up in expensive cars and wearing the latest fashions featured at Nordstrom's flagship store and at Frederick & Nelson, the society matrons flocked not only to ask Raoul about his merchandise but also to listen to stories of his adventures.

Manzanita often got off the bus on Eastlake Avenue after a hard day at the bank, walked a few blocks to the shoreline in the omnipresent spring rain, only to find the first floor of her residence overflowing with what she considered "silly women." Raoul kept odd hours in his shop — opening the doors at 6 P.M. For him, it was a social time, but his wife and stepdaughter would have preferred to have a family dinner and some quiet evenings.

The sounds of women's laughter floated up the stairs, and Manzanita heard her husband's deep, rumbling voice pontificating on one subject or another. When she saw certain women returning night after night, Manzanita felt waves of jealousy. Raoul always explained that he meant nothing by flirting with potential customers and said he didn't have the slightest sexual interest in any of the women, but Manzy wasn't so sure.

She had been with him long enough to know that he often exaggerated and enjoyed the attention he got from women. She had heard him exaggerate right up to the thin edge of an outright lie. More often than not, the truth wasn't in him. When it suited Raoul, he could tell a lie as easily, perhaps more easily, than he told the truth.

Manzanita had left her ex-husband four years before, so besotted with Raoul that she lived with him without marriage for two years until her cuckolded husband threw up his hands in defeat and gave her a divorce. Bill Mearns had allowed her to take Dolores with her but kept their two younger daughters with him. Manzanita had given up a lot for Raoul; she loved him and she would do whatever she had to do to keep him.

Holding court in his shop, the big man, who stood almost six feet three inches tall, with broad shoulders and a barrel chest, was undeniably handsome and extremely masculine. Raoul Guy Rockwell often told his customers of his exotic past. In retrospect, how much of it was true is questionable.

Raoul said that he was a native of Saint-Tropez, France, and spoke of being a third-generation antiques dealer. He told his eager listeners that he had come to America in 1940, when he was seventeen. Even then, his genius was so obvious that he was accepted as a freshman at the University of California almost immediately. Although he was native to France, Raoul explained, his natural talent for languages was responsible for his fluent English. Indeed, he had no trace of a French accent by the time he moved to Seattle.

After he graduated from the University of California, Raoul said, he had spent a six-year tour of duty in the U.S. Army as a second lieutenant, engaging in battles on many fronts. This didn't quite mesh with the dates he gave: World War II had ended shortly after he graduated, and the Korean

War hadn't yet begun. But it was technically possible for him to have participated in the last days of the Second World War.

Where he *really* was between 1945 and 1958 remained shrouded in the mists of time and Raoul's expansive imagination. Some who asked enough questions or who had a suspicious mind hinted that Raoul might have attributes that suggested he was a poseur and a flimflam man. But there was no question at all that he was brilliant, knowledgeable in his field, and a captivating storyteller. And he seemed harmless enough as he enjoyed his small kingdom on the shores of Lake Union in the center of Seattle.

Those who bought his antiques believed they had scored extremely valuable treasures and took great pride in them. His long-suffering wife put up with his flirtations, and his stepdaughter spent most of her time on the University of Washington campus, already moving away from her life with her mother and Raoul, looking forward to being on her own.

Dolores herself was quite beautiful, becoming more so as she matured. She apparently got along well with her stepfather, and she didn't date or stay out late at night.

If she disapproved of the women who clustered around Rockwell, Dolores kept it to herself. She was very close to her mother, and so far in her life, her fate had been entwined with Manzy's.

And that was Dolores's tragedy.

By March 1960 the Rockwells' marriage seemed to have fallen apart. Neighbors could not help but notice a lovely middle-aged blond who arrived at the antiques shop close to midnight several evenings each week. She drove a long Cadillac convertible and often wore expensive furs. When she slipped into the antiques shop, she left a cloud of Chanel No. 5 in her wake.

This woman may have been the final insult to Manzanita, who must have realized that a lot more than conversation about antiques was going on. Quite suddenly, Manzanita abandoned her home and husband. The manager of the bank where she worked was puzzled that such a dependable employee would quit without so much as giving notice. But Manzy Rockwell had. At the same time, Dolores Mearns stopped going to her classes at the university.

A couple who lived next door to the Rockwells had formed close ties with them. They were sure that Manzy would have talked with them before she left, but she never mentioned that she was about to leave "Rocky."

They were hurt at first and then worried. They knew Manzy was often annoyed by Raoul's flirtations and his tendency to spend more energy on his antiques than he did on her, but they had believed the two of them were in love. Sometimes they had laughed about it — who but Manzy would have put up with Raoul's pomposity and pretense? They often said he needed her. Manzy grounded him and was the voice of reason in their marriage.

Their neighbors suspected that there were even times when Raoul would have gotten into financial trouble without his wife's bookkeeping and steady salary. As much fun as Manzy Rockwell was, she was the one who paid the bills, took Raoul's clothes to the cleaners, helped out in the antiques shop, and generally held things together.

And suddenly she was gone. Simply gone. And so was Dolores.

The couple next door asked Raoul where Manzanita and Dolores were, and he said they had gone to Vancouver, British Columbia — some 150 miles north of Seattle — to visit relatives. But weeks passed and the two women didn't come back.

Finally, Raoul told them that he had made up an excuse for Manzanita's departure to hide the fact that she had left him. He was humiliated. He seemed almost heartbroken as he explained he'd hoped for weeks that they would reconcile, but he had finally realized that she wasn't coming back.

"She doesn't love me anymore," he said bleakly. "And Manzy closed out our joint bank account. She took every penny I've saved for the shop and to buy more antiques. She even burned all my business records before she left! I'm having a terrible time trying to figure out my income tax return."

Their neighbors saw that Raoul was really depressed. He was drinking heavily, and he didn't seem to care about the shop anymore, letting days go by without opening his doors for business. They were surprised; they'd always believed that if either Rocky or Manzy deserted the marriage, he would have been the one to leave. But he seemed to be the classic betrayed husband, bereft and anchorless. The late-night visits from the beautiful blond continued, but even they didn't seem to cheer him up.

Finally, though, Raoul pulled himself together. He filed for divorce from Manzanita on grounds of "cruelty and desertion." In Washington State, an uncontested divorce was final in three months. Raoul would be a single man by late July 1960. Manzanita didn't come forward, and the Rockwells' divorce proceedings moved ahead.

Once more, Raoul grew enthusiastic about his business, and he proudly announced to his friends and patrons that he had been awarded a Fulbright scholarship that would enable him to travel to Portugal and Africa to study the religious significance of Ashanti weights. Current theory was that the prized objects had been hand carved and then finished with a lost wax process introduced by Portuguese sailors.

"I don't agree with that," he submitted confidently. "My research thus far suggests that the weights were used as native charms long before Portuguese ships arrived on the African Gold Coast, and I intend to prove that."

Photos of Raoul Guy Rockwell holding some of his Ashanti weights appeared in several newspapers, accompanying feature articles on the fascinating collector. Rockwell had a very impressive résumé and he never hesitated to share it with reporters. He was a natural as far as the media was concerned, and he reveled in the publicity, posing patiently.

But Raoul Guy Rockwell's fame had only begun.

On July 26, the decree of divorce — unopposed by Manzanita — was granted. She and Dolores were thought to be somewhere in Canada, having cut their ties to Raoul and Seattle completely. According to him, they had plenty of money, since Manzanita had wiped out all his savings. But he was rebuilding his life.

Actually, he had rebuilt it far more rapidly than anyone expected. The day his divorce was final, Raoul announced that he was engaged to marry a most attractive fellow antiques dealer: Mrs. Evelyn Emerson, forty. Evelyn was petite and blond and, like Raoul, divorced. She had fallen in love with him very quickly, thrilled with his intellect, his exciting future, and his sheer masculine appeal.

She was not, however, the woman in the Cadillac convertible. She was younger, slimmer, and her hair was much shorter, cut and permed into a cap that surrounded her petite features. And Raoul had chosen Evelyn to face the future with him.

Although they had originally planned to marry on September 1, the couple was so smitten with each other that they had a marriage ceremony on July 29 in Evelyn's family's living room only three days after the divorce went through. Raoul had been single for just seventy-two hours.

Evelyn came from a socially prominent

and wealthy Seattle family. Her mother and stepfather, Germaine and Clifford Winkler, were delighted that she had found love again with Raoul Guy Rockwell. They were impressed with his cosmopolitan air and his business sense, and he was wonderfully considerate of Evelyn. The couple had many interests in common, and Evelyn was looking forward to traveling with him to Portugal and Africa as he pursued the project funded by his Fulbright scholarship.

It would be a honeymoon trip as well as a research trip that would add luster to Raoul's reputation as an antiques dealer.

To make their trip even more perfect, Raoul told Evelyn, friends had financed his purchase of a yacht, the *Ibsen,* and it was seaworthy enough to allow them to sail to Portugal and Africa. When they returned, he would sell the yacht and repay his wealthy benefactors.

Evelyn quickly sold her antiques shop and placed her remaining inventory in an auction house, planning to give all of her proceeds to her bridegroom as they started their life together.

The Winklers were honored a few days later when Raoul approached them about joining him in a business venture. He had located a treasure load of rare Indian artifacts and antiques in Canada. He had immediately put down a $500 deposit with the person who let him in on the deal, and he assured his new in-laws that he already had commitments from two Seattle art collectors who were anxious to pay him more than $16,000 for the rare Indian paintings and carvings.

But Raoul's funds were temporarily tied up, and he didn't have the $8,000 he needed to close the sale in British Columbia. His missing ex-wife had taken all of his liquid assets, and, although he had his own inventory of antiques set to be auctioned off by Seattle's top auction house, he said they hadn't sold yet.

(In 2007, the amounts involved would be hundreds of thousands of dollars — but $16,000 was a big chunk of money in 1960.)

Germaine Winkler assured her new son-in-law that she had the cash to help him. He demurred at first, and finally agreed to accept a loan from her *only* if she and Evelyn would let him give them each a $2,000 bonus when he sold the Indian objects to the collectors who were waiting anxiously to buy them.

When Germaine acquiesced to this, Raoul Guy accepted her check for $10,000. She made it for $2,000 more than he needed because she wanted to be sure he had enough when he went to Canada.

It would be a dicey deal in many ways. He didn't want to go through customs with the Indian artifacts; there would be too many questions, taxes levied, and some laws might actually forbid the removal of certain tribal icons from Canada. For those reasons, he said, he hesitated to fly or to drive between the two countries. He planned to rent a fishing boat for his return trip, bringing back his purchases by way of the open sea.

He wasn't worried at all about American customs agents; he assured Germaine and Evelyn that he counted many of them among his close personal friends. But he just couldn't envision what the Canadian customs officers might do.

It was August 3 when the newlyweds ate dinner at the Winklers' Magnolia home. They enjoyed a wonderful meal and it was a happy night. However, Raoul was concerned about the extra $2,000 Germaine Winkler had added to her check to him. He wanted to sign a check right there giving that money back to her; he needed only the $8,000. But he patted his shirt pocket and found it empty; since he didn't have his checkbook with him, he said, he would give her a promissory note later.

His new mother-in-law assured him that wasn't necessary.

Raoul confessed that he was worried about leaving Evelyn alone while he was away in Canada. They had been staying at an upscale hotel since their marriage, but he was still uneasy about leaving her. "Would it be presumptuous of me if I asked you to have her stay with you while I'm gone?" he asked Germaine and Clifford. "She isn't feeling that well, and I wouldn't worry if I knew she was here with you."

"Of course she can," Clifford Winkler said. "We would love to have her stay with us."

Raoul promised his new bride that he would be back in Seattle by August 6 — or August 7 at the very latest.

She hated to have him leave, even for that long. They'd been married for only six days, and she was completely in love with him. She had begged to go with him to Canada, but he told her he wouldn't even consider risking her life; there was the possibility of danger not only in negotiating the purchase of the rare Indian treasures, but in getting them back across the U.S. border. She was much too precious to him to risk harming even one hair on her head.

Reluctantly, she agreed once again that it

would be wiser for her to stay with her family. Soon enough, they would be on their honeymoon in their new yacht. The *Ibsen* was currently moored in a marina in San Francisco, Raoul explained, and they would fly there, pick it up, and be off on the greatest adventure of their lives.

Raoul excused himself after dessert and brandy, saying he had to go to his office to work on some details for the September cruise to Portugal. He called a few hours later, though, saying it was imperative that he leave for Canada at once. "I've just learned that there is another bidder on the Indian artifacts," he told Evelyn hurriedly. "They're prepared to offer twice the agreed-upon price: $16,000! I have to get up there to complete the deal I've been promised."

"Of course, darling," Evelyn said. "Go. I'll be fine here with my parents."

Raoul reiterated his promise to his new bride that he would be back in Seattle in four days at the most.

Evelyn waited for Raoul's return with some concern, knowing that there might be trouble with the other buyers who had suddenly surfaced. Raoul had even hinted at "pirate types" who might waylay him when he was out at sea.

That made her anxious, but she grew really frantic when six days passed with no word from him.

She realized that she didn't know any of her groom's intimate friends, but she did know that Raoul's attorney was Jeffrey Heiman — he had handled the divorce from Manzanita. She called Heiman, fighting to hold back tears as she told him that her husband was missing. "I don't know anyone else to call," she said softly. "I'm so sorry to trouble you."

Heiman thought she was overreacting, and he attempted to reassure Evelyn when she told him that Raoul had been gone since Wednesday, August 3. It was now August 9. He hadn't even called her to let her know that the deal had gone as planned and that he was okay.

When Evelyn confided that Raoul had over $10,000 that he had changed into Canadian currency before his flight out of Seattle-Tacoma Airport, Heiman, too, wondered if he had been the victim of foul play. The next day, the lawyer made a missing persons report to the Seattle Police Department.

"He was either on a United flight — #669 — or a TransCanada Flight — #148 — leaving Seattle on the third about 9 P.M.," Heiman said. "I tried to verify that he was on the passenger list on one or the other of those planes, but they didn't have his name on their manifests."

Sergeant Herb Swindler of the Crimes Against Persons Unit was given the chief responsibility to investigate the possible disappearance of Raoul Guy Rockwell. Swindler looked a great deal like actor Richard Widmark, and once he started on a case, he didn't let go until he found the answers he sought.

When Sergeant Swindler got this assignment, he had no idea that it would consume his life for many years to come.

Swindler arranged to interview Evelyn Emerson Rockwell. Dabbing at her eyes with a lacy handkerchief, she told him everything she knew about her husband's trip north across the border. "He called me from the airport that night — August 3rd," she said worriedly. "He told me he was leaving on a 9:05 P.M. plane and he had to rush to get on board. He planned to come home on a fishing boat sometime the following weekend, but I haven't heard one word from him since he called me from a pay phone at the airport."

Swindler also checked with the airlines that flew out of Sea-Tac on Wednesday at nine. He learned that if Rockwell was on that plane, he either had reservations under a different name or had missed his flight.

When Herb Swindler contacted Raoul Guy Rockwell's bank, the Pacific National Bank's branch near the University of Washington, they remembered him very well. "He recently cashed a $10,000 check written by Mrs. Winkler," the branch manager said, "and withdrew about $3,000 from his own checking account with us. That left a small balance in the account."

"He took it out in Canadian currency?"

"No, it was in U.S. money. His wife's name — Manzanita — was still on the joint account."

Rockwell's attorney was surprised to hear that. "After the divorce, I advised him to take Manzanita's name off that account," Heiman told Swindler. "She never came back. I understood he'd sold all his antiques at Bushnell's auction and collected that money, and he wouldn't want her to withdraw that money from their account. But it looks as if there wasn't enough left in there for him to worry about."

Swindler realized that the popular collector of antiques was virtually cutting his ties to Seattle, apparently planning a whole new life with his bride.

But where *was* he? He was carrying $13,000 in cash, a very large amount of money.

The situation became even more mysterious when the Seattle police investigator checked on Rockwell's means of transportation. He didn't own a car; he'd been renting one, and it had been turned in to the rental company at Sea-Tac Airport. But their records indicated it hadn't been returned on August 3, when Rockwell was supposed to be flying to Canada; Rockwell had driven it to the rental office on August 4, a day after he'd told Evelyn he was running to catch a plane.

And from that point on, he had disappeared.

Where had he been during the previous night? Just in case it hadn't *really* been Rockwell who returned his car, Swindler questioned the clerk at the rental kiosk, asking for a description of the man who'd dropped off the keys.

"Very tall, great smile," she answered. "It was him all right. I know Raoul Rockwell, and I'm positive it was him who brought the car back. And our ledger shows it was the morning of August 4."

So Rockwell clearly hadn't gone to Canada Wednesday night. Nor was his name on any flight lists to Vancouver or Victoria the next day.

Swindler suggested that the local newspapers might be helpful in locating Rockwell. Evelyn Emerson Rockwell and her mother, Germaine Winkler, agreed to speak to newspaper reporters in the hope that articles on the front pages of the *Seattle Times* and the *Post-Intelligencer* might bring forth some information about Evelyn's missing husband. Even though it embarrassed her to appear in the papers as an abandoned bride, Evelyn was willing to try anything to find him. She was terrified that he might be lying injured — or worse — somewhere in the fields that surrounded the airport.

With all that cash in his briefcase, Raoul was a prime target for thieves. Just because he'd returned his rental car, that didn't mean that he ever left the airport area.

Evelyn's picture appeared in the papers, a petite woman in a pastel dress with satin piping on the sleeves and a modest neckline, a double strand of real pearls around her neck. She begged readers to call her or Jeffrey Heiman or the Seattle Police if they had any knowledge of where Raoul might be. She was a lovely-looking woman, and it was hard to understand why her bridegroom would have deliberately left her alone so soon after their wedding. The reporters who interviewed her tended to think something dire must have happened to him.

On the evening after the articles appeared, Sergeant Herb Swindler got another call from Jeffrey Heiman. Heiman sounded as if he had suffered a severe shock. Raoul's attorney had believed he knew his client well. Now, he wasn't nearly so sure.

"I just got the strangest phone call," Heiman told Swindler, "and I don't know what to think of it. It was from this woman who lives on Queen Anne Hill — her name's Blake Rossler* — I've seen her picture on the society pages often."

"And?" Swindler asked impatiently.

"And she's telling me that she flew to San Francisco with Raoul Rockwell on August 4th, and he abandoned her there and disappeared."

"She's sure it was Rockwell?"

"She's positive. She's known him for a long time."

"That is strange," Swindler agreed.

"She's willing to talk further to me, but she wants me to bring a detective from your unit with me when I go to her house."

Herb Swindler was busy tracking down more flight lists — this time to San Francisco — so Homicide detective Gail Leonard was assigned to accompany Rockwell's attorney to Blake Rossler's upscale home. Despite his name, Gail Leonard was male, and a veteran Homicide investigator.

Blake Rossler was an absolutely beautiful woman, and Heiman and Leonard believed her when she told them that she and Raoul Guy Rockwell had been enjoying an affair for some time, even though she was still "technically" married. She said she had known "Raoul Guy" for five years, and they had become very close friends, sometimes meeting at his gallery, but more often arranging for discreet time alone. She wasn't embarrassed in the least to admit her infidelity; rather, she was seething over the way Rockwell had tricked her and then abandoned her.

"We were having lunch on the sixteenth of July," she recalled, "at a restaurant downtown. It was after Manzanita left him. And suddenly Raoul asked me to go to Portugal with him. At first I thought he was joking, but he said he was serious. He asked me to take some time to think about it, and then give him my answer.

"Several days later we went swimming together, and he asked me again about Portugal. I realized then he was very anxious for me to leave my husband and go with him, and I did think about it. When we met for lunch a few days later, I gave him my answer. I was about to leave on a vacation in Palm Springs, but I had decided to go away with him to Portugal if he would agree to wait for me to get back."

Rockwell had assured her he would wait.

Blake Rossler had returned from her vacation at the end of July.

"I called Raoul to tell him I was back, and we spoke of our plans for the Portugal trip. He told me he would stay in close touch with me."

Asked about Evelyn Emerson, Blake said that as far as she knew, Evelyn was just another antiques dealer in Seattle, and Raoul had no romantic interest in her. He had been so ardent and persuasive that she couldn't imagine he might be interested in any other woman.

"You didn't know they were engaged?" Gail Leonard asked. "That they were married last week?"

Blake looked astounded. *"No!"* she said. "Of course not. He barely knew Evelyn."

"When did you hear from Raoul again?" Jeffrey Heiman asked. Neither he nor Leonard had relished telling Blake that Raoul and Evelyn had gotten married on July 29.

"He called me on August 2nd," Blake said, her voice trembling with shock. "He had the plane tickets for us to fly to San Francisco. He also called me on August 3rd. We were going to California, where we would pick up his yacht, and we were scheduled to leave the next day."

"Where was he calling from?"

"Tacoma. I would imagine he had moved out of his place on Lake Union. I'm not sure, though. Everything was happening so fast."

It certainly was. The men who were questioning her were incredulous that the missing Raoul Guy Rockwell had managed to convince at least two women that he adored them — all within the same time frame. He'd been divorced for only four days, had married Evelyn Emerson, and had obviously been prepared to take Blake Rossler to Portugal with him, by way of San Francisco. But he'd also told Evelyn that the trip to Portugal was to be *their* honeymoon! And on the night his bride thought he'd left for Canada, he'd apparently been staying in a motel in Tacoma, Washington, twenty-six miles south of Seattle.

Blake said she had packed in a hurry, prepared to walk out on her husband on the fourth of August, leaving just a note to say good-bye. She said that she hadn't wanted to leave him in a precarious financial position, though, and that Raoul had promised to give her $1,000 so her husband could cover some debts she had run up recently.

"Raoul called me early the next morning

and asked if I could be ready to leave my house by 10:45 A.M. — that was Thursday, the fourth. I was all packed so I told him I could do that, and I took a cab to the airport. We caught a twelve-thirty United flight to Portland."

"Under Rockwell's name?" Gail Leonard asked, his normally serious detective's voice betraying his own incredulity. This guy Rockwell was amazing the way he played women — like puppets on a string.

Blake shook her head. "No, he bought our tickets as 'Mr. and Mrs. Rogers.' I assumed that was in case my husband tried to follow us."

After spending three hours in the Portland, Oregon, airport, they had boarded another flight — this time on Western Airlines, bound for San Francisco. Rockwell had given Blake a $50 gold coin and a wedding band — which was far too small for her. "He told me we could get it sized to fit me later," she said.

Still using their aliases as Mr. and Mrs. Rogers, Raoul had checked them into the Mark Hopkins Hotel in San Francisco, where they occupied a posh suite, but only for one night. The next day, they moved to the St. Francis Hotel, but again to a lovely room.

"It was 1127," Blake said, her voice a little faint now as she seemed to absorb that she might be the victim of a major hoax.

The romantic trip began to disintegrate when Blake became ill with a severe sore throat. "Raoul took me across the street to a doctor," she recalled, "who thought I needed to be seen by a specialist."

Raoul had agreed. "The next morning," Blake said, "Raoul told me that he had made an appointment with a Dr. James Whitman, who was on the staff of the University of California at Berkeley. His medical offices were supposed to be in the Alumni Building there."

Blake said that she felt ill and feverish as her lover called a cab, gave her $6 for the fare, and told the driver to take her to the Alumni Building.

"I was supposed to wait *in front* of that building until Dr. Whitman contacted me. I did think it was odd that I wasn't just supposed to go up to the throat specialist's office, but I did as Raoul instructed. I stood there on the street from 10 A.M. until 11."

No one came up to her, and when she went into the building, she couldn't find a Dr. Whitman on the directory posted near the elevators. Confused and feeling more ill all the time, Blake Rossler took a cab back to the St. Francis Hotel.

When she went up to room 1127 and opened the door with the extra key the desk clerk had given her, Blake said she'd been stunned. Raoul wasn't there, and he hadn't even left her a note.

It was almost like the familiar story of a couple who check into a hotel in a strange city or foreign country. When one leaves for some errand or other, the other comes back to find the lover missing. In this scenario — made into several movies over the years — no one admits to ever having seen the lover.

But the staff at the St. Francis Hotel acknowledged that they had seen "Mr. Rogers" when he and Blake had checked in the previous night. They had also seen him when he had left the building with her and put her into a cab a few hours earlier.

Blake said she'd found their room virtually empty of any sign they'd been there. Raoul had taken all of his clothes, except for a few soiled items left behind. He had also taken the gold coin and the wedding ring he'd given her.

She had no choice but to gather up her own things, slip out of the hotel because she had no money to pay the bill, and call her husband to ask him to wire money so she could buy a plane ticket home.

At the airport in San Francisco, Blake dropped all the dimes she had into pay phones as she called the hotel room where she had spent a lovely night with Rockwell. The phone rang emptily for the first half-dozen calls.

"Finally, on my last try," Blake recalled, "a woman answered the phone. She had a youngish voice. When I asked for Raoul, she said she had never heard of Raoul Guy Rockwell. I suppose it could have been a newly registered guest, but now I even wonder if he picked up some other woman and brought her back to the room."

Blake said she had hung up the phone and boarded the plane for her return trip to Seattle — ill, disappointed, and apologetic. Since she'd been gone only two days, she'd been able to come up with an explanation about why she'd gone to San Francisco.

"My husband didn't ask too many questions, and he forgave me for leaving without telling him where I was going. He may not have wanted to know . . ."

Blake said she had no idea where Raoul Guy Rockwell was now, but she certainly hoped he was someplace uncomfortable. Gail Leonard told her that she wasn't the only woman he had left behind. Beyond Evelyn Emerson, the investigators had heard rumors of other betrayed women. Blake was astonished.

"I thought I knew him," she said bitterly. "I guess I didn't know him at all."

"Maybe none of us did," Jeffrey Heiman concurred.

Evelyn Emerson Rockwell was even more shocked than Blake Rossler had been. She had been agonizing over what might have happened to her new husband, and now she knew that he'd deserted her for another woman — and abandoned *that* woman too. From the moment they'd met in his shop in February, she believed that she was special to him, and she'd never doubted his intentions. He had told her how miserable his marriage was, and that he was doing his best to leave his wife without hurting his stepdaughter too much. She thought he was a man who didn't want to hurt anyone, even his "selfish wife."

But now it dawned on Evelyn — and on Germaine Winkler — that Rockwell had disappeared with $10,000 of Germaine's money!

Evelyn had known him only six months. Looking back now, she realized that she knew virtually nothing about his background, his birth family, whether he'd been married before Manzanita. She felt horrible about her mother losing so much money and that they'd both been made fools of. It had been like a lovely dream — one that turned into a nightmare.

Herb Swindler learned that Rockwell had done some shopping on July 30. He bought a set of expensive luggage at a downtown Seattle store, and three days later — just a day before he said he was going to Canada to collect the Indian artifacts — he spent $80 on a pair of silk pajamas and some underwear for himself. He also spent $49.50 on a woman's handbag and asked to have it gift-wrapped. If he didn't give it to Evelyn Emerson or to Blake Rossler, who *had* he given it to?

There was undoubtedly a third woman in his life during that hot summer of 1960, but she never came forward. If, indeed, she *could* come forward. Every bit of information that turned up about Raoul Guy Rockwell sparked even more questions.

Things got worse for Evelyn Emerson Rockwell, the devastated bride.

Of course, Gail Leonard and Herb Swindler began to wonder about what had really happened to Manzanita Rockwell and Dolores Mearns. It seemed odd that Manzanita hadn't taken any money from the Rockwells' bank account, although Raoul had told everyone that she had. The records at the Pacific National Bank showed that the only withdrawals in the past five months had been made by Rockwell himself. The couple's friends hadn't heard from Manzanita or from Dolores. The bank where Manzanita worked was given no notice, and Dolores left school without withdrawing, losing all the tuition she had just paid. It was as though the earth had swallowed them up sometime near the end of March.

Bank records showed that Raoul and Manzanita had opened their account on December 11, 1958. On March 29, 1960, the balance was $199.73. On April 4, Rockwell had deposited $147.88, bringing their balance up to $347.61. There were no large checks drawn on the account, although Raoul had cashed the check from Bushnell's Auction for the sale of his antiques stock at his bank in early August. If Manzanita had wiped him out, how had she done it?

On September 2, 1960, Manzanita's former husband, William Mearns of Vancouver, Canada, filed a missing persons report on his ex-wife and daughter. He and Manzy had three daughters together; the younger two girls were in his custody, while Dolores had gone with her mother after their divorce. Their divorce was amicable, Mearns said, and Manzanita had faithfully visited her younger daughters at least once a month.

"But they haven't heard from her since March 12th," Mearns told Seattle's Missing Persons detectives. "Ordinarily, she would have come up for a weekend in mid-April, but they didn't hear from her at all. One of our girls called the Rockwell house in early May and talked to Raoul. When she asked about her mother, he said she was away on a trip, and he asked to have me call him. But when I did, he told me that Manzy had taken Dolores out of college and the two of them had left him.

"He said she had called him the next day," Mearns continued, "and that she asked him to pack all of her clothes and send them to Bekins Warehouse to put in storage, but he said his lawyer told him not to do that."

Her two husbands had agreed that if either of them heard from Manzy, they would notify the other. About ten days later, Rockwell had called Mearns to see if he'd heard anything, but he hadn't. Rockwell said he hadn't either.

Although Mearns had been concerned about his daughter Dolores, he wasn't really worried. "Manzy left me the same way when she ran off with Raoul," Mearns said. "She just took off without so much as a note. I didn't hear from her for nine months — not until she wanted to arrange for the visits with our younger girls."

It was now five months since anyone had seen Manzy Rockwell. Maybe she had had enough of Raoul's womanizing, and had chosen to leave him just as she had walked away from her first husband.

But maybe not.

The Crimes Against Persons detectives fanned out to talk with those who had known the Rockwells. They found several people who had heard Raoul Guy complain that his wife had stolen more than $5,000 from the antiques gallery's cash registers.

Detective Carol Hahn interviewed Karen Yanick, who lived next door to the now-missing couple. She said that she last saw Manzy on March 31.

"She was coming home from work, and everything seemed to be normal with her. I know I saw Dolores the day before, and she was so excited about registering for spring quarter — she'd gotten into the classes she wanted. Neither of them acted as though they planned to leave Seattle."

And yet, on April 3, Raoul had come to the Yanick home and said that Manzy had left him. "He was doing his income tax," Karen Yanick told Carol Hahn, "and he couldn't make his books tally. He said he had asked Manzy to help him and she just said, 'See my lawyer!' and wouldn't explain what she meant. I guess she gave him the name of her lawyer, and he said he went to find him — and couldn't. Then, when he got home, Manzy and Dolores were gone."

The very next day, Rockwell had gone to the Yanicks' again. This time, he said that there was somewhere between $3,000 and $4,500 missing from the books. And $800 in cash missing.

"I thought this was kind of odd," Karen Yanick said, "because Manzy told me that they were really in debt — that's why she went back to work at the bank, to try to catch up on their bills.

"We invited Rocky over to dinner several times over the next week or so, and he was so sad and worried. We even took turns staying with him at the antiques shop during business hours in the evening so he wouldn't be so lonesome. And then he just stopped opening the shop very often."

Karen said that Manzy Rockwell had worked days at the bank downtown and evenings in the shop — unless the "society women" showed up, and then Manzy would go upstairs because she couldn't stand to watch her husband flirt with them. "That made her so unhappy."

Dolores, too, had tried to help the Rockwells' financial situation by paying her own way in college. She signed on as a Kelly Girl temp in February, and then went to work full-time for the Pacific Northwest Company, managing to work and still go to her classes at the university.

Karen Yanick paused. There was more to tell, things that might sound crazy. She and her husband had begun to wonder about some of Raoul's behaviors.

"Maybe we just had overactive imaginations," she said. "But we noticed that one of the windows under their building was open, and it never was before. It was right next to the septic tank. And later on, maybe as late as June, there was a really terrible, foul odor coming from their house. It was so bad that we asked Rocky about it. He said it was only some crab that had spoiled, and he threw it into his garbage can."

Detective Noreen Skagen checked out the women's clothing left behind in the Rockwell residence. Karen Yanick helped her sort through Manzanita's and Dolores's things. There were numerous dresses, suits, coats, blouses, skirts, shoes, and purses. Noreen (who would one day become an assistant Seattle Police chief and then the U.S. Attorney in the Seattle District) wondered what might be missing. Karen Yanick said the only item of clothing that she could see *wasn't* there was a rust tweed dress that Manzy often wore.

Manzanita was a skilled seamstress, and Skagen and Yanick found a wool skirt that was half sewn, along with an almost-finished coat she had been making for Dolores. There was a pair of green high-heeled pumps that Karen recognized.

"Those are Dolores's," she said. "I remember how proud she was of them when she bought them last spring."

With an ominous sense of foreboding, the two women went through a barrel in a corner of the back bedroom. There they found full bottles of hair spray, barely touched containers of face cream, expensive perfumes, lipsticks. Dolores's newly purchased schoolbooks for her university courses were there, too, along with her purse. Her identification was inside; there was cash in her wallet, and all the ordinary things that most women kept in their purses.

"Why would she leave her purse?" Karen Yanick asked, and then gasped, suddenly suspecting why.

As the Seattle Police investigators spread out further with interviews of friends and clients of Raoul Guy Rockwell, they heard similar stories from all of them — except that they were never quite the same in the details.

Raoul had apparently tailored his anecdotes to suit whomever he spoke to.

He had told another couple who had socialized with Manzanita and him that she had left her packed bags behind, instructing him to have a moving company pick them up. When the husband, Robert Lane, dropped by at the end of May, Rockwell had sharply refused to let him go upstairs, giving him vague excuses why he couldn't do that.

It was rapidly becoming obvious that Raoul Guy Rockwell had had a slightly different story for almost everyone about where his wife and stepdaughter were. The amount of money that Manzanita was supposed to have stolen varied with each telling. Sometimes he said her attorney's office was in the south end of King County — in Kent — and sometimes he gave a Bothell address in the north sector.

He was fairly consistent, though, about describing his missing ex-wife as a thief, a woman out of control, unfaithful, determined to desert him, and leaving him in a snarl of financial entanglements.

One customer, a man named George

Sparr, told Gail Leonard that he had known Rockwell for three years. He confided that he had been horribly embarrassed sometime at the end of March to be present when Manzy and Rocky had a fight. "They were extremely insulting to one another," Sparr said, "and I edged my way to the door and slipped out, feeling that this was a private matter and not something I should be witness to."

"Did you see Manzanita after that?" Leonard asked.

"No. I went back sometime around April 16th, and Rocky told me Manzy and Dolores were gone. Apparently, while he was up in Bothell trying to find Manzy's attorney, he said, she was busy burning all of his irreplaceable papers in their fireplace. He told me that she had stolen thousands of dollars from him, messed up his income tax, and yet she left all of her jewelry behind — even her engagement and wedding rings. He showed me a note she supposedly left, instructing him to put all of her things in storage.

"But that's the odd thing," Sparr continued. "A couple of days later, I noticed some of Manzy's jewelry in a display case in the shop with a For Sale tag on them. I bought a pair of rare cherry amber earrings for only $5, and I took a friend to the shop later and she bought a necklace that was also under-priced."

Sparr had asked for the key to the Rock-wells' upstairs apartment so he could use the bathroom, and then asked "Is Manzanita upstairs?"

"What did he say?" Leonard pressed.

"He looked as if he'd seen a ghost, and he said, 'What the hell do you mean by a re-mark like that?' He was totally spooked, and he called me four times the next day, leaving messages for me to call — that it was urgent. When I did call him back, he asked me again why I had asked if Manzy was upstairs."

Rockwell had been alternately accusing and confiding with Sparr. He told Sparr that Manzanita was following him, and had trailed him to the apartment of a woman friend.

More and more odd things happened, Sparr said. Some weeks after Manzanita and Dolores left, Sparr had noticed that the heavy cement cover of the home's septic tank had been shifted. "When I went there later, though, it was sealed tightly."

Some of the witnesses Gail Leonard and Herb Swindler talked to came close to cat-egorizing Raoul Guy Rockwell as a Blue-beard, while others found him charming — if a little eccentric — a man caught in a marriage with a neurotically jealous woman. One couple even confided that Rockwell had told them that Manzy was seeing another man and that he was disturbed because none of their friends had told him about it.

"How could we tell him?" the wife said. "We didn't know anything about that. We never saw Manzy with anyone but Raoul. She adored him."

But Raoul Guy continued to describe his absent wife as a crazy woman, one who had made his life a living hell and then left him in disastrous financial straits.

One very reliable source disputed that Manzanita Rockwell *had* been reduced to a "basket case." In 1960, Dr. Sheldon Biback was a very popular and respected obstetrician-gynecologist with offices in the University District. Manzanita Rockwell was one of his patients.

When Noreen Skagen talked to Dr. Biback, he recalled an office visit he'd had with Manzanita on March 30. She had come to him in a state of extreme agitation, so anxious that she asked him to prescribe a sedative. That was not how Biback had viewed her in their past appointments, and he sensed that she was dealing with a reality that would make most women upset. She told Biback that she had suspected her husband of being unfaithful for some time, and she had followed him to another woman's house. There, she had confirmed her worst suspicions.

"I can't live this way," she confessed to her doctor, "and I told Raoul that I knew about his affair, and I wasn't willing to accept that and pretend it wasn't happening. I'm going to have a showdown with him to force some kind of a decision. I love him and I'm going to fight for him because I believe our marriage can be saved."

Dr. Biback told Noreen Skagen that he had found Manzanita Rockwell a "rational and reasonable woman." Even though she had been very distracted by her situation, calling herself "a basket case," she hadn't seemed at all crazy, or even vindictive. She was simply a woman who was ready to face a very real problem and try to do what she needed to to win back her husband's affection.

Biback hadn't heard from her again. But then, apparently no one had, except for Karen's brief sighting of Manzy as she came home from work the next day.

Manzanita had been Biback's patient for some time and he pulled her chart when Detective Skagen asked for her description.

"Manzanita was five feet five inches tall," he read, "and weighed 122 pounds. She had auburn hair and a fair, freckled complexion."

Dolores had been required to have a physical when she applied to the University of Washington, and Dr. Gilbert Eade had her chart in his office. She was five feet five and a half and weighed only 112 pounds.

Who the other woman in Raoul Rockwell's life was was anyone's guess. It could have been Evelyn or Blake, or perhaps one of several other women. Apparently Rockwell had been adept at carrying on many liaisons at the same time without any of his paramours knowing about the others.

By the time Detectives Noreen Skagen and Carol Hahn, and the Rockwells' neighbor Karen Yanick, had finished their inventory of Manzanita's and Dolores's abandoned belongings, they had listed 640 items! Everything from clothing to makeup to treasured personal belongings filled three boxes, three trunks, and three barrels. These were delivered to the property room of the Seattle Police Department on the second floor of the Public Safety Building to await any further developments on the women's disappearance or, less likely, instructions from Manzanita and her daughter.

The missing women had obviously left with only the clothes on their backs.

Without their purses.

Without their makeup.

■ ■ ■ ■

As summer faded into autumn, 1960, Raoul Guy Rockwell was still missing. His home and gallery sat empty, a looming gray building that no longer attracted eager collectors but looked more dreary with every day that passed. Rockwell's vibrant and charismatic personality had made it popular; now Seattle detectives sensed that it held some terrible secrets.

It was probably fitting that the most popular movie at the time was in its first run at Seattle's Paramount Theater. *Psycho* starred Janet Leigh (albeit briefly, as her character soon perished in the infamous bloody shower scene) and Tony Perkins as the Bates Motel manager. The mansion behind that motel hid Perkins's character's secrets.

It was also a looming gray building. And Leigh's character also disappeared completely.

Herb Swindler and Gail Leonard were not optimistic about the safety of the women who had vanished so completely from Raoul Guy Rockwell's life, and indeed from life itself. No one had heard from them. They had left no paper trail at all, hadn't tried to cash checks, contact banks, written letters to their daughters/sisters. They hadn't even taken their identification with them.

But where were they? The investigators in the Crimes Against Persons Unit sent out requests to other law enforcement agencies in the Northwest requesting information about any women who might have been in accidents or checked into hospitals — perhaps suffering from amnesia — or, in the worst possible scenario, been found dead and were currently listed as Jane Does.

Nineteen sixty, of course, was long before the high-speed communication of thirty to forty years later. There was no central clearing agency in the state of Washington or, for that matter, in the United States. Computer-generated fingerprint matching lay far in the future, as did DNA and other sophisticated blood and body fluid correlations to identify victims or link them to their killers. There were no computers in police departments, no Internet, no cell phones.

Even so, Homicide detectives were successful in closing the vast majority of their investigations and seeing convictions in trials the old-fashioned way: with hard work, canvassing, and brainstorming.

But this case was a challenge. It wasn't going to be easy to find Manzanita and Dolores. Or Raoul Guy Rockwell himself.

On September 1, 1960, the probers received information from a sheriff's office far from Seattle, on the other side of the Cascade Mountains. Wenatchee, Washington, was the seat of Chelan County, some 150 miles east of Seattle, a small city known for its apple blossom festival each May and the verdant fruit-growing orchards that spread out endlessly in the region.

Dick Nichols was the Chelan County sheriff in 1960, a genial man whose staff usually dealt with drunken fights in taverns and migrant camps, illegal marijuana patches, and the occasional homicide. The Columbia River roared close to Wenatchee, its banks crowded with towering poplar trees that protected the orchards from windstorms.

Nichols phoned the Seattle Homicide Unit lieutenant on duty to ask if the Seattle cops were aware that the severed legs of a female had been recovered from the Columbia River in nearby Grant County in May and June.

"Why don't you contact Deputy W. E. Dunstan in the sheriff's office in Moses Lake?" Nichols suggested. "They've got one of the legs, and the other is here in our county. Dr. Robert Bonafaci, our coroner, is a pathologist and he has it."

The floating legs were a gruesome find.

They could have come from a woman anywhere in Washington, or even from the Canadian border cities just beyond Okanogan County, which lay north of Chelan County. The Columbia was a wide river, full of dangerous rapids, carrying all kinds of debris as it coursed south.

Detectives Gary Honz and "Buzz" Cook drove to Wenatchee to pick up the severed legs and transport them to Seattle so that longtime King County coroner Dr. Gale Wilson could examine them. Along with the legs, they received photographs and slides that Dr. Bonafaci had taken, and four X-ray films.

While Honz and Cook were in Wenatchee, Detectives Bill Panton and Vern Thomas found some fascinating news at Cook's U-Drive, the car rental company Raoul Guy Rockwell patronized. A records search there showed that he had rented a GMC panel truck on April 6, four days after anyone had seen Manzanita and Dolores. He drove it away just before two that afternoon, and returned the vehicle on April 7 at 9 A.M. The odometer indicated that he had driven 319 miles. The round-trip distance to Wenatchee is exactly 306 miles.

On September 3, 1960, Dr. Wilson submitted his report on the two legs found in the Columbia River. In his opinion, they had come from the same person: a Caucasian female who had been approximately forty years old and about five feet five inches tall. She had probably weighed close to 130 pounds. Her feet had very high arches, and the second toe on the first leg was longer than the big toe, which had an obvious bunion on the outside surface; the little toe had a wide gap between it and the fourth toe, and turned under.

One of the legs had been found in a wooden box. That limb had been sawed off at midthigh and then broken. The second leg had been cut and broken closer to the knee.

There was a nylon stocking in the box, a Micro-Mesh, seamless type, sandy beige color, size 9 1/2. That wasn't much in the way of physical evidence but it was something. Perhaps they could find its mate or other hose of the same make and size.

The Grant County Sheriff's Office said that the first leg had been located by a family picnicking on the shores of the Columbia on May 30. A professor of anthropology at Washington State University in Pullman concurred that it belonged to a female of middle age, white, and possibly about five feet seven and a half. She had type O blood.

The second leg had surfaced in the Columbia on June 22, two miles away — in Quincy, Washington — and been spotted by a man living in a trailer court there.

The measurements of the disembodied legs seemed to fit the description given for Manzanita Rockwell. Manzanita had told one of her friends that her blood was type O, although that wasn't noted in Dr. Biback's chart.

To get still another evaluation of the floating legs, they were packed carefully and sent to Dr. T. D. Stewart, curator of the Division of Physical Anthropology at the National Museum in Washington, D.C.

He found that the radiographic detail of the two femoral ends (where the thigh bones ended at the knees) were so similar that they had undoubtedly come from the same individual. The bones were of a mature person, but still rounded enough at the joints, he said, to verify that the person was in "early adult life" — around thirty-five to forty.

If this was all that was left of Manzanita — and there was no proof of that — Dolores Mearns was still missing.

On September 6, Sergeant Herb Swindler and Detectives Bill Panton and Carol Hahn obtained a search warrant for the entire building at 2512 Fairview Avenue. It was the first foray of one of the most sweeping searches the Seattle Police Department had ever — or would ever — carry out.

As they examined the walls of the kitchen, they detected several dark stains that appeared to be blood near the stairway that led up to the attic. Further investigation disclosed numerous suspected bloodstains on the stairway itself, the cardboard underliner on the steps and other cardboard attached to the walls, the wooden pillar at the bottom of the staircase, and a south wall made of plywood.

These stains *would* prove to be human blood when they were tested in the police lab, and the type was O-positive. The manner in which the blood was smeared on the cardboard side of the stairway suggested that a person — or a body — had been dragged up the staircase shortly after a wound had been inflicted. Swindler spotted two small reddish brown hairs and one white hair caught in a large blood smear. They were not human hairs, but rather, they had come from a cow.

That was an oddity in an already peculiar case. Swindler learned later from the missing women's friends that the two had shared a favorite brown-and-white cowhide belt, one item of clothing *not* found with their belongings.

Swindler did find a long reddish brown hair on the underside of the third step; it would prove to be microscopically alike in class and characteristic to similar hairs taken from Dolores Mearns's pink hairbrush.

Manzanita's red hair was dyed, and some of it was found on the stairs and in her hairbrush. There were also pink and white woolen fibers, as if from sweaters, trapped in the swaths of blood.

As the searchers reached the attic, they found a virtual abattoir there: drops, smears, stains, soaking blood. Only halfhearted attempts had been made to hide it. Rugs had been piled on top of some stains, and fabric with dark stains had been jumbled together, as if to hide them. Bizarrely, someone had tried to cover up bloodstains by swabbing blue paint over them. When the paint was still wet, scraps of wallboard, plywood, and tar paper had been stacked on top of it.

If the effort was meant to permanently hide the evidence of massive blood loss, it failed. So much of the red stuff had been shed that the blood seeped through the floor joists onto paper covering the ceiling just below. Just south of the blue-painted area, Swindler found a white enamel pan, its bottom stained halfway up with brownish red stains. There was little question that a body or bodies had been dissected here in the dim attic; there were innumerable particles of dried blood, bits of human tissue, and bone fragments left behind.

The blood and tissue was all type O.

A broken tooth, a lower canine, lay near the stairwell. It would be identified as coming from someone about twenty years of age.

There were empty packages that had once held large plastic bags, the remains of a roll of thick plastic, and some lengths of rope and twine.

There was no way to look at the dreadful physical evidence except as the handiwork of a mad butcher.

Friends had told the detectives that Raoul Guy Rockwell had plunged into weeks of heavy drinking — unusual for him — during the prior April. Still, he hadn't appeared to be drunk. Now, during a reinterview Detective Panton had with Karen Yanick, she commented on that. "Rocky said, 'If I could just get drunk so I could forget it for a while,' but he never explained what it was he wanted to forget."

Karen recalled that Rockwell had moved his bed from the kitchen area to a front bedroom in late April. "He used to use that for a place to refinish furniture, but he said he couldn't sleep in the kitchen alcove anymore."

As Swindler, Panton, and Hahn surveyed the ghastly mess in the attic, they could understand Rockwell's need to forget. Even if the man was a psychopath, whatever had happened here would give anyone nightmares. It certainly looked as though he had killed both his wife and his stepdaughter and dragged them up to the attic, where he dissected their bodies.

"But he went ahead with his divorce to bolster his alibi," Swindler said sardonically, "and it didn't slow him down when it came to romancing other women. He just went on with his life."

There was more evidence to find.

Swindler and Leonard hadn't forgotten the information that the Rockwell house's septic tank cover had been ajar for a short time during the previous spring, and then sealed tightly. When they had collected the thousands of pieces of evidence inside the old house, they knew that the next step was to open up the septic tank, cutting through the freshly cemented seams.

It was not a pleasant thought.

But it had to be done.

Deputy Chief Frank Ramon, who had taken over the intense probe into the fate of Manzanita Rockwell and Dolores Mearns, arranged to have a Seattle City Engineering sludge truck and a skin diver standing by as the septic tank was opened. As the contents of the tank were pumped out, what looked like human body parts came into view. Dr. Gale Wilson would later verify what they were:

1. A uterus with a small portion of the vaginal vault attached. It measured 8x5x4.5 centimeters, and it contained numerous small fibroid tumors. (These benign tumors are quite common in young women.)
2. The upper portion of the right ear of a human, which had been hacked off clumsily.
3. A kidney, with adipocere attached. (Adipocere is a soaplike substance that sometimes forms when human tissue is submerged in water or other liquid for some time.)
4. Five pieces of colon, and mesentery (the lining of the inner abdomen).
5. One section of lung.
6. One section of muscle.

7. One partial kidney.
8. Two sections of rib, one partially burned, with sawed ends.
9. An ulnar bone (one of two bones in the forearm).
10. A radial epiphysis (the growth ends of the other forearm bone).
11. Four phalangeal bones (hand bones).

There were also numerous hairs, paintbrushes, and other household debris.

Dr. Wilson said that it was his opinion that all of the tissue and bones had come from a human female approximately eighteen years old.

This suggested, of course, that Dolores Mearns had never left the old gray house on Fairview Avenue at all.

In the twenty-first century, given the amount of physical evidence and the massive circumstantial evidence the investigators had turned up, the case against Raoul Guy Rockwell would quickly result in an arrest warrant. But in 1960, the King County prosecutor's office hesitated to charge him. Type O blood is the second most common type in humans, and the science of winnowing out subcategories in crime labs was not done half a century ago. DNA hadn't even been heard of.

Hairs and fibers could only be classified as "microscopically similar." Were the legs found in the Columbia River the earthly remains of Manzanita Rockwell? Were the pitiful bits and pieces of some female body found in the septic tank all that was left of Dolores Mearns?

With DNA, a criminologist would have been able to say that they definitely were — or were not. But armed only with a common blood type, any prosecutor would face obvious attacks by a defense team, who would surely insist that there was no proof that they belonged to either of the missing women — or that they were actually deceased.

While searchers continued to scour the Rockwells' former home, other detectives questioned acquaintances of the missing couple in an ever-widening circle. They also reinterviewed those they had talked to before.

In the weathered building that no longer had any charm at all, given the grisly things they had already located there, detectives wearing protective coveralls and rubber gloves bagged and labeled a mountain of evidence, much of which would be sent to the FBI lab for further examination: hairbrushes from each women (Manzanita's held strands of her hair that were dyed auburn at the ends but were her natural brown at the roots); panties stained with menstrual blood (Dolores's — she also had type O blood); a pair of Micro-Mesh nylons still in a package from the H. L. Green Company; women's shoes sized 7 1/2; a .22 caliber expended long-rifle bullet, apparently fired through the box spring of a mattress in the bedroom; a box of .22 caliber bullets; a pair of men's slippers, size 13, soaked in dried human blood; and a meat-saw frame and two meat-saw blades.

Human tissue, blood type O, was found in the recesses of the meat-saw frame. A check with the Seattle Blood Bank was lucky; Raoul Guy had donated blood there, and *his* blood type was the relatively rare type B.

Detectives located the hardware store where the meat saw had been purchased, but the owner did not recall who had bought it. The district manager of the H. L. Green Company verified that the stores had had a special sale on the Micro-Mesh stockings after buying fifty dozen pairs from the Liberty Hosiery Mills in Gibsonville, North Carolina. The closest store to the Rockwells' home and business was only steps from the corner where Manzanita transferred from one bus to another as she commuted from her bank job. She had probably bought several pairs of hose there in March.

That information still wasn't enough to secure an arrest warrant.

There were no fingerprints — no intact fingers, for that matter, of the missing women. The phalangeal bones found in the septic tank were determined to be from the fingers of a young person — someone under twenty.

All through the rainy autumn of 1960, the intensive probe into the disappearance of Rockwell's wife and stepdaughter continued. It wasn't headline news, however. Rather, it meant dreary overtime hours put in by dogged detectives who found out fragments of information that might be helpful.

The big news that fall was national: John F. Kennedy and Richard M. Nixon had their first televised debate, with Kennedy winning it running away; Nixon's image without makeup was that of a pale man who needed a shave badly.

Ted Williams retired from baseball, hitting a 420-foot home run against the Baltimore Orioles in his final game and receiving a standing ovation.

Nikita Khrushchev made his infamous shoe-banging speech at the United Nations General Assembly, and Clark Gable died of a heart attack at the age of fifty-nine.

On that very day — November 16 — Detective Panton contacted a couple in Vancouver who had been close friends of Manzanita Rockwell's. Fortuitously, Jim Garner was an anthropologist for the Vancouver City Museum. He and his wife, Bea, had visited the Rockwells at the antiques gallery six months earlier on April 2, 1960. It had been a short visit — only a half hour — that took place about ten-thirty that night. It was a kind of pop-in visit and the Garners were testing the waters to see if the Rockwells would welcome company so late.

"I could see that it wasn't a good time for us to drop in," Garner recalled. "Manzy and Rocky were having a squabble, and they both seemed upset even though they tried to hide it. We just made excuses, saying we had to get on the road north."

"Did you ever see Manzanita after that?" Panton asked.

"Never. Rocky called me about two weeks later and asked if we had seen Manzy. When I said we hadn't heard from her, he told us that they had had a fight that started that night Bea and I stopped at their place, that Manzy and Dolores left, and they stole a lot of money from him."

It was virtually the same story that Rockwell had told everyone who had known his wife. Rockwell had embroidered a bit more on it by saying that he had seen his wife talking in hushed tones to a strange man who had come into their shop, and he believed she had run off with him.

Because Jim Garner *was* an anthropologist, he made an excellent witness who could describe Manzanita's figure — particularly her legs.

He remarked that they were unusually stocky for a woman with a slender torso and upper body. She had thick ankles, and a large muscular swelling that began on the back of her calf and continued downward.

"She almost had what people call 'piano legs,'" Garner said.

Bea Garner nodded in agreement. "She always wore pointy-toed shoes that were too small for her feet, and her skin kind of puffed out over the tops."

They both agreed that Manzanita's legs had been atypical, a feature that most people would remember about her. Jim Garner agreed to look at photographs of the severed legs found in the Columbia River, although Bea Garner demurred.

Garner nodded. "I think those are Manzy's legs," he said. "See there? The thickening in the ankles? The feet are those of someone who wore shoes too small for her, and the toes curl under from wearing pointed shoes."

Panton talked with Bill Mearns, Manzanita's ex-husband. Before he looked at the photographs, he too described her legs as having very thick ankles that hardly narrowed at all below the calf. And he also gave details of her deformed toes. "It looked as though she had bunions on the outside of her big toe joints, and her little toes looked bunched up."

When Panton brought out the leg photos, they were *exactly* as Mearns had described them, just as Jim Garner had described them.

Until Panton's trip to Vancouver, the Seattle detectives had believed that Manzanita and Dolores had probably been killed on March 31, on the evening after they had come home from work and college.

But the Garners had visited them two days later. Bea Garner felt guilty, she said. "I had the feeling that Manzy wanted to tell me something that last night — but she never did."

Bea recalled that her friend had been wearing a rose-colored sweater, a light skirt, nylons, and black shoes. That was important because the search of the stairway up to the attic had turned up those odd pink and white fibers under a step's edge that hadn't been explained.

Now, detectives suspected that Manzanita had been killed shortly after the Garners left on April 2, undoubtedly dragged up the stairs either before or after death, her sweater and skirt catching on the rough wooden steps.

Charles O. Carroll, a onetime football great at the University of Washington, had been the King County prosecuting attorney for many years. It was an elective office, and Carroll had proudly maintained a conviction rate of well over 95 percent in all those years. There were times when detectives took cases to the prosecutor's office, only to be disappointed because they were sent back to find out more. While they were willing to take a chance on an acquittal, the prosecutor hesitated to risk that; if a killer should be acquitted, double jeopardy would attach and he could never be tried again. And then there was the political angle, too: a winning prosecutor is more likely to get reelected.

In the Rockwell case, there really were no bodies — at least not bodies that could be absolutely established as belonging to Manzanita Rockwell and Dolores Mearns. A murder conviction without a body had not yet been accomplished in Washington State. Indeed, it would be forty years or more before that happened.

Instead of a murder warrant, Charles O. Carroll filed a grand larceny charge against the still-missing Raoul Guy Rockwell, on the evidence of the bunco scheme that robbed Mrs. Winkler of $10,000.

If Rockwell should ever be picked up, that charge would hold him.

There were times when Herb Swindler wondered if Rockwell was dead, perhaps a suicide when the apparitions of what he had almost certainly done appeared in his dreams. Nobody had heard from him.

And then, on September 29, 1960, Detective Gail Leonard received a two-page letter that had been mailed to the Winklers. It was dated way back in March, and was signed by someone named Major John Riley.

Riley waxed enthusiastic as he described Raoul Guy Rockwell as a "great man" and he listed various outstanding honors he had received in the past, and spoke of a distinguished background. A handwriting expert examined the letter, whose postmark was blurred and unreadable, and declared that the signature purported to be Major Riley's was actually that of the man known as Raoul

Guy Rockwell. Maybe Rockwell was planning to return to his disillusioned bride. But he didn't show up in Seattle.

Additions to the murder investigation case continued to pile up in October and November, but they were mostly affirmations of earlier statements. Yes, Manzanita and Dolores had both worn the distinctive wide brown-and-white cowhide belt, Manzanita's toes were very strange, and she had told several people she had type O blood. The Royal Canadian Mounted Police tested Bill Mearns and his surviving daughters for blood type, and they all had type O. Manzanita had been dyeing her hair auburn for about eight years.

Some would argue that there was more than enough evidence to convince a reasonable potential juror that the missing Raoul Guy Rockwell was responsible for the deaths of his wife and his stepdaughter, and that he had employed extraordinary means to cover up his crimes.

Charles O. Carroll did not agree with that point of view.

Herb Swindler, Gail Leonard, Bill Panton, John Leitch, and the rest of the Seattle Police Homicide detectives were not really surprised at the information they got when a California woman contacted them. She explained that she knew Raoul Guy Rockwell well, although Rockwell was not his real name. "His name is Muldavin," she said. "I'm married to his older brother, Michael."

The family name had always been Muldavin, and Raoul Guy had been born Guy Muldavin on May 8, 1925. Sometimes he gave his birthday as October 27, 1923, but that was a lie. He wasn't in his mid-forties; he was only thirty-five. He hadn't been born in Saint-Tropez, France, either, but in Brooklyn, New York. Michael Muldavin was three years older and was currently living with the female informant in San Diego, California.

The matriarch of the family was Sylvia Muldavin, who spoiled her younger son, Guy, outrageously, doting on him and taking him on trips and cruises. She found the boy charming and brilliant. In 1936, Sylvia and Guy had taken a cruise to Cuba on the S.S. *Iroquois,* returning to the Port of New York via Miami on April 21. The ship's manifest listed their address as 2865 West Twentieth Street in Brooklyn.

Rockwell's sister-in-law said that Guy had never been in the army because he had an ear condition that made him 4F. Nor had he gone to the University of California. He had gone to boarding school and attended a few months of drama school during the Second World War. At that time, he had changed his name from Muldavin to Rockwell, and added "Raoul" because he planned to have a career on the Broadway stage and it sounded better. He didn't have even the equivalent of a high school degree, much less a college degree.

"Guy was married once before Manzanita," his chagrined sister-in-law said. "They had a son, but when they divorced, his first wife got custody of the boy."

The Michael Muldavins had received a phone call from Guy from San Francisco on either April 6 or 7. That would have been two days after he abandoned Blake Rossler in the Golden Gate city.

"He promised he was coming for a visit," the woman said, "but he never showed up. He also told us he was going to Ribera, New Mexico, where his mother lives, and he was going to travel with her to New York to visit relatives. But Sylvia says he didn't meet her as he promised. You really can't count on Guy — he lies."

That much the detectives already knew.

They had checked on Rockwell's Fulbright scholarship and found that it never existed.

The Fulbright Foundation had never heard of Rockwell or his amazing collection of Ashanti counterweights.

His sister-in-law promised to notify the Seattle investigators if she heard from Guy Muldavin Rockwell.

But when the elusive antiques dealer surfaced, he was way across the country from San Diego. Just after Thanksgiving 1960, the FBI and New York City Police had located him and arrested him on the grand larceny warrant and other charges.

Sergeant Herb Swindler booked a flight to New York immediately. He believed that if he could engage Muldavin-Rockwell in a conversation, he would be able to elicit a confession that would tie up the double-murder investigation successfully. Although Swindler would be involved in any number of high-profile investigations throughout his long career in law enforcement — including the Ted Bundy case — no one who knew him would deny that tracking "Raoul Guy Rockwell" was *the* most important case in Swindler's life.

"I met him in unfamiliar territory," Swindler told me. "The New York cops were anxious to talk to him, but they gave me an interview room and some time alone with him. He came so close to telling me what I needed to hear."

It was December 2, and the Christmas lights were glittering on the tall tree at Rockefeller Center when Herb Swindler was at last only a few feet away from his clever quarry. He built up to the hard questions slowly, aware of the big-city detectives waiting their turn in the hallway beyond the small room where he sat with the fugitive.

Swindler spread out the 8-by-10 glossies that his team had taken during their many searches of Rockwell's property.

"What happened?" Swindler asked. "Can you explain what happened? It's had us baffled for months now, and you're the only one who can tell us."

Swindler was deliberately playing to Rockwell's massive ego, giving him yet another chance to pontificate — to be the expert, the man with the key to an intricate maze of facts. He could see that Rockwell-Muldavin was tempted to reveal long-held secrets but that he was trying to censor his comments.

"I'm morally guilty of Manzanita's and Dolores's deaths," he said slowly. "I was the only person living with them, and the only person who might have had an opportunity to commit these crimes."

Swindler waited, but Rockwell stopped talking.

The bulldog detective laid out another photograph; it was a close-up of Manzanita's severed leg.

Rockwell's whole body shuddered as he stared fixedly at the terrible picture. "I know what Manzanita's leg looked like," he said. "And I know that Manzy and Dolores are dead."

"You told a lot of stories after they disappeared," Swindler said. "They didn't match up that well, but it seems as though you know what really happened to them."

"Let's not be coy," Rockwell said sarcastically. "How could those stories be true? You know, too, that they're both dead."

Now Rockwell became somber, his face changing into a mask of despair. "I want to die, you know," he said sadly. "I have nothing further to live for, and I am willing myself to die. I would never allow myself to be in a position to hang. Never."

Swindler felt he was the only audience for a performance by a consummate actor, a complete con artist. Rockwell told him that he would reveal the entire story of what had happened the prior April, but not during his lifetime. "I will write it all down in my will."

"Why won't you tell me now?" Swindler pressed.

"I need advice on several moral issues that are involved."

It would have been laughable, Swindler thought, if the situation wasn't so serious. Raoul Guy Muldavin-Rockwell discussing what was moral. He had conned and robbed and undoubtedly killed to get what he wanted, sometimes hurting people for no reason at all except to prove how clever he was. How could he now be discussing morals?

The prisoner dropped tidbits of confessions, doling them out like small prizes, enjoying the power he had to stop talking whenever he chose, knowing that Swindler was so eager to hear the truth. He admitted that he had forged his wife and stepdaughter's names to endorse the paychecks that came in the mail after they disappeared. Swindler knew that was true from the handwriting expert's report.

"I sealed the septic tank with cement," Rockwell said. "After they vanished, there was a terrible, foul odor coming from it."

Herb Swindler felt they were right on the edge of a full confession when there was an impatient knocking on the door of the interview room.

"We were so close," he said a long time later. "And those New York cops said they needed the room — right then. I had no choice but to stop the interview at that point. I've never been so frustrated."

On December 5, Swindler and FBI special agents Joe Fox and Frank Donnelly had another shot at Rockwell. Once again, the suspect admitted to "moral guilt" for Manzanita's and Dolores's deaths. But he would go no further. "I'll tell you all about it," he promised, "as soon as I talk to a Jesuit priest in Seattle."

And then he shut up.

Returned to Seattle in Swindler's custody, Raoul Guy Rockwell met with a Jesuit priest on December 7 and December 9. Their conversation was, of course, privileged. What Rockwell said to the priest is unknown.

After conferring with the priest, Rockwell spoke once again to Herb Swindler, this time in the Seattle Homicide Unit. He refused to talk about his probable crimes, breaking his promise to tell everything after he had talked with a Jesuit.

What he did say to Swindler undoubtedly summed up who Rockwell really was, and his total lack of conscience.

"They are dead," he said forcefully, "and I'm alive, and that's what's important."

Raoul Guy Muldavin-Rockwell was never

charged with the murders of Manzanita Rockwell and Dolores Mearns. Nor did he serve time for the theft of $10,000 from the woman who was his mother-in-law for a very short time. He disappeared from the Seattle scene, and few people who live there today even recognize his name. As infamous as he was forty-seven years ago, the winds of time have swept away his dilapidated buildings, his alleged crimes, and his memory.

Public records show that a man named Guy R. Muldavin was married on February 16, 1974, to a woman named Teri in Washoe County, Nevada. And a man named Milo Guy Maltby married another woman named Teri in Clark County, Nevada, on May 4, 1981.

Was it really Raoul Guy Rockwell, still charming women? Quite possibly. He would have been forty-nine in 1974, and fifty-six at the second civil wedding.

Sylvia Muldavin, Rockwell's mother, died on July 23, 1972, in Santa Clara, California, at the age of seventy. His brother, Michael, passed away in Ribera, New Mexico, on January 1, 2005.

And unless he pulled off his own disappearing act, Guy Muldavin's death at the age of seventy-six is recorded as having occurred in Salinas, California, on March 14,

2002. He took a lifetime of secrets with him to the grave, never to be revealed.

Sergeant Herb Swindler rose through the ranks of the Seattle Police Department, eventually becoming the captain in charge of the Crimes Against Persons Unit. Before he retired, Herb gave me a hundred pages that detailed his work on the Raoul Guy Rockwell case.

There, I found that every piece of evidence his team had picked up was listed carefully in Swindler's own handwriting, all the overtime hours he had worked. The single-spaced typed summary of Case #60–495–379 that he wrote about the mysterious double-murder case is on lined paper, yellowing with age now, and curled at the edges, but it is all there, bringing back the grotesque horror of 1960. The detectives who searched the somehow-haunted building that housed Guy Rockwell's antiques store marked the pages with their initials. I'm sure that all of them remembered this case for the rest of their lives.

I promised Herb Swindler that one day I would write about Raoul Guy Muldavin-Rockwell, the killer who got away. And now I have. Sadly, Herb passed away in 2005 without ever seeing a truly satisfactory ending to the case he wanted so much to solve. But he gave "Rockwell" a run for his money, and the city of Seattle was rid of one of the most outrageous con men ever to settle there.

And of course, neither Manzanita nor Dolores ever came home again.

The
Truck Driver's
Wife

During the years I wrote for *True Detective* and several other fact-detective magazines, it sometimes seemed that I spent half my life in Homicide units around America. I attended the King County Sheriff's Office's Basic Homicide School for two weeks, and I went on many ride-alongs with various law enforcement officers: the Washington State Patrol, Seattle Police Department, Pierce County Sheriff's Office, and even the Seattle Fire Department's Arson Unit: Marshal 5.

It was the best way I could understand what cops and investigators actually *did* when they left their offices and headed out into the field after Roll Call or Show-up. As any other civilian must, I had to sign forms that said I wouldn't sue any of these departments if I should be injured during my ride-alongs.

Fortunately, I never got hurt, but I often

came home smelling of smoke after riding a shift with Marshal 5's arson investigators. For years, I carried a card, issued by the fire chief, that gave me blanket permission to enter any burning building I chose to. After my first experience inside a fire site that had been "tapped" (fire extinguished and situation under control), I didn't relish entering an arson site. Even when the flames were out, the smoke was almost suffocating. The men who investigated possible arson fires had once been firefighters themselves and seemed inured to the acrid fumes as they hastened to check the premises for signs that a fire had been deliberately set.

But I never got used to the smoke — not even after I rode with Marshal 5 for more than three hundred hours.

The men who had spent years in the fire department sometimes tested my gullibility with anecdotes and stories that couldn't possibly be true. I usually caught on quickly, but there were times I wasn't sure if they were teasing or telling the truth.

Like Homicide detectives, arson investigators look for minute clues that will give them something they can prove in a trial. They have the added challenge of sifting through *burned* material that is often unrecognizable. They begin at the roof and work down, removing layer after layer of what were ceilings, walls, curtains, furniture, rugs, floors, papers, trash, and — if they are lucky — gasoline cans or candles not quite burned, which mean a clumsy and stupid arsonist has been there.

Marshal 5 investigators taught me about professional arsonists who could set up a fire that would start long after they were on a plane out of town. They explained that neophytes were often seriously burned — or even killed — when they threw a lighted match into a room doused with an accelerant, thinking they could slam the door before the inferno got to them.

They didn't expect the instant explosion that usually followed.

I think the most intriguing tales involved human beings who simply caught fire for no explainable reason. Was it possible that some chemical change occurred within a living body that caused it to burst into flames without any outside cause?

Some of the old-timers said it was, and recalled finding the remains of people who had apparently caught fire while they sat in an easy chair. They died quickly as tremendous heat was generated.

The story of Dorothy Jones may be a case

of spontaneous combustion. I have pondered it for many years, and I am still not
sure what happened to her.

At the age of forty-four, Dorothy Jones was the envy of many of her friends. She was an extremely attractive African American woman with an exceptional figure that any twenty-five-year-old would have been proud of. She had a longtime husband and there were rumors that she also had an attentive lover. She had a wide circle of friends, both trusted female friends and business associates who admired her. They were loyal to her. Initially, none of them were anxious to talk about Dorothy's private life when detectives came around asking questions.

She had a good income, and she and her husband shared a neat and comfortable house in the south of Seattle. They had no children.

Five days before Christmas 1976, Dorothy was busy running a number of errands. She was looking forward to a trip to San Antonio, Texas, to spend the holidays with relatives there. Her husband was an over-the-road truck driver, and her friends thought she would probably meet up with him at his mother's house in the Alamo city. He'd been gone on a long trip — more than a month — and he was to deliver a load of furniture in Texas, and then they would reunite for a leisurely holiday.

But that wasn't going to happen. Dorothy never made it to Texas. Somewhere in Dorothy's complicated life, a killer waited for her. Whether it was a human murderer who had his or her own reasons to want Dorothy dead, or a more amorphous killer — some sort of natural or unnatural phenomenon — would be the question.

The death of Dorothy Jones was one of the strangest occurrences I ever encountered.

There is no question at all that she was seen alive and vibrant on the evening of Monday, December 20, 1976. Less than an hour and a half later, she was dead, literally roasted, on the charred bedroom of her home.

What happened to Dorothy seems impossible. It could not have happened.

And yet it did.

The Seattle Fire Department received the first call on the 911 line at 6:24 on the evening of December 20. The caller blurted that flames were belching from an upstairs window of a house on Thirty-first Avenue South. Firefighters from Battalion Number 5 leapt aboard their waiting engine and roared to the address with sirens keening. They arrived within a few minutes. They could see the smoke pouring from the upper windows and curling around the roof when they turned the first corner, but when they entered the house, the downstairs looked completely normal, untouched by either flames or smoke.

Firefighter Gordon Ochs ran through the downstairs rooms and followed wisps of smoke up the stairway. That stairwell was full of superheated air.

As Ochs approached the bedroom on the west side of the center stairway, he saw that the door to that room was open approximately eight inches. But as he pushed on it, he felt so much resistance that he had to put his shoulder against the door with great force in order to gain entrance.

The smoke in the room was thick and black; no one could have made it past the top of the stairs without a mask. Ochs's eyes swept the room rapidly, and he saw that the three windows in the smoke-clogged room were unbroken. When he opened the nozzle on the inch-and-a-half hose line he carried and cold water hit the room, the windows shattered.

He was able to extinguish the fire in the room rapidly; the flames seemed to have been most concentrated on and around the king-size bed. The fire had been intense and fast-burning, so hot that the plastic cabinet of a TV next to the bed had literally melted into a grotesque caricature of what it once was.

The bedroom walls were blackened with clear-cut fire Vs rising above the bed's headboard, but their lower portion was untouched.

Now Ochs could make out the form of a woman who lay just inside the door. She was totally naked. She rested on her back with her left leg wedged between the seat and the base of a swivel chair, her face turned slightly to the right.

There was no question that she was dead. Indeed, a postmortem examination would show that her body — particularly her full breasts — had literally been cooked by the fierce heat in the room.

With the discovery of the woman's nude body, the fire on Thirty-first Avenue took on new dimensions. Marshal 5, the arson squad, always responded to fire death scenes to determine whether the cause was accidental or deliberate. Now, Inspector Jim Reed and Seattle Police detective Bill Berg, who was on special assignment with Marshal 5, were alerted. They headed up Seattle's Yesler Street toward the fire site. Seattle Police detective sergeant James Whalen of the General Assignments Unit that handled arson cases joined them.

The flames were gone, but the house still reeked of smoke as Jim Reed walked through the front door. He saw that there was no fire damage at all on the first floor. The home was nicely decorated and immaculately kept. It was almost eerie; from the appearance of the downstairs rooms, it seemed that whoever lived here had stepped away for only a moment or so. The living room was very neat. Reed looked automatically for ashtrays and found them, but they had been emptied and washed. The evening paper lay unopened on a chair near the front door.

There was a TV tray next to a recliner, and it held a familiar red-and-white sack from Kentucky Fried Chicken. Jim Reed cupped his hand around the sack and found it was still slightly warm. It couldn't have been there for long. When he peered in, he found an order of chicken for one person.

A set of car keys and a pair of sunglasses

lay on the floor next to the staircase, and two piles of mail were stacked precisely on a side table. One pile had been opened; the other envelopes were still sealed.

As Reed stepped into the kitchen, he felt the presence of the woman who lived in this house even more. Amazingly, there was a saucepan of corn on the stove. It had cooked down so that it had only just begun to scorch slightly on the bottom.

The double sink was filled with water. The sink on the right held warm soapy water, and the one on the left, filled with cool water, held women's clothing, delicates that required hand washing.

The woman upstairs had to have come home within the hour and set down her chicken dinner to wait while she cooked some corn to go with it. She had, perhaps, run the kitchen sink full of soapy water and rinsed out some clothes while she waited. She hadn't even had time to open the paper or read her mail. Now, she lay dead upstairs. It was unreal.

Seattle Police officers F. Aesquivel and A. Thole strung up yellow police tape to cordon off the parameters of a possible crime scene and stood guarding the house and yard while the investigators worked inside.

Inspector Jim Reed headed upstairs. The

hallway outside the fire room had sustained very little damage, only some surface blistering on the ceilings and walls. The bedroom beyond, where the woman had died, had similar damage to most of the walls and ceilings — nothing deeply burned at all, just surface burns.

In the fire room, there was a king-size bed against the south wall, a nightstand next to it, a swivel chair, a nine-drawer dresser with a blackened mirror, and the melted TV set on its metal stand. The light switch controlling the single ceiling fixture was in the off position. The only electrical outlet was behind the dresser.

The room was carpeted with thick shag carpeting, and it was this carpet that had pushed against the door, making it difficult for Ochs to open it.

Even though most of the fire room was uncharred, Dorothy Jones's body had been exposed to such intense heat that her skin had begun to "sleeve" on her legs, forming a thin shell that could be slipped off like a glove. Both of her nostrils were full of soot, and so was her ear on the side that was exposed to the room.

Jim Reed and Sergeant Jim Whalen bent over the dead woman, searching for some sign that she had been attacked, possibly even killed, before the fire began, but they could detect no wounds whatsoever on the part of her body that they could see. Reed took several photographs before Whalen carefully turned her over.

The mystery only grew. There were no wounds on the nether side of her body either — nothing at all to indicate why the woman hadn't simply gotten up and fled the flames. Perhaps an autopsy would show why. Deputies from the medical examiner's office removed the dead woman, and the investigation continued.

Reed surveyed the bedroom. There was no damage to the shag carpeting. Fire burns upward, and this was to be expected. The mattress was not burned on top, although the sides were scorched. This tended to eliminate smoking in bed as the cause of the fire. Besides, the ashtray on the nightstand next to the bed held only fire debris, no cigarettes or tobacco residue or ashes.

The nightstand itself was scorched, the telephone atop it melted. The stand and the television set had been only a few inches from the bed.

The two investigators lifted the mattress off its metal frame. The carpet beneath it was consumed, with the most damage just under the center of the bed. The floorboards there were charred.

They carried the mattress out to the front yard. There, under strong auxiliary lighting, they could see that Dorothy Jones's wallet, checkbook, and savings deposit book were entangled in the bedding. But robbery didn't appear to be a motive: the wallet held $280 in cash.

When the mattress was flipped over, a mass of fire damage came into view. The worst charring was in the center and on the left edge where the foot of the bed would have been.

It seemed obvious that the blaze in the room had not started accidentally — at least not from the usual reasons that arson investigators expect. They had found nothing beneath the bed that could have started the fire — no wires, small appliances, heating pads, electric blanket controls, candles, matches. Nothing. It was as pristine under Dorothy's bed as in the rest of her house.

Jim Reed checked the television set. Although the case was melted, the interior wiring appeared intact and undamaged. The on-off knob was also melted, but he removed it and found that the control shaft was in the off position. It was plugged in behind the dresser and the cord was in good condition.

The two detectives moved to the east bedroom just across the hall. Here, there was no fire damage whatsoever. The room was furnished much like the fire room, and it was as tidy as the downstairs. There was a jewelry case on the dresser, and it was full of both costume pieces and expensive rings and necklaces. There was an open packed suitcase on the bed. Clothing bags holding suits and slacks hung nearby — as if someone was about to take a trip. A pair of white women's slacks, a silk blouse, and a lacy bra were folded perfectly in a neat pile on the bed.

Josh Nathan,* the neighbor who had called in the first alarm, paced outside, waiting to talk to the two investigators.

"Me and the wife always look after Dorothy and Carl's place while they're away," he said. "He's a long-haul trucker, and he's out on the road all but one or two days a month. Dorothy's usually here alone."

Nathan said that he had picked up his parents at the Sea-Tac Airport earlier in the afternoon, and then picked up his wife on the way home. Shortly after they arrived home, he had glanced out the window and seen the flames.

"I called 911 and my wife ran over there. She told me the front door was unlocked and I went in. I found the corn just starting to burn and I turned the stove off. The lights were on downstairs, but I didn't see any upstairs. I didn't go up because the smoke was so heavy."

The Nathans had seen Dorothy's car outside her house, but no other cars nearby, and they were sure no one had left the house — at least not after they got home.

Working in the front yard of the Joneses' house on this increasingly chilly December night, Jim Reed and Detective Bill Berg carefully rebuilt the mattress from the fire room, sifting debris as they worked. They found the remains of a brassiere caught in there, too.

The burn patterns on the mattress confirmed Reed's first impression. He had thought that the fire had been caused by someone holding a flame under the bed at the center and near the foot. But that would have been a very tight squeeze for anyone who wasn't really thin.

Or who didn't have exceptionally long arms.

But why? Moreover, Dorothy Jones should have had time to jump out of bed and escape the inferno before anyone under the bed could wriggle out from the narrow space beneath it.

But of course she hadn't.

Jim Reed, Jim Whalen, and Bill Berg worked far into the early morning hours on the baffling case. At eight the next morning, day-shift arson investigators took over. Marshal 5 veterans Jack Hickam and Gary Owens attended the postmortem on Dorothy Jones. King County medical examiner Donald Reay performed the autopsy, and he was a pathologist who always looked for even the smallest sign that signaled an unnatural death.

Perhaps there was some preexisting condition that had rendered Dorothy helpless to escape the flames. Maybe she had suffered an injury not easily detectable the night before. She could have been strangled or suffocated, and the bruise marks from the killer's fingers or the petechiae (broken blood vessels) could be hidden beneath her burned skin.

But Dr. Reay found nothing beyond a small bump over her right eye, and there was no hemorrhaging beneath it. Reay opined there was a slight chance that the bump had come from a blow to her head that might possibly have knocked her out momentarily — but hardly long enough for her to lie there unconscious and die from smoke inhalation. And he didn't really think she had sustained even that.

Her flesh had no needle marks, and the blood tests would come back with negative readings on blood alcohol and a wide spectrum of drugs. Reay acknowledged that there *were* "dozens" of more obscure drugs that could have been administered and gone undetected.

The blood from Dorothy's heart chambers was bright cherry red, an indication of carbon monoxide poisoning. There was a 61 percent concentration of carbon monoxide in her blood, more than enough to kill her, but that was a result of the fire.

The official cause of her death was "death by asphyxiation due to inhalation of products of combustion." Her severe burns had been sustained after her death.

In the end, her autopsy showed that Dorothy Jones had not been strangled, shot, knifed, beaten, or smothered. There was no obvious reason why she hadn't fled the burning room.

Yet she had not.

Evidence of rape or recent intercourse showed on the vaginal swabs taken. A test for acid phosphates showed that there was semen present in her vaginal vault, which turned the swabs reddish purple. Dorothy had engaged in sexual intercourse shortly before her death. The man involved had no sperm cells in his ejaculate; he had had a vasectomy to render him sterile. According to criminalist Ann Beaman of the crime lab, intercourse had taken place within two to four hours before Dorothy died; an active woman will not retain semen in the vagina longer than that.

Jim Reed set out to find out everything he could about the victim — how Dorothy had spent her last hours, her lifestyle, the human relationships that might have led to her murder. He was to discover an extremely complex woman, one who was different things to different people.

One of Dorothy's elderly in-laws told Reed that she had passed by the Jones house at four that afternoon and she was positive that Dorothy's 1974 Cadillac was not parked in front at that time. "Dorothy's the only one who ever drives that car," the woman said. "If it wasn't there, that meant she wasn't there."

A woman neighbor recalled seeing Dorothy come home just after 5 P.M. on December 20. At 6:20, she was dead. That narrowed the time frame to what should have been quite workable for the investigators. These two witnesses substantiated that the crucial time period was less than an hour and a half.

An hour and a half to come home, start dinner, remove her clothing, make love, or perhaps submit to a rape.

And die.

Dorothy's husband's aunt had nothing but good things to say about her. "Dorothy's always been good to me," the woman said. "She usually drove me to work every morning and she was always calling me to be sure I was all right. I talked to her Sunday morning and she told me she was going to the Esquire Club that night and would be out late. Then, on Monday morning, she said she was too tired to drive me to work. I tried to call her Monday night at five-fifteen and there was no answer. When I tried a few minutes later, someone picked up after three rings. But no one spoke. I heard some rustling movement and then the phone just got hung up. I tried again and the line was busy."

Asked if her niece-in-law had any male friends, the woman shook her head. "No. Ohh, no — I don't think so. Dorothy's a very nice girl."

Jim Reed called the doctor whose name was on a prescription bottle found in Dorothy's home. It was for a sinus condition.

Nothing dark or mysterious about that. The doctor recalled that Dorothy had been in an auto accident in October 1975 and had sustained back and neck injuries.

"She also complained of blurred vision."

"She ever have dizzy spells?" Reed asked.

"No — not that I know of. She never told me about any condition that might have caused her to lose consciousness or faint."

Dorothy had received a settlement from an insurance company after that accident — something around $10,000.

Maybe that settlement could explain Dorothy's magnificent wardrobe. She had 115 blouses (the cheapest estimated at about $60), 50 pairs of slacks, 37 dresses, 24 nightgowns. And she had shoes, boots, and accessories to match. Although her husband surely made a comfortable living as a long-haul trucker, it hardly seemed adequate to clothe his wife like a movie star.

Carl Jones himself arrived in town at 2 P.M. on Tuesday, December 21. Marshal 5 Inspectors Hickam and Owens met him at the house where his wife had perished only the day before. Jones, who had been delivering a load of furniture in Dallas the previous night, was shocked and incredulous about his wife's baffling death.

He said he had arrived in Dallas the previous day, unloaded his van, and driven to his mother's house in San Antonio. That was where he was when he got the phone call from a neighbor late Monday night telling him that Dorothy was dead.

"I got the first flight I could today to fly home to Seattle," Jones said tearfully, clearly overwhelmed by his loss.

Asked about his marriage, he said that he and Dorothy had been together for sixteen years, ever since she divorced her first husband. They had had no children. Their marriage had been a good one, although they actually spent very little time together since he was on the road four weeks a month. He seemed about to say more but stopped speaking, too grief-stricken to go on.

Jones said he felt the whole picture surrounding Dorothy's death was "fishy." He could not understand how anyone could have gotten into their house without Dorothy's consent, and she was much too smart to be tricked by anyone.

"Dorothy never stayed ten minutes alone in the house without locking all the doors," Jones said. "It was reflex action for her to turn the locks behind her."

He confirmed the investigators' impressions about Dorothy Jones being a woman of precise habits, almost fanatically neat.

"She always slipped off her shoes at the door, and she put on bedroom slippers. After that, she took her street clothes off in our spare bedroom and folded them real careful."

That was just as the arson detectives had found them.

"How about in the house?" Jack Hickam asked. "Did she sometimes walk around without clothes — after she locked the doors?"

"No way. She was a very modest woman. She *never* walked around naked!"

The next questions were more difficult. Hickam and Owens tried to be tactful as they approached the question of Dorothy's possibly having a boyfriend when Jones was out on the road.

"I never suspected she had one, nothing like that — although we were separated so much of the time because of my job. I just don't know. I'd hate to think that was true."

On December 28, Jim Reed received a call from Carl Jones. He said he had gone to his home at 8:25 in the morning and found the front door ajar and a back door wide open.

Jones said he couldn't stand to live in the house where his wife had died, and he was preparing to move. He had had the couple's belongings packed by a commercial mover. All the nonfurniture items from the downstairs had been sitting in boxes in the living room. The upstairs rooms were not yet packed. Someone had entered the home — although not forcibly — and thoroughly ransacked it.

"I locked the place up myself at six-thirty last night," Jones told Reed, "and I don't know of anyone else who has a key. Only me and Dorothy."

Oddly, Jones said, he hadn't found anything missing.

"I can't be sure of everything Dorothy had, of course, but the only thing that seems to be gone are some wooden kitchen tools."

Criminalists from the Seattle Police Department dusted the living room and obtained some good latent prints from the underside of a marble coffee table.

In the mid-seventies, unfortunately, the Automated Fingerprint Identification System (AFIS) didn't exist. Most people didn't know what a computer was, and there certainly weren't state or nationwide clearinghouses where computers had huge banks of known prints. The FBI's Crime Lab filed single fingerprints from their "Ten Most Wanted" felons on the run, but that was all. Unless the detectives found a suspect whose fingerprints could be compared to those retrieved from the coffee table, they were virtually useless.

Beyond those few latent prints, they had no clues they could link to whoever had entered the home the Joneses had rented for nine years, or any discernible motive. If Dorothy Jones *had* been murdered, maybe her killer had panicked, remembering some item in the house that would point to him, and returned to retrieve it. It couldn't have been a set of inexpensive wooden spoons and spatulas.

And when Carl Jones first got home, he had searched the house and hadn't found anything that didn't seem to belong there.

Jim Reed talked with the manager of the Kentucky Fried Chicken franchise that was identified by the number on the receipt. He learned that the receipt found in the carry-out bag in the victim's living room on December 20 showed that the food had been purchased in the fifty-fifth sale of the day.

"According to our usual pattern that should have fallen somewhere between three and four-thirty," the manager estimated.

So Dorothy was alive at three, alive at five. Where had she spent the rest of her day? There were many facets of the investigation that didn't fit with Carl's aunt's description of her as "a nice girl."

On January 3, Carl Jones came into the Marshal 5 offices that were located in Station 10 near Seattle's historic Pioneer Square.

His face looked strained as he told the arson investigators that he had been asking questions, and gotten some answers that he really didn't want to hear. He had come to the conclusion that his wife hadn't been completely faithful to him.

"I've heard some rumors," he said. "They say that Dorothy was seeing some guy — some businessman. His name is Dante Blackwell."*

At Jim Reed's request, Jones looked over the address book found in the scorched bedding, and he pointed out other names there that he didn't recognize. There were seven.

As it turned out, they had no significance. Investigators traced those people and found them to be only casual friends of Dorothy's.

On January 5, Jim Reed and Jack Hickam called on Felicia Brown,* one of Dorothy's oldest friends. Felicia knew considerably more about Dorothy's day-to-day life than anyone in the investigation so far.

"Dorothy came by my beauty shop about noon on December 20th," Felicia recalled. "She often dropped by the shop in the late afternoon to say hi, but we aren't usually open on Mondays. She just happened to see me. She was very excited about her trip to Texas, and she was on her way to buy a Christmas present."

Felicia, too, characterized Dorothy Jones as a creature of habit, who kept to her own routines. "Usually, after she stops in here, she gets the paper and goes home to supper."

"You don't know that she went home after her visit to you? Hickam asked.

"Not for sure, but she probably did."

Felicia said that she and Dorothy had gone to the Esquire Club on Sunday night. "We don't go out often — or rather, I don't, because I have a family to look after."

Dorothy, on the other hand, had no children and a husband on the road all the time. Felicia said that Dorothy was an avid horse race aficionado and that she spent a lot of time at Longacres, Seattle's popular track.

"She always checked the papers for out-of-town results," she added, "and she went down to Portland Meadows in Oregon, for the races there."

When the arson investigators asked her about the man rumored to be Dorothy's lover — Dante Blackwell — Felicia Brown nodded. "She was always talking about

Dante. I can't really say how serious they were. I know Dorothy sometimes had men over for a drink, but that was pretty casual. She used to know a soldier that she wrote to, but I don't think she's seen him in years."

Asked what Dorothy Jones had been wearing on Monday, Felicia recalled that she'd worn white slacks, a silk blouse, a velveteen jacket, and brown shoes. Those were the clothes found folded on the bed in her spare bedroom just after the fire.

Jim Reed wanted to know more about the elusive Dante Blackwell. Reed, Gary Owens, and arson inspector Bill Hoppe called on yet another of Dorothy's friends — Lita Bowen. Lita said she'd known the dead woman for five years, and that they'd been very close friends for the past year and a half. They attended numerous functions together — bingo, dances, horse racing.

"We went to the dances at the Esquire Club, and we played bingo four nights a week unless something came up. We went Mondays, Wednesdays, Fridays, and Saturdays. Dorothy would drive to my house, park, and I'd drive to bingo, or else she'd pick me up. We always called first to make arrangements, and if we couldn't reach each other, one of us would go first and save a seat. We always got there at six so we could sort the cards before the crowd came."

Lita Bowen knew Dante Blackwell well. Dorothy had started dating him in September, and sometimes the three of them went out together.

"Dante got married after he started dating Dorothy, but it didn't seem to bother her, or slow him down," she said. "Their relationship didn't change."

Lita gave her opinion that Dorothy's marriage wasn't as happy as Carl Jones claimed. "Dorothy just got tired of him being gone on the road all the time. In fact, she filed for divorce."

"When was that?" Bill Hoppe asked.

"On November 27th."

"Did Carl Jones know about Dante Blackwell?"

"I don't know if he was aware of him, but I'm fairly sure that he knew Dorothy had filed for divorce."

"Was Dorothy afraid of anyone?" Reed asked.

"Well — I do know at least two people who have threatened her. One night, we were at a dance at the club with Dante, and this man came up to Dorothy on the dance floor. I've seen him at the track, but I don't know who he is. I heard Dorothy say to him, 'You would be better off to hit your wife or your mother than me.' Dorothy seemed to be very afraid of him — so much so that she asked me to wait when I took her home that night, and every night after that. You know, wait until she got inside safely. She even asked me to find someone to live with her because she was afraid to be alone."

"Did she tell you of any threats she received?"

"The only one I know of came from one of Dante Blackwell's ex-girlfriends," Lita said. "It was around the week of December 13th to the 19th. This woman told Dorothy to keep away from Dante or she'd kill her. But Dorothy just laughed about that, knowing he had a wife too! She wasn't worried about some woman who was all mixed up about who to be jealous of."

Asked about the woman's name, Lita Bowen didn't know it. All she knew was what Dorothy had told her.

Lita said that she had thought a lot about something that had happened on Sunday night/Monday morning, only about fourteen hours before Dorothy Jones died.

"I went out Sunday night, and Dorothy had plans to go to the Esquire Club. When I got home at four in the morning, there was a message that Dorothy had called me at three. I didn't call her back because I was exhausted and I figured she'd just called to tell me that she'd had a good time or something. I decided to call her when I woke up. Well, she called my apartment again at three on Monday afternoon to say she wanted to talk to me. She told my roommate to tell me she'd gone to see about some shoes for Carl and would be back shortly. I called her at five, five-thirty, and five-forty-five. But nobody answered. I figured she'd changed her mind about going to bingo so I went without her. I didn't find out she was dead until the next day. Now, I really wish I'd called her at 4 A.M. on Monday morning. Maybe I could have saved her life or something."

Witnesses had seen Dorothy Jones about to enter her house at 5 P.M. on Monday afternoon. Yet she didn't answer any of the calls made to her between five and six. Someone had picked her phone up once during this time — at about 5:20 — but whoever did that didn't say anything, and the receiver had been replaced. Was someone waiting inside for Dorothy — perhaps someone who would not permit her to answer her phone?

Lita Bowen verified further that Dorothy Jones was almost paranoid about keeping her doors and windows locked. She reiterated that Dorothy didn't smoke and discouraged smokers. "She said, 'You can smoke

— but don't blow it in my face,' so nobody felt comfortable smoking in her house. And she never allowed ashtrays upstairs in the bedrooms."

It was January 11 when Inspector Jim Reed found Dante Blackwell, the man rumored to be Dorothy Jones's lover. Blackwell, forty-three, was a handsome and expensively dressed businessman, somewhat flamboyant and very confident. He didn't deny that he and Dorothy had been intimate friends. He said he had been dating her for four months and paying some of her bills.

"I gave her $300 to buy her plane ticket to Texas," he said. "She was very excited about the trip. She had lots of friends there, and she loved to travel."

"When did you see her last?" Reed asked.

"Monday — that last Monday. She came into my store. We'd been to the Esquire Club until two-thirty the night before. She was on her way home when I saw her in the store. She said she was going to see the shoe man and said she wanted to buy me a pair of shoes, too. When I told her I didn't want any, she said she could buy me a present if she wanted to, so I told her to do what she liked. Then she left, but she called me from home about five. She was upstairs and I could hear the TV. We only talked a minute or two."

Blackwell said that Dorothy was afraid of something, and that she planned to have her door locks changed. He didn't know, though, specifically what she feared. Asked about the man who'd threatened her at the club, Blackwell shook his head slightly. "I think that was just a guy who wanted to date her and she told him to forget it, but I don't think she was upset about it — or scared."

Blackwell said that man had a reputation as a woman beater, and Dorothy didn't like him.

Dorothy had told Dante that she planned to place her valuables in the trunk of her car and park it at his house while she was in Texas over the Christmas holidays.

Blackwell, too, said that Dorothy was a very modest woman who never walked around naked. "She wouldn't even walk from the bedroom to the bathroom without slipping on a robe."

Lita Bowen had said that Dorothy hadn't allowed ashtrays in her bedrooms, but Blackwell explained the one arson investigators had found next to her burning bed.

"She put it there as a favor to me," he said. "I like to smoke — after . . . well, you know."

Dante Blackwell said that Dorothy had had three expensive diamond rings that she routinely wore. This was surprising because she certainly hadn't been wearing them when she died, and they had not been found in her jewelry chest. For some people, rings worth a few thousand dollars might have been enough motive for murder.

Blackwell had a solid alibi. He said he had been at his store continually from the time Dorothy stopped in in midafternoon on Monday, and until after the fire was reported. His employees would substantiate this. He also agreed to a lie-detector test about his relationship with Dorothy Jones.

The next step for Jim Reed was to locate "the shoe man" whom Dorothy planned to visit on the afternoon she died. He found a dealer who sold shoes from his home, located a few blocks from Dorothy's house. The man verified that she had been there sometime around three-thirty on Monday afternoon to pick up some shoes for her husband's Christmas present. She had told him she was leaving for Texas on December 23 and would be gone for a week.

So the timetable tightened up. According to statements of those who had seen Dorothy Jones, it went like this:

Noon: She visited Felicia Brown in her beauty shop, and then left the shop to pick up a Christmas present.

2:30: She visited her lover at his store and left to buy shoes.

3:00: She called to leave a message for Lita Bowen, but didn't talk to her.

3:30: She picked up shoes for her husband.

3:00–4:30: She bought fried chicken for one, and the evening paper.

5:00: She was seen entering the driveway of her home.

5:00–5:10: She called her lover and talked a few minutes.

5:18–5:20: Her aunt in-law called Dorothy's home; someone answered without speaking and then hung up.

6:24: The fire was reported. Dorothy was declared dead fifteen minutes later.

Sometime during Monday afternoon, Dorothy Jones had engaged in an act of sexual intercourse, either willingly or by force. This could have occurred between noon and three, or even after she arrived home. Her schedule left little time for an assignation — unless her partner *was* lurking in her home when she arrived there or was someone she knew well enough to admit willingly.

Still, it seemed doubtful that Dorothy Jones had been a willing partner for a sexual assignation; if she had been, she surely would have turned off food cooking on the stove before she walked upstairs to the bedroom.

In any homicide case, detectives look first at those closest to the victim. In this baffling case, they learned that her husband had been distraught over Dorothy's free-spending shopping and her obsession with gambling, but he had never been known to make any threatening statements about her. Carl Jones apparently had had no knowledge that his wife was seeing another man. He found that out only after her death.

Further, a check with his employer, a cross-country moving company, elicited records that verified that Jones had been on the road constantly in the past thirty days — and when she died. There was simply no way he could have detoured to Seattle at the time Dorothy died in their house fire. Carl Jones had been en route from Alexandria, Virginia, to Dallas, Texas.

On February 8, Jones gave a taped statement to Inspector Jim Reed about his marriage. He wanted to be frank. He said he hadn't seen Dorothy since before Thanksgiving. He admitted now that things had gone very wrong in his marriage. In fact, the last time he'd been in Seattle, he'd stayed at a friend's house due to their strained relationship.

"*I* was the one who filed for divorce — and that was before *Thanksgiving,*" he said with a sigh. "I'm sorry I didn't tell you that before, but I guess I thought all along that we'd make up."

Asked if his wife's life had been insured, Jones shook his head. "She only had about $1,100 worth of insurance — not even enough to pay for her funeral."

On February 11, Jones passed a lie-detector test.

Reed verified that Dorothy Jones had only minimal insurance. She had had a couple of savings accounts. Her husband was unaware of these accounts; their balances totaled a few thousand dollars. Still, she hadn't made the payments she was supposed to make on Carl Jones's semi rig.

Dorothy had had numerous charge accounts, and she apparently had plenty of money available to her to buy clothes, go to the horse track, and to dance clubs. Dante Blackwell had given her money; maybe someone else had.

Carl Jones told the investigators that he had uncovered some rumors that his wife had been a "pickup" girl for marijuana sales, but he hadn't learned any names of the people she had allegedly dealt with in illegal drug sales. No one else who knew her had linked her to drug trafficking, and she herself certainly had not been a drug user.

It seemed like a red herring.

Bizarrely, many pictures of Dorothy Jones had emerged. The wife who had been happy in her marriage for many years — at least until recently; the good friend and considerate relative; the immaculate housekeeper; but also the gambler, the glamorous seductress, and possibly even the drug runner. She *had* been a complicated woman.

And it was quite possible that there were facets of her daily life that she revealed to no one. Still, neither the arson investigators nor the Homicide detectives had found anyone who had a compelling reason to want Dorothy dead.

Jim Reed talked again to Dante Blackwell, and brought forth new information. Before Blackwell got married, Dorothy had been a frequent visitor to his home. During that period, Blackwell recalled, he had received a number of weird phone calls.

"When I answered, a man's voice would say, 'Where's your girlfriend? Did she dump you?' When Dorothy answered, there would only be breathing.

"I figured that the man was probably someone whose voice Dorothy would have recognized."

On March 10, Dante Blackwell took several polygraph examinations and he, too, passed them all cleanly. Just like Carl Jones, he clearly knew nothing more than he had told the investigators.

If the fire in the Joneses' home had burned even ten or fifteen minutes longer, Dorothy Jones's death would probably have been listed officially as accidental. But the fire was discovered in a short time, thanks to her neighbors. Arson investigators felt it was a deliberately set fire, although they were not sure exactly how that was accomplished. Their most likely method was a candle or match or other heated object held underneath the mattress of her bed.

Somehow, someway, Dorothy had been unable to leave the room, where she died of smoke inhalation. How she was rendered incapable of saving her own life would remain a huge question — even until today, some three decades later.

Her autopsy revealed the slight bump on her head. Perhaps she had been given a drug that could not be detected in the postmortem exam or in all the tests afterward, something that crime labs rarely tested for.

The most likely drug that would have quickly paralyzed her and been difficult to detect on autopsy (because small amounts are normally present in the human brain) would have been succinylcholine. It is a drug routinely used in surgery to relax muscles so that a ventilating tube can be inserted into the windpipe. But it also takes away the ability to breathe or move, so oxygen must be available instantly, administered by an anesthesiologist.

It would have been almost impossible for anyone other than a medical professional or someone with access to a hospital to obtain. In the history of crime — distant and current — there are several infamous murder cases involving succinylcholine, *all* of which were carried out by medical professionals.

It is one of the cruelest ways to kill someone. Although the victims of succinylcholine poisoning cannot move even to blink an eye, they are fully conscious. They cannot will their lungs to expand and draw in air, and they suffocate.

Dr. Carl Coppolino, a Florida anesthesiologist, served twelve years in prison for the 1965 murder of his wife, Dr. Carmela Coppolino. He had allegedly used succinylcholine to render her powerless. In 1984, Genene Jones, a San Antonio, Texas, nurse who became known as "the Angel of Death," was sentenced to 159 years in prison for the murder of a toddler in her care and the poisoning of several other children, who survived. Her drugs of choice were succinylcholine and heparin (a powerful blood thinner).

More recently — in July 2006 — a critical care nurse in Nevada named Chaz Higgs was arrested and charged with the murder of his wife, Kathy Augustine, who just happened to be the elected controller of the state of Nevada, a powerful and very attractive woman. Reno detectives said that Augustine had died after being injected with succinylcholine, although it was first believed that the popular forty-two-year-old politician had suffered a heart attack.

The mark of an injection of this drug can be hidden in a mole or birthmark, and certainly, Dorothy Jones's burned flesh would have obliterated it.

But it was just a theory; as far as anyone knew, she had no intense involvement with a doctor or any other person in the medical field.

Still, it was only natural to look for far-out methods in the death of Dorothy Jones. The common methods just were not indicated. There were none of the eye and lung hemorrhages that would have pointed toward strangulation. And she had not fought a killer; her long, well-manicured nails were unbroken.

And why was Dorothy nude? She had had sexual intercourse on the afternoon she died, but with whom? In 1974, of course, it wasn't possible to extract DNA from the ejaculate her partner left behind.

Someone — possibly a killer — came back to the scene of her death one week later and searched her house frantically. But for what?

Was Dorothy Jones killed by a jealous lover? A jealous woman? A drug dealer who "burned" her (literally) for "burning" him (figuratively)?

And $280 in cash was left behind, but her diamond rings were gone. Odd.

Was there another man that Dorothy planned to be with? She had talked to her girlfriends continually about Dante Blackwell, and even hinted that she had agreed to a divorce because of him, although he'd married another woman a few months after their affair began. Was all that talk only a smokescreen to hide a man she really cared about, perhaps a man of wealth and reputation whose name had to be kept silent? Had he been frightened at the thought that she was about to expose him, demanding more from him than he'd planned to give?

Such a man might well have had a duplicate key to her home, might have waited while she changed her clothes, started supper, even as she made a phone call to Dante Blackwell. Perhaps they made love for a final time — although Dorothy would not have known how final it was. And then this secret lover had killed her, deliberately setting a fire beneath her mattress.

Perhaps.

Maybe this unknown man believed he had gotten away without leaving a trace of himself, and then found, to his horror, that he'd dropped something — something that could inexorably be traced back to him. That would account for the "break-in" on December 27. Had he found what he sought?

After considering all the possible scenarios, there is one other that has to be addressed. It is possible that Dorothy Jones wasn't murdered at all — that she succumbed to the strange phenomenon of spontaneous human combustion (SHC).

The theory that there are certain conditions inside a human body that will cause it to suddenly catch fire is as old as the Bible, although it is impossible to validate the incidents therein. In 1763, a Frenchman named Jonas Dupont wrote a book called *De incendiis corporis humani spontaneis,* exploring several case studies of people who had literally burst into flames.

Dupont became interested in the subject after the husband of a woman named Nicole Millet was acquitted of her murder by a judge who was convinced by arguments that she had perished by spontaneous combustion.

A far more familiar author, Charles Dickens, used spontaneous human combustion to dispatch a drunkard in his 1852 novel, *Bleak House.* When critics mocked him, Dickens retorted that he had thoroughly researched the subject and found thirty cases where human beings had literally burned to death from some source inside their own bodies.

A century later, the charred remains of a St. Petersburg, Florida, woman named Mary Reeser, sixty-seven, were found in her apartment on July 2, 1951. Photographs show that all that was left of her body — beyond ashes — was her skull and her unburned left foot, still wearing a black satin slipper. Her neighbor, worried about her, had touched the doorknob to her apartment, found it hot, and called the police. A four-foot circle around Mary Reeser's body was burned black.

The police investigators concluded that Mary, a heavy woman and a smoker, who had worn a highly inflammable rayon acetate nightgown, had accidentally set fire to herself. But the medical examiner wondered how heat believed to have reached 3,000 degrees hadn't burned the whole place down. Although the ceiling and walls were covered with soot, the room was not burned at all.

Hapless Mary Reeser became the poster girl for spontaneous human combustion.

Six years later, Anna Martin, sixty-eight, of West Philadelphia, was discovered in her home, completely incinerated except for her shoes and a small portion of her torso. The medical examiner estimated that it would have taken temperatures above 1,700 degrees to accomplish this. And yet newspapers only two feet from the burned body weren't even scorched.

There are dozens of similar, carefully documented cases of spontaneous human combustion, and even one victim who survived. A man named Peter Jones was saved by rescuers who smothered the flames. He later recalled feeling no pain, saying, "I didn't feel hot at all — I only saw smoke."

There are no absolutes in discussing the phenomenon, which has been attributed to everything from mass hysteria to old wives' tales to electric short-circuiting within the body to punishment from God.

Experts in this bizarre subject have suggested that the elderly, particularly women, are more likely to spontaneously combust. Overweight people and alcoholics are thought to be prime candidates. But there are also thin people who are teetotalers who have reportedly caught fire with no outside flame starter.

I have been told a few times about a firefighter or an arson investigator who came upon a woman sitting in her living room in an easy chair with her entire torso, save for her genitals, burned away. Her legs and arms were intact, and so was the room. But when I tried to track this story to its source, I was never able to find the one person who saw this. It became more of a folktale than a credible first-person report.

One researcher offered a checklist to determine if SHC should be considered in a case of death by fire.

- The body is normally more severely burned than one caught in a usual fire.

- The burns are not distributed evenly over the body; the legs and arms are untouched while the torso is severely burned.
- Small portions of the body remain unburned.
- Only parts of body have burned. SHC victims have burned up in a bed without the sheets catching fire, clothing is barely singed, and inflammable materials only inches away remain untouched.
- A greasy soot deposit covers the ceiling and walls, usually stopping four feet above the floor.
- Although temperatures of about 3,000 degrees Fahrenheit are normally required to char a body so thoroughly, frequently little or nothing around the victim is damaged, except for the exact spot where the victim ignited.

The fact that Dorothy Jones was so severely burned in such a short time while the rest of her house and most of her bedroom were not makes one wonder if she could have been a victim of spontaneous human combustion. Although she was pleasantly buxom, she wasn't overweight, and she didn't drink to excess.

The shag carpet in her bedroom was not burned except for the spot right under her body. The mattress she lay on was burned beneath her body, the rest untouched, except for one spot at the foot of her bed.

SHC is only one theory among many, and probably not the cause of her death. But still, I wonder.

Marshal 5 investigators Jim Reed, Jack Hickam, and Bill Hoppe went over the incredible circumstances of Dorothy Jones's death again and again, trying to find the one clue that had to be there. It was, ultimately, to be an exercise in frustration, and yet they still worked on the case whenever they could.

Time moved on and they all retired. Jack Hickam, who was "Mr. Arson" in Seattle, the ultimate expert in determining the cause of fires, passed away in September 1994 after a long illness. Jim Reed lost touch with his fellow investigators from Marshal 5. I still see Bill Hoppe often, and he remembers the case well. But he believes that no one ever unlocked the mystery of what happened to Dorothy Jones.

It is a challenge to try to figure out what might have taken place during that vital time period — *only one hour* — during the Christmas season 1976. Was there a man that no one knew about who stalked Dorothy? She was afraid of someone, but even her closest friends didn't know who.

With the almost miraculous outreach of the Internet, perhaps one day I will hear from someone who knows the answers. If there was a human killer, he may be long dead now. Or he may have been dealing with a nagging conscience for thirty years and want to unburden himself. Or herself.

I think someone does know, and my e-mail address is listed in the back of this book . . .

■ ■ ■ ■

THE
CONVICT'S
WIFE

■ ■ ■ ■

The standard reaction to murders featured on the nightly news is, "They seemed like the nicest family. I can't believe something like that could happen in our neighborhood!"

The case that follows has extra pathos because the people involved had almost no neighbors or friends. No one really knew them at all. They wandered across America, looking for someplace they could live without paying rent. The men involved had a choice in the way they lived their lives, but the woman and the small children didn't.

And how they must have longed to have some stability and to be able to count on where they would be the next year — or even the next month. The pieces of their world continually blew away in the winds of change like so many particles of milkweed or dandelion fluff. Nothing was permanent and they could never know what tomorrow might bring.

They journeyed toward the Pacific Ocean from their Midwestern roots. In an odd kind of way, the woman named Doris Mae was as defenseless as the pioneer wives who followed their men west in covered wagons 150 years earlier. Some will argue that she made immoral choices, and she did.

Others will understand that she probably had no one to turn to.

The brothers Light grew up in Illinois and they lived by their wits; sometimes they lucked out, but as often as not, they ended up behind bars. Steadily building dubious reputations that made their names well known to lawmen all over the state, what they lacked in brains, they made up for in persistence. George Allen Light was six years older than Larry Max Light and he had a head start in crime, but Larry began young and soon caught up with George. Indeed, some said he surpassed him. Their crimes were the sort that take only modest ingenuity: car theft, strong-arm robbery, assault, burglary. Their faces became familiar behind the walls of the state pens at Joliet and Pontiac and Menard.

If they were unpopular with police agencies, they were sought out as gang members in the street subculture where aggressive behavior was a badge of honor. In 1959, when he was only nineteen, Larry Light was "rushed" by the gangs as assiduously as any prom queen at a sorority tea.

He chose one gang and, as a sort of initiation, was sent to "call on" the leaders of the gang he had turned down. The social call soon disintegrated into a brawl. Larry punched out the rival gang leader, but he spun around when someone leapt on his back spitting and scratching. He couldn't see who it was, so he blindly swung his arm behind him. His fingers activated his switchblade knife, and he stabbed his attacker.

The grip on his back loosened and the soft moan of a female shocked the tangle of thugs who were still fighting. Larry Light had just fatally stabbed the gang leader's "old lady." While the gang members tried to stanch the dying girl's bleeding, Larry slipped away and ran to the first hiding place he could think of.

As he hid out, he pondered his problem, which was twofold: He had already seen enough of the inside of reform school and prison walls to last him a lifetime, and he didn't want to go back. More than that, he knew he was a dead man if the avenging mourners of his victim found him. He wasn't even twenty yet, and this wasn't exactly how he'd planned his future.

Larry's chances for survival weren't very good to begin with, and the odds dropped to zero when his brother, George, twenty-five, was questioned by detectives. George was pretty uptight whenever policemen approached him. He'd been into so much heavy stuff that he was afraid he was about to receive what convicts and cops called "the Big Bitch." In most states, after conviction on three felony charges, repeat offenders could be sent to prison for life as habitual criminals.

George's family loyalty was never all that trustworthy before Larry killed the raven-haired young woman, and now he sang like a bird when he was asked who stabbed the gang leader's girlfriend. In return for his fingering Larry, George benefited from some plea bargaining that would keep him out of prison — at least for the moment.

George went free, while Larry drew a thirty-five-year sentence for murder and was bused off to Joliet Prison. He was furious over George's betrayal, and he had plenty of time to think about it as he sat in his cell. His brother had snitched on him to save his own skin. During the endless dark nights at Joliet, Larry made certain promises to himself. It might take a long time, but he vowed that George was going to get what was coming to him for his transgressions. All prisoners detest snitches, and snitching on a man's own brother broke almost every rule of prison ethics.

George Light's face was as battered as any prizefighter's, the results of his propensity to use his fists, especially when he'd been drinking. He was certainly not the answer to an average maiden's prayer, but fourteen-year-old Doris Mae found herself drawn to him. Being with George seemed safer to her than where she was. He had a pretty good job as a truck driver, and that meant stability to her.

George Light was her ticket out of a home where her life was totally miserable. Doris was tiny and slender, and she had a face like a bruised pansy. She had no education, no skills, and clearly no talent at all about judging men. George was nicer to her when they were dating than any men she'd known so far, and she linked her fortune to his.

Despite her frail body, Doris Mae was soon constantly pregnant. She bore five children in rapid succession. When George was in jail — a frequent occurrence — she and the children lived on welfare payments; when he was out, she often served as his punching bag. If she had felt trapped before, Doris

Mae was *really* trapped now.

Nobody knew exactly why, but in 1970 George packed up his family and headed west to the state of Oregon. Maybe things were getting too hot for him in Illinois. Their trip was reminiscent of desperate families escaping the Dust Bowl in the thirties. They had barely enough money for gas and baloney sandwiches along the way, and no money at all to rent a house when they reached their destination.

Salem, Oregon, in the fertile Willamette Valley, looked like paradise in the spring and summer, and George assured Doris Mae he would find them housing. His selection of a home was expedient and economical, if not luxurious. He spotted a deserted farmhouse near Salem on the Powers Creek Loop Road. It was a two-story structure, with a sagging porch, broken windows, and a yard overgrown with weeds. When he peeked in the windows, he deduced that it had obviously been empty for a long time.

George kept his ears open as he drank a beer at a local tavern, and with careful questions, he found out the farmhouse was owned by someone who lived out of state and never came around. He smiled when he heard that, and he soon moved Doris Mae and their five children into the abandoned house.

The old car that had barely gotten them to Oregon soon died. George parked it over an abandoned open well so the kids wouldn't fall in. Doris Mae was discouraged when she surveyed the creaky old house, but her husband told her they would have to live there until he made a stake.

She had lived in a dozen or more places since their marriage and this leaking farmhouse was just another in a string of dumps. She put cardboard over the windows, stuffed newspapers in the cracks where the wind whistled through, set out pans where the roof leaked, and tried to make the best of it. It was kind of pretty outside by the grove of fir trees, and she noticed there were cherry trees that might blossom in the spring. Maybe she could even start a garden if they stayed that long. But they never stayed anywhere long, so she didn't count on it.

George got a job in the lumber mill in the hamlet of Molalla. It was twenty-four miles away, but he got a ride to and from work from a generous neighbor. The money from his mill job wasn't bad and he could have taken adequate care of his family — except that he spent money for liquor first and groceries second.

George Light was not a man who became cheerful and amenable when he drank. Not at all; he was a mean drunk. Doris had long since learned to dread the sound of his footsteps after he'd lingered at the tavern. She weighed 95 pounds, and George weighed 160, and if she said or did the wrong thing, she could expect a new crop of bruises or a black eye that no amount of makeup would cover. It was a way of life for her, and she did her best not to irritate him.

She enrolled their three older children in the closest grade school and spent her days with the two babies, one of whom was only a few months old. She lived a lonely and solitary life. About the only time she got out to talk to people was when she shopped at the Lone Pine store for groceries.

And then a Christmas Eve visitor changed the direction of Doris Mae's life, not to mention George's.

Larry Light, thirty now, had been recently paroled from prison after serving almost eleven years. His parole papers stipulated that he was not to travel outside the state of Illinois, but he ignored that edict, figuring that no one was going to chase him all across the country. He decided to surprise his brother and sister-in-law and join them in Oregon for Christmas 1970.

Laden with presents and several fifths of whiskey, Larry knocked on his brother's door. If he still harbored resentment toward George for his betrayal, it wasn't obvious. The brothers seemed to get along all right, and Larry soon moved in with George and Doris, stashing his sleeping roll in an attic alcove.

Larry had been a long time without female companionship and he was powerfully attracted to his fragile sister-in-law. Although Doris was twenty-nine years old, she still looked like a teenager. The years with George should have aged her a lot more than they had, but the damage had been done more to her spirit and soul than to her outward appearance. Her hair was still dark brown, untouched by gray, and hung almost to her waist. Her brown eyes were clear. There was only a faint hardness — or maybe it was tension — in her facial expression attesting to her years of disillusionment.

Larry studied her quietly as she moved about, doing the myriad chores required in a house with only the most rudimentary conveniences. She had to haul water from an outside pump, wash clothes by hand, carry in wood, and try to keep the dark rooms clean without the benefit of a vacuum sweeper.

George didn't help her. When he wasn't working, he was either off at the tavern or sitting at the kitchen table nursing a bottle of whiskey. If he paid her any attention at all, it was to criticize her and bully her or demand his husbandly rights in bed.

Doris was not unaware of Larry's eyes following her. It was exhilarating to know she could still attract a man after so many years with no money to spend on herself. Larry wasn't as good looking as George, and he looked older even though he was six years younger, but unlike her husband, Larry was kind to her. He paid her little compliments and rushed to help her carry the laundry out and bring the wood in. She even allowed herself to flirt a little when George wasn't looking.

She knew that Larry wasn't a much better deal for a woman; he had a police rap sheet longer than George's, and he was a drinker too. Between them, the two men could easily put away a fifth or two every night, and Larry enjoyed honky-tonking as much as his older brother.

For a week or so, the two brothers got along, but as the winter storms keened outside, the thin veneer of civility that existed between George and Larry began to crack like the paint on the old farmhouse the trio shared. Liquor served only to bring the hostility closer to the surface. Now, when George gave Doris Mae the back of his hand, Larry intervened, and that made George even angrier. He'd been knocking her around for years and it was none of his brother's business.

Shortly after the New Year — in January 1971 — George got arrested for driving while intoxicated and without a license. This time it was George who drew a jail sentence. With George locked up, Doris Mae and Larry were thrown together even more. It was pleasant for her to share the home without having to put up with George, even though the presence of the five youngsters didn't give them much privacy. Maybe they talked about beginning what would be a most dangerous affair, but they didn't become intimate at that point; they only became allies and the very best of friends. Doris Mae felt as though she had someone on her side at last — someone who would protect her from George's rage.

Pete Getchell,* one of George's new friends, noticed a closeness between Doris Mae and her brother-in-law when he dropped by the farm one night. He wondered what was going to happen when George got out of jail. Pete knew you couldn't hide the kind of attraction Doris Mae and Larry had for each other — even if they hadn't consummated their passion yet.

When George walked out of the Marion County Jail in Salem a few weeks later, the threesome continued to live together as they had before, but tension hung in the air like a palpable thing. George kept smacking Doris, and Larry kept objecting, with most of their arguments occurring in a haze of alcohol.

Maybe George was getting worried, or maybe he had something else in mind, but sometime early in February, he bought an old double-barreled shotgun and propped it against a wall between his bedroom and Larry's. He showed it to his good friend Pete but didn't explain why he'd bought it. Pete hoped that maybe he only wanted to hunt game to feed his family.

Around the first of March, Larry Light got involved in a tavern brawl. He had objected to something the members of the country-western combo performing either said or sang, and he waded in swinging with a beer bottle. Just as he'd done eleven years earlier, he hit a woman, but not fatally this time. One of the musicians' girlfriends got in his way, and when Larry was drunk or angry — or both — he attacked first and looked to see who he'd attacked later.

Like his brother before him, Larry was booked into the Marion County Jail in Salem. While Larry was incarcerated, Doris Mae was a familiar sight at the jail every visitor's day. His brother, George, didn't show up at all.

In fact, George didn't report for work, either.

Nor was he seen in the taverns he was so fond of. He wasn't so popular that anyone missed him very much, but a few people at the lumber mill wondered why he hadn't called in sick.

On the first night of spring, March 21, 1971, Silverton firemen answered an alarm that sent them to a run-down farmhouse on the Powers Creek Loop Road. Flames had licked through the roof by the time they arrived and they could hear the terrified screams of children inside.

The firefighters raced to break into the smoke-filled house and groped for the youngsters. Fortunately, they found and rescued Doris and George's five children. By the time the fire was finally extinguished, a gaping hole five feet in diameter had been burned through the roof.

The older youngsters said that they were all alone in the place. Their uncle was in jail and their mother had gone out for a while; they didn't mention their father at all.

Doris Mae drove up and burst into hysterical crying as she saw the charred ruins. She was assured that her babies were safe at a neighbor's house down the road.

Doris was reprimanded for leaving young children alone, and she was contrite, promising that it would never happen again. She hadn't been gone long at all, she said, and thought her older children would be okay looking after the babies. Clearly, a terrible tragedy had been averted.

It was only a week later that the fire alarm sounded again and the address given was the same farmhouse. The Silverton fire crew raced back to the Light residence, fearful that this time they might not reach the children in time. This fire was not as severe as the first, however. Sparks from the crumbling chimney had ignited the roof again, but Doris had been at home and called for help right away.

The firefighters felt sorry for the slender woman who lived alone in a house that was clearly unsafe and without even the smallest human comforts. For the children's sake, and hers, too, they condemned the property and told her she would have to move out. She nodded her head distractedly when they asked her if she understood.

On April 3, however, when Chief Larry Carpenter checked back, he found the house still occupied. Once again, he gave Doris Mae notice that she had to move out of the red-tagged house. No one realized that the Light family were only squatters, and that they hadn't even been paying rent.

The next day, the house was empty.

Chief Carpenter contacted the out-of-state owner and explained that the property was a menace. He suggested that it should be razed before anyone was injured — or killed. The owner, surprised to hear anyone had been living there, agreed at once.

On April 18, the Silverton firefighters burned the house, the sheds, and accumulated trash in a controlled training exercise. Nothing remained but the old car atop the well and some charred beer cans.

Spring winds danced over the burned weeds and blew curls of ashes into the air.

But soon nature regenerated the property. Lupines and California poppies and buttercups bloomed amid the ashes, and the old farm with its firs and cherry trees became a thing of beauty instead of an eyesore. Doris Mae never got to see how pretty the land there could be, despite her hope that she could stay there through the spring and summer and plant a little garden.

Where she had gone was anybody's guess. Sadly, nobody knew her well enough to wonder.

The Lights had disappeared as quickly as they'd arrived, and folks in the region thought little of them. Pete Getchell missed his friend George Light and wondered why his old buddy had moved on without even saying good-bye. He mentioned it a time or two in the taverns and was finally semiconvinced that George had simply fallen back into his wandering ways.

More than three years later, by August 19, 1974, the Lights were only dim memories around the Powers Creek Loop Road. But in the Marshall County Jail in Lacon, Illinois, on the eastern shore of the Illinois River, a prisoner wrestled with a burning conscience he hadn't even known he had. He peered out the bars at the flatland shimmering in the heat of the August afternoon and in his imagination saw, instead, the old farmhouse and cherry orchards of Oregon. It was a strange thing; he'd made it clean away, and now his damned conscience was nagging him. He'd done it partly for revenge, partly because he wanted the little woman so much — and now the revenge had turned to ashes in his mouth and the woman was gone.

In the intervening years since he'd pulled out of Oregon with Doris and the kids, Larry Light had come close to dying. Even though he was only in his early thirties, his heart had gone bad on him. Despite all the trouble he'd caused, the state of Illinois had paid for his open-heart surgery while he was in jail for parole violation. He felt somewhat better, but he still had to take heart medication all the time. He was suddenly aware of his own mortality, fearful of dying with a terrible burden on his soul. And here he was in jail again on a theft charge. He couldn't even sleep. When he closed his eyes, he kept seeing George's face the way it was at the last.

Larry rattled the bars and called to Marshall County undersheriff Russ Crew: "I gotta talk to somebody in Oregon — Salem, Oregon."

Crew listened as the prisoner insisted. "Look, it's about a murder out there. Believe me, they'll be interested in what I have to say."

Crew and Sheriff Moe Berg questioned Light closely to see if he was up to something, but he kept insisting that he had to talk to Marion County sheriff's detectives. The Marshall County lawmen put a long-distance call through to Salem and reached Captain Richard Bay. "This man says he killed his brother out there back about three or four years ago. Says he left him in the ground and that he's probably still there."

Bay said he would check on men missing in Oregon, and on any records there for the Light brothers, promising to get back to Berg as soon as possible.

But Richard Bay failed to locate any information on unidentified bodies matching the description of George Light, the purported victim, that had been found near Salem. That didn't mean, though, that there wasn't one still lying undiscovered. He passed the information on to Lieutenant Jim Byrnes, who was the chief of detectives in the Marion County Sheriff's Office. Byrnes placed a conference call to Lacon, Illinois. Byrnes talked to Larry Light while Sheriff Berg listened in. Byrnes carefully advised Light of his rights under Miranda before he began to question him.

Larry Light insisted that he had killed his brother, George, with a shotgun after an argument sometime early in 1971. "Then I buried him out in back of the house," Larry blurted. "He's about two feet down, wrapped in a blanket."

"When you shot him, was he facing you?" Byrnes asked.

"He was facing me — then he turned. I shot him in the head — left ear."

"What type of gun?" Byrnes asked.

"A sixteen-gauge shotgun."

Larry explained that he and Doris Mae, George's wife, had covered George with a blanket as if he were asleep and waited until the next morning to bury him. "It only took about half an hour to bury him; the dirt was real loose. George shouldn't be hard to find."

Byrnes jotted notes on the pad in front of him, as Larry gave specific directions to the body. He described a shed in the back of the farmhouse that was approximately ten by twenty feet. "George is next to the middle of the shed on the north side."

It was a most unusual confession for Jim Byrnes; the killer was thousands of miles away, only a disembodied voice on the other end of the phone line, but he spilled out information in a tumble of words like water bursting from a dam. Once started, he was unstoppable.

"I'm curious. Why are you confessing this now after all this time?" Byrnes asked.

"Because it was my brother I killed and I have had this on my mind for three years and I want to get it over with as it has bothered me."

Byrnes assured Larry Light that his crew would search the area he had described and that he would hear back from them as soon as they had something definite.

Jim Byrnes called Marion County district attorney Gary Gortmaker and told him about the information that he'd just received from Illinois. Then he checked local records for any mention of George or Larry Light. He found that they had both served terms in the county jail in early 1971. George had been there first — in January. Larry had served thirty-three days of a ninety-day sentence in March and was released on the first of April to return to Illinois for parole violation.

The FBI rap sheets on the two men listed scores of felony offenses.

Byrnes saw a notation that a Silverton police officer — Bill Laws — had followed up some rumors about George's disappearance. Laws had gone so far as to question Doris Mae Light, but she told him that George had abandoned her and the children and that she had no idea where he was. The poor woman was living in abject poverty with a pathetic bunch of little kids, and Laws didn't doubt that she had been abandoned.

It was early in the morning in the third week of August 1974 and the dew still clung to wildflowers on the old farm property when ten searchers arrived. Jim Byrnes, Captain Dick Bay, District Attorney Gary Gortmaker, his assistants Robert Hamilton and Richard Morley, Marion County detectives Larry Lord and Jan Cummings, Corporal Ron Boedigheimer, Deputy Jim Lovin, and Oregon State Crime Lab technician Richard Brooke began their search of the isolated property on the Powers Creek Loop Road. The buildings were gone, the undergrowth thick and tangled. It was a far different place than Larry Light remembered.

Was there really a body lying here, undiscovered? It hardly seemed possible. All the landmarks that could have helped them were gone. The investigators poked beneath the weeds, searching for the foundations of the house and sheds that had once stood there. Jim Byrnes figured that the shed Light described had to have stood beyond a lean-to used for storage.

They would begin with a backhoe. Cautiously, the operator broke into the ground, scraping the topsoil off until the red Oregon dirt was exposed in an ever-widening circle.

At first, only rusted cans and old beer bottles surfaced. But thirty minutes after the backhoeing began, the shredded corner of what appeared to be a rotting blanket came into view. A chill came over the investigators, one that defied the burgeoning warmth of the day.

The backhoe was pulled away; now the digging would have to be done by hand. Whatever clues might remain from the events of three years ago would be fragile, too easily destroyed by anything but the most meticulous hand search. Byrnes and Bay bent to the onerous task beneath a blazing August sun.

Working in a carefully roped-off area, Byrnes found a broken segment of desiccated bone fragment. It was too large to have come from an animal. It was a piece of human skull. Next, he and Bay discovered wadding and a few pellets from a shotgun shell. Two hours after the first find, Byrnes located the upper teeth of a human being.

George Light, the punitive husband, the Judas brother, had lain in this quiet ground decomposing for more than three years. Just as his brother, Larry, had predicted, his entire skeleton was there, still clothed in a shirt and blue jeans — the material virtually intact while the flesh beneath had rotted.

Byrnes attached a tag, "Light, George, 8-20-74, #74-7731," to the femur bone of one leg.

They had searched for more than nine hours, and it was after five when the scene was cleared, the skeleton removed, leaving Boedigheimer and Lord to complete the diagramming of the exact spot where the grave had been unearthed.

Jim Byrnes made reservations to fly back to Illinois to talk to Larry Light in person, while the other investigators followed the trail the Lights left behind in 1971.

Jan Cummings and Ron Boedigheimer talked to Pete Getchell, the only friend George had made in Oregon. Getchell said he'd bought George's horse from Doris and Larry after George had "took off," and he tried to recall the last time he'd seen his friend. He remembered dropping into the farmhouse sometime late in February and finding the three Lights engaged in one of their increasingly frequent battles. Doris had run out of the house with George right after her.

"He smacked her a good one and she screamed and ran back in the house while Larry tried to break it all up."

Getchell said he'd gone back a day or so later and Larry and Doris told him that

George was taking a nap.

"I told them I had to talk to George, and before they could stop me, I went and looked in the bedroom. I saw him stretched out on the bed. There was a blanket tucked up tight under his chin; he had his jeans on, and his boots were there on the floor beside the bed."

Jan Cummings suspected that George might have already been dead when Getchell peeked into the bedroom. "How did he look?" she asked. "Like a normal guy sleeping?"

"Well, George's face looked awfully bruised up, and it was kind of all red and swollen," Getchell said. "But I figured it was just because of another fistfight. Him and Larry was always swinging at each other."

Suddenly Getchell realized what Jan Cummings had suggested. He looked at her and breathed, "You ain't telling me George was dead when I was looking at him?"

Jan Cummings nodded. "What did they tell you when George disappeared?"

Pete Getchell's face turned pale green. "They said he took off for Chicago — just like that," he said. "And I believed them, didn't even think otherwise. And I bought the horse when they also took off for Illinois. I don't know what happened to that old gun.

It was a real old one, like maybe fifty years old. Maybe it got burned up in the fire."

Cummings and Boedigheimer checked at the Lone Pine grocery store and learned that Larry and Doris Mae had been in to cash a check sometime in the first week of April 1971. The store owner said that he hadn't had enough money in the cash register to cash a check so large. "It was one of those IBM checks like the welfare gives — almost $400 worth. They never did come back to pay us what they owed us — let's see, here it is: $31.42."

That welfare check was probably why Doris Mae had stayed in the old house even after it was condemned. She and Larry needed that money to get out of Oregon.

Halfway across the country in Sheriff Berg's office in Lacon, Illinois, Jim Byrnes faced the man who had confessed on the phone to murder. Larry Light was still anxious to shed himself of the burden of guilt he'd carried for three and a half years. He said he was willing to pay whatever penalty he had coming for killing his brother.

Byrnes realized that had Larry not confessed, George's body might never have been discovered. Somewhat ironically, the crime had been effectively covered up by the Silverton Fire Department when they burned the farmhouse and outbuildings.

Now, Larry spoke about his obsession with his brother's wife, and his anger over the way George treated Doris Mae. And yes, he admitted that he had still harbored resentment over the way that George had snitched him off to the police on the murder charge in 1959. During the years he spent in prison, he had planned so many times how he would settle that score. Had he consciously followed George to Oregon so that he could wreak revenge? He honestly didn't know. At first they had gotten along, during the Christmas holidays at the end of 1970. But when George was so cruel to Doris Mae, Larry said, it "kind of set me off."

"And I *knew* I was going to kill him after he hit me between the eyes with a beer bottle."

"When was that?" Byrnes asked quietly.

"It was sometime in January or February back in 1971. I can't say for sure when. I guess it was three or four days later that I shot him.

"I recollect that it was on a Sunday when it happened. Doris Mae had shown me where the shells were kept for the old pump shotgun after our first bad fight. I was sitting at the kitchen table drinking whiskey when another argument started. When George threw a lamp at me, I went for the gun. Doris saw what was going to happen and she rushed the children out back, except the baby might have been on his table in the kitchen."

Larry Light narrowed his eyes as he seemed to envision the scene in the old farmhouse. Byrnes realized it was no longer a hot day in August in Illinois — it was a winter night in Oregon some three years earlier.

"He told me I'd better get started killing him because he was going to beat me up. I got up and walked into the front room and I was right by the stairs leading upstairs. He threw a lamp at me and I just reached in and grabbed the shotgun and shot him."

"Had you been thinking about what you were going to do?"

"Yeah. I knowed I was going to kill him if he started it again."

Larry remembered that he had fired from the hip as George threw up his arms in a futile gesture of self-defense.

"I dragged George onto the bed and tucked the blanket around him. There was a lot of blood pouring out from behind his left ear. I think he died right away."

Larry Light said that Doris Mae had just finished cleaning up the blood on the bed and the floor when Pete Getchell dropped in unexpectedly. The two of them had huddled in the kitchen anxiously as they listened to Pete trying to talk to George. They were "scared to death" that he would figure out George wasn't taking a nap at all, but was lying there dead. But Pete never caught on. He kept having a conversation with a dead man.

The next day, after the children had gone off to school, Larry had wrestled the now board-stiff corpse of his brother out to its shallow grave. Doris's only part in the impromptu burial was to hold the back door open for him.

In the days that followed, they had both turned to liquor to sublimate the horror of what had happened. That hadn't been a good idea at all because that was when Larry had gotten so drunk that he got involved in the tavern brouhaha. "And I had to go to jail for a month — and leave Doris Mae out there alone, except for George in the ground."

One can only imagine what that month was like for Doris Mae, isolated in the farmhouse, alone at night when the March storms flailed at the windows and the wind howled in the treetops, all the time knowing that her husband's body lay buried a few feet from her back door.

On February 25, 1971, Doris had a terrible scare when police officers came to her door.

But they had only wanted her because she'd failed to answer a traffic citation. She was mugged and printed but released. No one said anything about her husband, and she didn't volunteer anything.

Jim Byrnes figured that Doris Light had probably been looking over her shoulder for three years too, waiting for the past to catch up with her. Larry said he didn't know where she was.

"She left me," he said.

With the terrible secret they shared, it just hadn't worked out between them as far as romance went. "I don't know where she is now."

Byrnes finally located Doris Mae Light in Chester, Illinois. When he knocked on the front door of the last address he'd found for her, he recognized her at once from her traffic violation mug shot. She was still pretty and very petite. But she gasped when he identified himself and she ran like a deer across the plowed field behind her house. She hid briefly at a small business where a friend worked, but then she agreed to talk with Byrnes.

First reading her her Miranda rights, the Oregon detective asked her about the murder.

"Who did I kill?" she asked faintly.

"Your husband, George, is dead."

"George isn't dead." She shook her head emphatically.

"We've recovered his body in Oregon."

"George went to the store," she answered in a curious non sequitur. "George was mean most of the time, but good sometimes. Larry said he wanted George dead, that he has hated him all his life."

"Did Larry kill George?"

Doris Mae didn't answer at first. Jim Byrnes sensed that she had buried the reality of George's murder so deeply in her subconscious mind that she was truly having trouble accessing it.

After a long silence, she answered almost mechanically. She remembered living in Oregon. George had been drunk one day and sent her to the store for cigarettes, but she had run out of gas on the way home. When she finally got home, she recalled that "George was gone."

It was as if she'd washed the whole thing away, unable to bear the truth, not an altogether surprising reaction.

Byrnes reminded her that the old Nash Rambler they'd been driving was still at the house. He asked her how George could have left; it was too far to walk anywhere.

She didn't have an explanation for that,

but even so, Doris Mae continued to insist that she believed George had merely left her. "When he didn't come back that night," she said, "Larry wanted to sleep with me — but I wouldn't. My husband left me, but I was still married."

Later, Doris said that they had finally had a sexual relationship. She admitted to Byrnes only that she'd always "thought" Larry had killed her husband but that she wasn't sure.

Maybe she was telling the truth — or maybe she was saying what she had to believe now or she would go crazy.

Back in Oregon, Pete Getchell, whose mind had been completely boggled at the thought that his last view of George Light was of a dead man, continued to recall the events after the killing. He'd seen Doris Mae and Larry a few days later and warned Larry, "George is going to kick your ass," after he saw Larry caressing Doris.

Larry had only grinned and commented cryptically, "I have already whipped his ass and sent him down the road."

Once the illicit duo had returned to Illinois, their affair was short-lived. Larry had been arrested for parole violation and went back to prison at Menard, and Doris and her children had settled in nearby Chester.

Both Larry and Doris were extradited to Oregon to face the charges for a long-hidden crime. On September 5, 1974, Larry Light pleaded guilty to a charge of second-degree murder (after dismissal of first-degree charges) and was sentenced to ten years in the Oregon State Penitentiary.

One week later, Doris Mae's first-degree murder charge was dismissed and she was charged only with being an accessory after the fact.

She pleaded guilty to the latter charges on November 5, 1974, and received a five-year suspended sentence. Consideration was given to the fact that she had five young children to care for.

All her life, Doris Mae Light ran from one unhappy situation to another in search of freedom to live a happy life, only to find herself more and more enmeshed. Suddenly she was free of both the men who had trapped her: the brothers who first coveted her and then bound her into a special kind of slavery.

Perhaps Doris Mae's compassionate sentence was a fitting end to one of the strangest murder stories in Oregon history. Where the years since have taken her, God only knows.

If she is still alive, she would be sixty-six years old.

■ ■ ■ ■

THE
CHEMIST'S
WIFE

■ ■ ■ ■

There are many obsessions that trigger human decisions; of them all, none may be as deadly as pathological jealousy. It can drive some to commit acts so despicable that they are incomprehensible to a rational individual, beginning with treating a woman as a possession. A woman in this kind of relationship is caught in a cage — as surely as if she were actually hemmed in by iron bars. Not only is she in danger, but so is anyone who might try to free her.

My mail and e-mail are full of desperate pleas for advice from women trying to move out of unhappy liaisons where they feel trapped or, worse, live in fear. What they once believed was true love was really their partners' need to control them. When they try to leave, they are threatened, demeaned, and even physically attacked.

How I have wished that I had answers and solutions for them, but the law has few remedies for women who are afraid, short of restraining orders to bar stalkers from approaching them — and those are really only pieces of paper with little clout. Even when the woman, her family, and her friends know in their hearts that tragedy lies ahead, police cannot arrest someone for what he *might* do. That would take away his rights.

Some women run away, hoping to disappear in a town or city far away, but that means leaving their families behind. Most don't have the financial resources to do that. If there are children involved, moving would mean the loss of grandparents, schools they are used to, a familiar life they trusted. And in custody disputes, it is often illegal to take children away from their fathers and refuse visitation.

The small percentage of wives or lovers who have been backed to the wall in terror and fight back, killing the men who have stalked them, don't walk away untouched. Even if they are not charged with murder and sent to prison, they inevitably suffer profound emotional damage, and they live the rest of their lives full of guilt and regret.

In the end, this seems to be an insoluble problem, one that might be avoided only if women could see beyond the romantic façade of a suitor who promises her the world while he is steadily separating her from her family and her friends.

The lover who insists that he loves a woman so much that he wants to be with her all the time — and tells his love object that she should want to be with *him* constantly — is almost always a burgeoning stalker.

When Emily Borden* encountered Terry Ruckelhaus* for the first time, she was just fifteen years old, albeit a mature-looking fifteen. She could pass easily for twenty. The attraction between the teenager and the twenty-six-year-old chemist was immediately apparent to anyone who observed that first meeting.

They met in Hawaii, where Terry worked for Emily's parents. Despite the eleven-year disparity in their ages, Emily was allowed to date Terry. Maybe her parents knew they couldn't stop the couple from seeing each other and hoped that Terry wouldn't seem so enticing to their daughter if they didn't make a big fuss about it. Perhaps they hoped the connection between the two would die of its own weight.

Then again, Terry appeared to be the kind of young man that any parent might covet as a future son-in-law. He was brilliant, clean-cut, and the scion of a wealthy Texas family. He looked just as young for his age as Emily appeared to be mature for hers. Anyone who didn't know their ages wouldn't have given them a second glance.

The Borden family originally moved to Hawaii from Alaska. When her parents closed down their Hawaiian business interests, Terry and Emily had been dating exclusively for six months and showed no signs of slowing down. Emily was adamant that she wasn't going to move away from the islands with her family and leave Terry behind. Only then did her parents realize that their gamble that she would grow tired of Terry hadn't worked. Emily insisted on remaining in Hawaii.

Her family wasn't at all happy with this idea, but it was extremely difficult — if not impossible — to argue with a sixteen-year-old girl in love. If they forced her to leave the islands, she would probably just run away and return to Ruckelhaus.

And Terry promised to take good care of Emily, assuring her family that she would be safe with him.

At first, things were fine, but soon their financial picture grew desperate. Although Terry had five years of college with majors in biology and chemistry, he found it difficult to find a new job. The young couple lived on unemployment for six or seven months. This didn't bother Emily; she was adept at making money stretch, and she enjoyed keeping their apartment immaculate.

There were a few obstacles that kept her from being truly secure, however, little warning flags that troubled her. First, there was Terry's temper. The slightest things could send him into towering rages. One day his car broke down and he threw a screaming tantrum about it. Emily was shocked at how angry he was, but then the storm clouds passed as quickly as they'd come. After all, she figured, he was worried about money and they needed their car so he could look for work. Terry was probably just reacting to the frustration of one problem piled on top of another.

When he couldn't find a job by mid-July that first year, they decided to return to the mainland and try their luck there. Terry's family in Texas welcomed them into their home and the young couple lived there for three months. Finally, Terry found a job performing lab tests on the effects of acid and weather corrosion on different structures. With his salary as a chemist, they soon had enough money to move into their own apartment.

They never had a formal marriage ceremony, but Emily considered herself to be married, at least under common law. She had all her identification documents changed to read "Emily Ruckelhaus."

Their lives should have been running smoothly now — but something was wrong. Emily knew she was a good housekeeper, but she was never able to please Terry. No matter how much she scrubbed and waxed, he continually complained that she kept the apartment like a pigsty. She sighed to her friends, "If he even finds two dishes sitting in the sink, he freaks out."

It wasn't just her housekeeping. She recognized that she often made him angry. Worse, she didn't even know why. He continually changed the rules about how they should live, and what he expected her to do. She never quite measured up.

When he was mad at her, Terry was like an enraged bull. She found it hard to keep any kind of a wardrobe together. During his temper tantrums, he tore at her clothing, literally ripping her blouses from her body. Time after time she stood there humiliated, her clothes in shreds.

Their quarrels took on a perverted pattern. Something Emily had said or done would set him off. Sometimes it was something as minuscule as her paying seven cents too much for a half gallon of milk. Terry would get an odd smile on his face and say, "Come on, sweetheart. We're going to have a little talk."

Emily dreaded what was going to come next.

Terry pulled the drapes and locked all the doors. Even their pet dog, Amber, recognized that something bad was about to happen and ran to hide under the bed.

And then Terry would beat his teenage "wife." He knocked her to the floor and kicked her, screaming, "God dammit, Emily, I'm going to kill you!"

He seemed to take sadistic pleasure in her terror and confusion. "What's the matter?" he taunted. "You're scared, aren't you? You're damned right you're scared."

And then he would go into a terrifying monologue about what a "mean S.O.B." he really was. Emily saw that he took great delight in reminding her of that.

Terry began to watch Emily's every movement. If she went to buy groceries, she had a time limit. If she didn't return within five minutes of her limit, he locked the doors on her and made her beg to be let in. Only when he felt that he had subjected her to enough humiliation would he let her in. Then Terry would make her sit across from him while he carefully checked the supermarket's receipt against what she had brought home.

Terry had no reason whatsoever to suspect Emily of going against his wishes or cheating on him with another man. In spite of the jealous rages and beatings, she still loved him with the kind of unwavering devotion a young woman feels for her first love. She kept hoping that they could somehow find their way back to the way they had been when they were first together. She tried to obey his rules — rules she didn't understand and that changed so rapidly that she could never keep up with them.

Terry succeeded in completely isolating Emily. She was far away from her own family, alone — except for Terry — in a strange city. She tried to believe that he would change, that she could live up to his expectations so the beatings and psychological torture would stop.

But her life only grew worse. One night, Terry threw her all the way across the room, and a huge gash opened on her knee when she landed on something sharp. Another time, he slapped her so hard with his open hand that her lip split, and then he grabbed her by the hair and methodically slapped her until her head bounced like a rag doll's.

As suddenly as he'd started, he stopped. He looked shocked as he gazed at her with obvious distress.

"I just realized I was beating the shit out of you," he said, begging for her forgiveness.

Emily took a job in Fort Worth — because Terry asked her to. They needed more money to pay their bills, he said. But then he resented the time she was away from him, and he was jealous of the men he believed she talked to at her job.

It became routine for her to show up at work with scars and bruises on her face. Her fellow employees and boss worried about her, but she brushed aside their questions. She was ashamed and she was frightened.

Terry had sayings he enjoyed repeating. "A good woman needs a beating every day," he said. He explained to her that he knew she still loved him, so it was all right for him to beat her.

Although Emily was no longer allowed to see her girlfriends, Terry had several male friends. Their opinion of women matched his. When he complained that he didn't trust Emily, one of his friends said, "Just put her on a chain."

"Well, she knows I love her," Terry said. He really believed that a woman would submit to anything as long as she was sure of her man's devotion.

In his own obsessive way, Terry thought he loved Emily. Had he not been filled with such emptiness and inadequacy, had his need for a complete love slave not been so all-encompassing, he might have been able to accept her love and to trust it. Initially, he had the total devotion he said he wanted — but he was destroying any love Emily had for him with his jealousy, his physical punishment, and the terrible emotional flogging he constantly administered to her.

Emily was seventeen years old, but she felt as if she were a hundred.

Like a butterfly trapped in a cigar box, Emily beat her wings hopelessly against her prison. One night, she rode her bicycle around the block a few times, only to come home and find Terry in one of his rages. *Where had she been? Who was she sneaking off to meet?*

Before she could open her mouth to answer, he was on her — hitting and kicking her in full view of a neighbor. When the neighbor started in their direction to stop him, Terry was even angrier at Emily, blaming her for "embarrassing me in public."

Then a time came when she was no longer allowed to talk to her friends on the phone. He was mad when he got a busy signal when he tried to call her. Foolishly, he ordered her to leave the phone off the hook so her friends couldn't get through, apparently not realizing that if she did that, he couldn't get through either.

Twice, her courage honed by especially rough beatings, Emily left Terry and ran to friends' houses. But she stayed away only overnight. He always tracked her down. Predictably, he was full of remorse, and sounded sincerely miserable when he promised to change.

Things would be different. He pleaded that he needed Emily. If she would only come back to him, he would never hit her again.

Still, nothing changed. As soon as she was home, the beatings began again. She feared that he really would carry out his threats to murder her, the awful things he voiced when he was in one of his maniacal rages and claimed not to remember later.

The final straw came with another beating. This time, however, it was not Emily who was the victim; it was her dog. They had been caring for one of Terry's relatives' dogs when Emily's dog crept out on the porch and ate the other dog's food, a perfectly predictable thing for an animal to do. But Terry had rules for animals, too, and this was unforgivable. He beat the helpless dog with a broom handle until Emily's tears and sobs mingled with the anguished howls of her pet.

Somehow, she saw Terry's cruelty and sadism more clearly when she herself wasn't the victim. With a flash of great clarity, Emily knew she couldn't stay with him any longer. She waited for her chance, and as soon as he left the house, she gathered a few clothes and her dog and she fled to her girlfriend's house.

Emily had managed to put a little extra money in their bank account. She planned to draw it out and head for her own family. Her grandparents and her aunts and uncles lived in Seattle. If she could get that far, she knew they would protect her. Then she could make her way up to Alaska and her parents.

But Terry was one step ahead of her. When Emily went to the bank to withdraw her half of the savings account, she found he'd put a hold on the account. She had faithfully deposited a hundred dollars out of each of her paychecks. It was her money. The bank teller studied the tense young girl in front of her and made what was perhaps a fatal decision. She told Emily that she couldn't take her money out without her husband's permission. "I'll call him and ask him," she said with a smile.

Emily's face blanched stark white, and she whirled and ran as the woman began to dial a number. She was caught, trapped, and there was no one to help her.

Her friend could give her shelter, but that was all. And her friends were afraid of Terry, too. They told Emily he was crazy.

It was only a matter of time before he tracked Emily down.

And that was exactly what he was doing. He knew that Emily was very close to her grandparents in Seattle, Bill and Florence Borden. He figured they might be a weak link in the protective fence around Emily. He called Florence Borden, who was seventy-five, and told her he had to talk to Emily. He explained that he was in a sanitarium getting treatment for "nerves," and that he knew he'd recover more rapidly if he could just talk to Emily.

Florence Borden knew where Emily was, but she didn't trust Terry. She knew her granddaughter had suffered a great deal at his hands. For almost three weeks, the elderly lady talked daily on the phone with Terry. He pleaded, cajoled, and tried to reassure her that everything was going to be all right.

"I'm here voluntarily," he said earnestly. "I signed myself in for treatment. I just want Em to know that I'm doing the right thing, and I want her to know that I love her.

"The doctors here tell me that my behavior wasn't my fault — it was caused by some pain pills I was taking for a bad tooth."

Florence Borden wasn't fooled. She knew that Terry had been acting crazy for a year and a half. She reasoned that pain pills prescribed only recently probably hadn't triggered his violent attacks on Emily.

Still, as the weeks went by, Terry wore her down. He was so convincing, so contrite. And he seemed to be sincere. At length, Emily's grandmother gave in, thinking that he really did love Emily, and she told Terry the address where she was hiding.

That was all he needed.

Emily returned to her friend's house that afternoon and her heart stopped when she saw Terry's Capri parked at the curb. Her girlfriend had tried to convince Terry that Emily wasn't living there, but he saw their pet dog and knew she couldn't be far away. He was determined to wait, and no amount of diversionary tactics had distracted him.

Emily knew she had no chance to get away when she saw Terry's car. Her heart pounded with fear, but she took a deep breath and entered the house.

Terry was contrite, as he always was when he wanted her back. He told her the same lie about having gone into psychiatric treatment. He said he realized he'd been wrong, and he vowed to change — with professional help.

"I won't ever hurt you again," he promised, his eyes glistening with tears.

But Emily didn't believe him, and she had also had a taste of freedom, even though it was freedom haunted by the specter of her eccentric lover. She wasn't fifteen any longer; she was eighteen and of age. She remained resolute in her decision to stay free. Her friends supported her. They warned her that she must never go back. However, she knew Terry had a gun, and she was afraid. Afraid to stay away. Afraid to go back.

Terry talked of their going back to Hawaii. Things had been better in Hawaii, he insisted. If they could just go back and start all over, he told Emily, he was sure it would be all right.

Emily encouraged him to go, hinting that she might follow him when she got all their things packed up. It was enough to satisfy him in that meeting.

Now that Terry knew where she was, he was a constant visitor, almost camping out on her friend's porch. One day he found Emily alone. He suddenly grabbed her by the throat, tightening his forearm against her larynx. He accused her of trying to ship him off to Hawaii so that she could run away once he was gone.

"But Terry," she argued desperately, "it was your idea to go back. You go. And I'll follow you."

He pulled out his revolver and held it to his head, threatening to commit suicide. Emily managed to wrestle it away from him and unloaded it. But they were at a standstill. She knew he could overpower her and take the gun back. He wanted the gun, and he said he was going to use it to kill them both.

To lead him away from the gun, Emily finally agreed to go to a motel with Terry, but only if he agreed to leave it behind. There, she told him, they could talk in private.

They talked for hours, and Terry seemed to agree to the plan to go to Hawaii. He would pack and leave the next day. She helped him pack enough clothes for the journey and was almost hopeful that he really intended to leave. She was lying to him, but she knew she had to.

Emily had tried everything else. A restraining order against him was now in effect. She had changed all her identification back to her maiden name. If he would just go, she could get away. By the time he got back, he wouldn't be able to trace her.

But Terry didn't leave the next day. Or the day after. Or the day after that. He found one reason after another to delay his departure. And he insisted on seeing Emily. When her friends refused to let him in to visit her, he threatened to break in — restraining order or not.

Emily faced him, wondering what tactic he would use now. But he was charming, persuasive; he said all he wanted to do was take her out for dinner one last time before he left for Hawaii. He said he had reservations to leave the next day.

"Just one dinner — at a really nice place?" he urged.

Emily finally agreed. She had been away from Terry for three weeks. She thought she had broken any legal bond to him, although she really wasn't married to him. Someone had told her that if she just changed her social security ID back to her maiden name, the common-law relationship would be dissolved.

Maybe it would be easier for Terry to accept if she agreed to one last meal together. She changed her clothes. Somewhat oddly,

Terry insisted that they take their dog along with them.

It was 10 P.M. on December 14, 1975.

Terry said that the restaurant was in Fort Worth and that he had to take Highway 287 to get there. But he kept driving and driving, and promising that the place was only a few miles farther. They passed innumerable restaurants. And then traffic began to thin out and soon they were in the country. Although Terry still said the restaurant was just around the next bend, Emily began to get suspicious.

He ignored her questions for a while, staring straight ahead. Finally, along a lonely stretch of highway, he pulled over and parked his car alongside the road.

Terry turned toward Emily and grinned, but there was danger in his eyes. "We're not going out to eat," he said. "I have a surprise for you. We're going to Seattle."

This was the last thing she wanted. Emily did hope to get to the Northwest and reunite with her relatives there, but she wanted to go alone.

"I don't want to go, Terry," she said quietly. "Please turn the car around."

Instantly, he became angry. He began to scream and slammed his fists around, frightening her badly. She tried to keep her voice as calm as possible, but he was wired, almost vibrating with rage.

Now he locked the car's doors so that she couldn't jump out. And he revved the engine up; the speedometer inched up to eighty miles an hour as they headed north.

Once they were on the road again, Terry became eerily calm. Emily didn't want to get him excited again so she said very little, censoring all of her remarks before she said them aloud.

She wondered if her friends would report her missing when she didn't come back. Maybe there was a chance the Texas Rangers or the highway patrol might stop them. But they passed several police units, and the officers inside didn't pay any attention to them.

They drove past the Texas border and across New Mexico without stopping. Finally exhausted, Terry pulled into a motel. But he wouldn't let Emily out of his sight for a minute. If she had thought she was a prisoner before, now she was really captive. He kept her beside him as he signed in at the motel's front office. She thought about signaling the desk clerk there but couldn't think of a way to do it. Terry would notice.

As long as she didn't argue with him, he

was calm. After they had some sleep, they continued on, heading northwest through Colorado, Utah, Idaho, and then into Oregon.

Something set Terry off as they approached Portland. They had been on their marathon trip for five days, and Emily was exhausted, more frightened with each day that passed. Suddenly, he shouted that he was going to turn around and drive until they ran out of money. He didn't care where they ended up.

She pleaded with him to keep going toward Seattle; they were only 180 miles away. She didn't want to hurtle through the countryside with him until they ended up in some godforsaken spot with no money. Maybe, if she could just get to her relatives, they could help her escape.

Terry finally agreed to keep heading north on I-5. It was a little after four in the afternoon on December 20 when they pulled up in front of Emily's grandparents' modest home. She saw them peering out the window in surprise, and then William and Florence Borden rushed out their front door and welcomed them with open arms.

Everything seemed normal for the first time in a week as Emily's grandmother bustled around the kitchen to fix dinner for her un-expected guests. Emily was still afraid but she relaxed a little as they ate the home-cooked food and sat in the warm kitchen.

They spent the next four days joining in her grandparents' preparations for Christmas and visiting her aunts and uncles. Terry could be so charming — when he wanted to. He told Emily's aunt that he had been stationed in Bremerton, Washington, when he was in the navy and he was looking forward to revisiting the navy yard and seeing the Seattle waterfront, too.

On Christmas Eve, Terry and Emily went shopping for presents. He bought a shirt for Emily's grandfather and a cutting board for her grandmother. They planned to open their presents Christmas morning and then go to Emily's aunt's house for Christmas dinner. Terry continued to act like a perfectly normal guest, and Emily relaxed a little more. She still wanted to "divorce" him, but he seemed so rational that she began to hope this could be accomplished without a lot of grief.

Christmas Day dawned wet and rainy — as it usually does in Seattle; exterior holiday lights all had halos that shimmered in the downpour.

In an extremely rare circumstance, even

the Seattle Police Homicide Unit offices on the fifth floor of the Public Safety Building were empty. There were detectives on call — there had to be — but Sergeant Don Cameron's four-man crew hoped devoutly that their phones wouldn't ring and that they would be able to spend the holiday with their families.

It was not to be.

The Patrol Division answered the first call. At twenty-eight minutes after two on Christmas afternoon, Officers Dick Gagnon and Al Smalley responded to an emergency call for help. Their patrol cars screeched to a stop in front of a small green-shingled house on South Myrtle Street. Within minutes, the rain-washed pavement in front of the house was alive with blue-and-white squad cars.

Don Cameron and Officer Bill Brooks arrived on the scene. They found a critically wounded seventy-five-year-old woman who was bleeding profusely from a wound in her throat. Ignoring her own injuries, she insisted on leading them into the house. They followed her along a narrow hallway to where a very old man lay motionless on a linoleum floor, the surface beneath him so awash with blood that its pattern was obscured.

More Homicide detectives and a Seattle

Fire Department paramedic unit pulled up. The holiday for Sergeant Ivan Beeson and Detectives Dick Sanford and Dick Reed was over. They could see that any Christmas celebrating had long since ceased in the little house on South Myrtle.

The old man was dead.

Bill Brooks took a nearly incoherent Florence Borden to Harborview County Hospital. It was difficult to understand her, but she kept saying that someone named Terry had "hurt Papa" and herself, and she was afraid that he might have hurt her granddaughter, too.

"Where *is* your granddaughter?" Brooks asked. He wondered if the child — or maybe she was a teenager — was lying injured, or even dead, back in the Bordens' house.

Florence Borden shook her head. "He kept knocking me down on top of Papa," she sobbed, "and then he grabbed Emily and made her leave with him. I'm afraid he's going to kill her."

The elderly woman was treated in the ER and then admitted to the hospital in serious condition from shock and blood loss. She had a jagged knife wound in her throat. It was a wonder she'd survived; the knife had barely missed her carotid artery.

Back at the Borden home, the Homicide

investigators surveyed the carnage. The one-story, two-bedroom home must have been immaculate before everything in the kitchen and hall area became sprayed and soaked with blood.

Dick Sanford had investigated many murders in his first year and a half as a Homicide detective, but he had never seen so much blood. He mentioned it to Dick Reed, who had more experience in the Homicide Unit than any of the eighteen detectives assigned there. Reed had seen other victims who had literally exsanguinated — bled out — but not often.

Trying not to notice the Christmas tree in the living room and the presents around it, they began to work the crime scene. Bloody footprints made a path down the hallway to the kitchen sink, and then out to the back porch, and back to the bathroom sink. The red stuff marked everything from the floors to the ceilings, on all the walls and doorways.

The frail old man lay on his side in the walkway just between the two bedroom doorways. He was fully clothed; his glasses were near his head. Someone had cut his throat, slicing through his jugular vein and left carotid artery. His life's fluid had poured out unchecked. He would have been dead from such a wound in a matter of a few minutes. It was such an ugly crime, made more so by the obvious vulnerability of the victim.

"He couldn't have put up any kind of fight," Dick Reed said. "His wife said he was eighty-three."

The Homicide crew sketched the scene, took measurements, and logged in numerous items of physical evidence they recovered, carefully sealing it and signing their initials.

And all the while, they tried to piece together what might have happened. They noted bloody fingerprints on a beige phone near the bed in the west bedroom. In the east bedroom, they found a white nightgown, a black lace scarf, and a green pullover shirt — all of them ripped to pieces.

The kitchen phone line was yanked from the wall.

The Bordens' daughter pulled up in front of the house and wandered in shock past the squad cars. She had come to see why her parents hadn't shown up for Christmas dinner. Barely able to speak, she was finally able to tell the detectives that the old man was her father: William Robert Borden. The gravely injured woman, who was currently in surgery, was her mother, Florence.

The shocked woman said that her niece Emily had been visiting her grandparents for the past several days. She had arrived from Texas with her common-law husband, twenty-nine-year-old Terry Ruckelhaus.

When they asked her about Ruckelhaus and where he might have gone, the woman tried to gather her thoughts. "He said he wanted to see the waterfront — that he'd been in the navy at Bremerton once. That's all I can think of."

She said that Ruckelhaus drove a maroon 1974 Capri. "I don't know the license number," she said, and then looked up, "No — *wait*. He said something about getting a ticket for a moving violation on the trip up here. Would that help?"

It quite probably would.

Reed called the Washington State Patrol and gave them Ruckelhaus's name, a description of the car, and the information that it had Texas plates. The WSP computers soon came up with the license number: Texas CXB-808.

Sergeant Ivan Beeson and Dick Reed called the ferry terminals on the Seattle waterfront. If Ruckelhaus really had it in his plans to return to Bremerton, a ferry would be the quickest route. Ferry officials reported that a maroon Capri with Texas plates *was* on board a ferry departing the Colman dock at 2 P.M. It was due to dock in Winslow on Bainbridge Island at 2:40.

The detectives alerted the Winslow Police, Poulsbo Police, and the Kitsap County Sheriff's Office that a murder suspect was on board the ferry and gave his description. Two police officers and a sheriff's deputy on the Bainbridge Island side of Puget Sound put on ferry workers' uniforms and waited at the dock for the ferry from Seattle to hove into sight.

As it eased into the slip, the three officers jumped on board and moved between the vehicles waiting to debark. Their eyes rapidly scanned the license plates as they searched for one from Texas.

They finally spotted it and saw that there was a couple inside. All the vehicles on board had been delayed from driving off the ferry, and drivers and passengers craned their necks in curiosity as the trio of officers surrounded the Capri.

They signaled to the woman passenger to flip up the locks. She looked nervously toward the driver, and then did what they asked. With weapons drawn, they ordered the driver to get out.

As the driver staggered from the car, a strong odor of liquor emanated from him.

He wore blue jeans, a yellow shirt, and a leather thong tie. There was a knife sheath on his belt, and the Bainbridge Island and Kitsap County officers found two knives inside the car.

The suspect put up no resistance as he was arrested. He appeared to be concerned about his "wife," Emily, who trembled with shock.

She identified him as Terry Ruckelhaus.

Handcuffed, he was transported to the Kitsap County Jail in Port Orchard. Kitsap County chief of detectives Bill Clifton read Ruckelhaus his rights and asked him if he knew what he was being booked for.

"No," he said. "I don't know."

"You're under arrest for murder."

Ruckelhaus insisted that he had no memory about what had taken place in Seattle.

"I can't even remember getting on the ferry."

Ruckelhaus said he was twenty-nine, but he looked younger. He had curly hair that hung close to his face in ringlets, even features, and a thick mustache. His eyes were glassy, almost blank. When Clifton read him his Miranda rights, he nodded and said he understood them.

While Ivan Beeson and Dick Reed were on their way to his Port Orchard office by ferry,

Bill Clifton talked to Ruckelhaus's young female passenger, Emily Borden.

She looked as though she had gazed into hell itself, but she made an effort to describe had happened at her grandparents' home earlier on this Christmas Day.

Emily told him that Terry had literally kidnapped her, forcing her to travel to Seattle from Texas. Everything seemed to be all right when they got to her grandparents' home and for a few days afterward. "But then my parents called me from Anchorage, Alaska," she said. "That's where they live, and I've been trying to get home to them for months now. I spoke to my mother, but Terry was sitting next to me, and he was giving me dirty looks so that I was afraid to say much."

"What is going on?" her mother had asked.

"I tried to keep my voice soft so he couldn't hear me. I told her that I would write as soon as I could, and explain everything.

"After we hung up, I went into the bedroom and Terry followed me, demanding to know what my mother said, and what I said to her. I told him my parents just said to say 'Hi' to him, and that they had wished him Merry Christmas. But he didn't believe that was all. He said what we did was none of my folks' business and he didn't want them butting in."

Terry had decided then that they had to leave Seattle, and he didn't want to go to her aunt's Christmas dinner. When Emily begged him to let her stay, he became enraged and started tearing her clothes off.

"He ripped off the new white nightie my grandmother bought me for Christmas. And then he tore up my scarf and a shirt.

"My grandmother heard us fighting and she opened the door and told Terry to leave me alone. He yelled at her to get out and slammed the door in her face."

A minute later, eighty-three-year-old William Borden had opened the door.

"He saw Terry holding me down on the bed, and he came in and tried to make him stop. After that, there was blood everywhere."

Ivan Beeson and Dick Reed arrived in Port Orchard to take custody of Terry Ruckelhaus and to take Emily Borden back to Seattle. She wanted to go back, but she begged them not to make her see Terry or put her in the same car with him. They assured her she wouldn't have to. Beeson drove the suspect back to Seattle around the land route that goes through Tacoma, while Reed accompanied Emily on the ferry.

Somewhat calmer now, Emily gave Dick Reed a complete statement about what had happened in the Bordens' home. When William Borden told Ruckelhaus to leave his granddaughter alone, the younger man whirled and shouted, "You're not going to stop me from taking *my* wife!"

"I didn't think my grandfather was stabbed," she said tearfully, "but he kind of looked down, and then I saw all the blood. Then he was on the floor and Grandma was lying on her back."

Emily said she couldn't do anything to help them. Terry had gone to the kitchen with a knife in his hand. His glasses were on the floor and she'd picked them up and washed the blood off the lenses. She didn't know why she'd done that. It was all so horrible, as if it couldn't really be happening.

"Terry told me to get the car keys. I saw my grandmother in the kitchen trying to get something to clean up my grandfather. She kept saying, 'My husband is dead. Emily, don't leave! I have to get help. Please call the police.' I wanted to help her, but Terry yelled, 'Mrs. B., no!' And he jerked the phone out of the wall."

Then he told Emily that they had to leave. Shocked and terrified, she went with him.

Emily said she felt guilty because her resistance to leaving with him had set the scene for her grandfather's knifing.

"I told him that he just couldn't keep dragging me all over the country. It was the first time I ever really stuck up for myself. My grandparents tried to save me, and they threatened to call the police. But after he stabbed my grandfather, I knew I had to go with Terry to get him away from there — so my grandmother could call for help."

Emily had called Amber, her dog, and they got in the car.

"Terry was shaking so hard that he had a hard time starting the car. He kept saying, 'Look what you made me do! Look what you made me do.'"

They started driving toward downtown, and Terry saw signs directing them to the ferry terminal.

"He was crazy — he kept babbling and telling me that now we both had to die, but we would meet again 'in the sea.' And then everything would be all right. It would all be different then. I was sure he was going to kill me, too. But there wasn't any way to get away from him once we were out of the house. He was right behind me, and he wasn't going to let me go."

Emily said she had asked Terry to get rid

of his knife, but he had only tucked it into the waistband of his pants. She begged him not to use it.

"He was covered with blood," she said with a shudder. "It was all down the front of him and his hands were red. My shoes were red, too, and I don't know why, but I felt compelled to clean them off. I tried to wipe the blood off when we waited in line for the ferry, but there was too much — so I slipped them off and put on another pair."

As their car inched forward in the ferry line, Terry Ruckelhaus had rambled on about how they could get married now and have children. But soon, he would switch to his theory that they would both have to die — to meet again in the sea someday.

Emily said she couldn't believe that no one noticed Terry, covered as he was with her grandparents' blood, but people seemed intent on their own errands on this incredibly gruesome Christmas Day. Terry had reached across her to take a bottle of Wild Turkey whiskey out of the glove compartment. He took a deep swallow, and she said she'd encouraged him to drink it, hoping that if he got drunk enough, he wouldn't be able to hurt her or anyone else after they landed.

"I was just hoping we would land," Emily

told Dick Reed. "With his wild talk about our being together in the sea, I was afraid he might force me to jump off the ferry with him."

Emily said she hadn't been able to let herself think about what had happened to her grandparents; she tried to hope that her grandfather had only been unconscious when they left. It didn't seem possible that anyone could be dead so quickly.

It was twenty minutes to ten that night when Detective Dick Reed and Emily Borden debarked from the Seattle-bound ferry and drove the three blocks to the Public Safety Building and the Homicide Unit. There was no place for the exhausted girl to stay. She couldn't go back to the bloody house on Myrtle Street, and her relatives were all at the hospital where Florence Borden was undergoing lifesaving surgery; the doctors who operated on her discovered that she had avoided the same death suffered by her husband by a mere fraction of an inch.

The detectives found a safe hotel room for Emily.

Their own day was far from over. It seemed to them that Christmas Day had gone on for a week. There was voluminous physical evidence to log in to the Evidence Room, and reports to type up. Beeson and Reed

417

checked with the hospital at 12:40 A.M. and found that Florence Borden was still in surgery, still in critical condition.

The two Homicide investigators booked Terry Ruckelhaus into jail. The next day, he would be formally charged with one count of first-degree murder and one count of assault in the first degree. The second charge might become another murder charge at any time as Florence Borden was holding onto life by a thread.

His bail was set at $100,000. The booking sheet listed Ruckelhaus as twenty-nine years old, five feet eight inches tall, 165 pounds, with brown hair and mustache, blue eyes. His occupation was listed as "chemist" and he carried a Hawaiian driver's license.

Ruckelhaus seemed removed from the Bordens' brutal stabbings, but he still claimed to be very worried about his "wife," Emily. It clearly hadn't dawned on him yet that he had committed such savage acts that Emily was lost to him forever.

Early on the morning of December 26, Detective Dick Sanford went to Winslow and processed Ruckelhaus's car. He found the bloody shoes Emily had removed during their flight to escape on the ferry. There was a large, very sharp buck knife in its case under the front passenger seat. It was similar to the buck knife arresting officers had removed from Ruckelhaus's belt as they took him from his car the night before. He had been well prepared with backup weapons.

On December 27, Emily Borden gave Sanford a taped statement about her life with Terry Ruckelhaus, detailing the romantic beginning that had disintegrated into an endless ordeal of beatings and terror. She recalled how many times she had tried to get away from him but had found it impossible. Terry told her continually that she belonged to him — in mind, body, and soul. He had told her he would always find her — and he had, tracking her down until the last, fatal trip to Seattle.

Would she agree to testify against Terry in a murder trial?

YES!

There was an icy resolve in Emily now. It was as if she had become so completely terrified that she had passed over into a place where Terry could no longer make her afraid. He was locked up, and she intended to see he would stay behind bars.

Florence Borden did not die. She beat all the odds and slowly recovered her strength. There would be some years left for her, but years without Papa, who had died before her eyes as she tried to save him. Still confused and unbelieving, she gave detectives a statement about what had happened. It coincided exactly with Emily's.

Terry Ruckelhaus underwent observation to determine if he was mentally competent to participate in his own defense in a court of law. He was found to be sane, and able to stand trial. That trial began on March 29, 1976, in Judge Jerome M. Johnson's courtroom in King County Superior Court. Lee Yates, a King County deputy prosecutor, presented the state's case in the nonjury trial.

Terry Ruckelhaus had an exceptional defense team. Two of the area's best-known criminal attorneys, Anthony Savage and Michael Frost, argued in his behalf. Many years later, Savage would defend Gary Ridgway, the infamous Green River Killer.

Savage argued for acquittal on grounds of mental irresponsibility, but Lee Yates's questioning of Emily Borden elicited a portrait of a man consumed with compulsive jealousy. Although Terry Ruckelhaus's obsession with her seemed psychotic, he had been fully capable of formulating carefully thought-out plans to kidnap her and keep her captive.

Emily's grandparents had gone out of their way to be kind and welcoming to Terry.

They had protested only when he began to hurt Emily.

And he had turned on them in a maniacal frenzy.

On April 6, Judge Johnson made his decision. Terence Roger Ruckelhaus was convicted of second-degree murder with no premeditation but with conscious intent to kill, and first-degree assault. He would not serve life in prison, although there were many who knew of this case who felt he should.

Thirty-two years later, Terry Ruckelhaus has vanished into society, leaving no records behind him with which to trace him.

Emily, too, has moved on. Today, she would be fifty years old, and Ruckelhaus, if he is still alive, would be sixty-one.

Emily Borden's liaison with Terry Ruckelhaus is a classic example of love slowly killed by sick jealousy. If Terry had ever allowed himself to trust her, to accept the affection she'd given him so willingly at the start of their relationship, untold tragedy could have been averted. But he smothered her love, binding her so tightly to him that she was suffocated and repulsed by his possessiveness. He spent years in prison while Emily picked up the frayed ends of her life. One thing was certain: she never wanted to see him again.

What Emily suffered at Terry's hands was, sadly, not unusual, and certainly not something that has stopped happening as women have won more rights over the decades since. Indeed, women who strike possessive men as uppity and too strong for their own good often invoke abuse. Except for the date of this murder, nothing has really changed. Every day, women are trapped in what domestic violence experts term the "circle of abuse."

A startling diagram designed to demonstrate how domestic violence occurs in an endless, seemingly inescapable circle is rimmed with the words "Physical Violence — Sexual — Physical — Violence — Sexual — Physical Violence."

Inside the ring of virtual terror are the behaviors that foreshadow domestic violence for women in every single demographic level of society:

Jealousy and possessiveness
Isolation
Emotional abuse, belittling comments
Intimidation and insults
Coercion and threats
Minimizing and denying the man's behavior

Blaming the woman
Using children as hostages
Demanding "male privilege"
Economic abuse

Many women who read Emily's story and the checklist above are going to recognize danger in their own relationships. I hope sincerely they will rethink their own engagements or marriages, and extricate themselves before they are caught too tightly.

It is never too late, though, even if they are legally bound to someone who treats them badly.

One factor *has* changed since 1976; there are far more groups and agencies where women who are afraid can turn. I hope that they will seriously consider contacting the closest domestic violence organization in the areas where they live. For those with Internet access, go to www. google.com and type in "domestic violence" to locate places that offer help.

At some point, the circle of abuse must be broken. I don't want to keep writing books and stories about women who have been hurt — or killed — by someone whom they once loved.

Let's all work together to break the circle.

THE TRUCK DRIVER'S WIFE

Dorothy Jones burned to death in this house — but how? And why?

Arson investigators spread the burned mattress sections on the lawn of Dorothy Jones's home. They tried to determine how an "impossible" fire had started, but nothing fell into place. Had Dorothy herself simply burst into flames?

Bill Hoppe, an arson investigator for the Seattle Fire Department's renowned Marshal 5 unit, had seen one case of spontaneous combustion; he wondered if Dorothy Jones's death was another.

Jim Reed, a member of the Marshal 5 arson investigation team, evaluates burn patterns in Dorothy Jones's home as he looks for the flames' point of origin. With Bill Hoppe, the arson detective tried to unveil some fatal secret in her life.

THE CONVICT'S WIFE

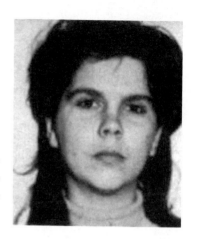

Doris Mae Light had a difficult life, but it got worse when her husband's brother came to spend Christmas — a surprise guest.

Larry Light had reason to resent his brother, George, and they both had good reasons to get out of the state of Illinois. Larry followed George and Doris Mae to Oregon, where they all lived together in an old farmhouse in the country outside Salem.

Lieutenant Jim Byrnes of the Marion County, Oregon, Sheriff's Office investigated the family triangle that appeared to have ended up as a duo. It was no wonder some people said the isolated farmhouse was haunted.

Long after he failed to appear at his favorite tavern, Oregon detectives discovered all that remained of George Light.

THE CHEMIST'S WIFE

Seattle Police Homicide detectives were called out from their homes on a rainy Christmas Day to investigate a tragedy. They found an elderly couple there, but the young couple who came to celebrate the holiday was gone.

Veteran Homicide detective Dick Reed and a uniformed officer take measurements at the home of Florence and Bill Borden. Reed and his sergeant, Ivan Beeson, would find themselves on an unexpected ferry ride as they tracked an elusive suspect.

Like any number of men who seek to possess the women in their lives, Terry Ruckelhaus would not allow his teenage girl-friend to leave him. What had begun as a wonderful romance in an island paradise ended in a savage attack on a vulnerable victim.

"Papa" Borden, 83, fought to save his granddaughter, but his opponent was fifty-five years younger than he was. He will always be remembered as a hero to his family and to the police who spent a stormy Christmas Day looking for his killer and, perhaps, yet another victim. The holiday season brings out the best—and sometimes the worst—in people.

THE MINISTER'S WIFE

In 2006, the Reverend Matthew Winkler and his wife, Mary Carol, lived in this house in Selmer, Tennessee, with their three small daughters. It was the parsonage furnished by the Fourth Street Church of Christ, where Matthew was the youth minister. The Winklers appeared to have a happy marriage. (CREDIT: BEVERLY MORRISON)

When neither Matthew nor Mary Winkler showed up for evening services at this church, the Fourth Street Church of Christ, on Wednesday, March 22, 2006, church members became concerned. Several men, friends of the Winklers, went to their home. What they found stunned them.
(CREDIT: BEVERLY MORRISON)

Above Left: *The Reverend Matthew Winkler was handsome, charismatic, and well versed in the Bible. He had moved up steadily in the Church of Christ as a youth minister, and looked forward to being the pulpit minister in his own church soon.* (Credit: Russell Ingle Photography)

Above Right: *Mary Winkler, always the perfect minister's wife, was very small, soft-spoken, and seemed to be in shock when police located her in Orange Beach, Alabama, where she had taken her three daughters for one last "happy time."* (Credit: Russell Ingle Photography)

Patricia and Allie Winkler leaving their father's funeral with flowers for remembrance. (Credit: Russell Ingle Photography)

Mary Winkler, holding hands with her defense attorneys, is arraigned and charged with the murder of her husband in March 2006. She looked like a terrified child in her orange jail uniform. Church members and townspeople alike wondered what could have happened in the Winkler household a few days before.
(CREDIT: RUSSELL INGLE PHOTOGRAPHY)

Steve Farese Sr. (left) and Leslie Ballin, one of American's "dream teams" of criminal defense, stepped forward to represent Mary Winkler. She clung to them and depended on them as her trial for her husband's murder lay ahead. (CREDIT: BEVERLY MORRISON)

In August 2006 Mary Winkler was released on bail. Her father hugs her as Attorney Steve Farese looks on. Mary lived with friends in McMinnville, Tennessee, and worked at a dry cleaning business while she waited for trial. Like most trials, there were delays. (CREDIT: RUSSELL INGLE PHOTOGRAPHY)

Mary at work at her job in the dry cleaning business in the fall of 2006. Her three daughters were living with their paternal grandparents. On New Year's Eve, someone with a camera phone took her picture as she sat at a bar, and every area media outlet carried it on the evening news. Some viewers were scandalized. (CREDIT: RUSSELL INGLE PHOTOGRAPHY)

Mary Winkler walks through a gauntlet of media cameras and reporters to the McNairy County Justice Complex on April 9, 2007. Opinion polls showed that locals were split almost fifty-fifty about whether she should be convicted in the murder of her minister husband or freed. (CREDIT: RUSSELL INGLE PHOTOGRAPHY)

Assistant District Attorney General Walt Freeland (left) shakes hands with defense counsel Steven Farese. They faced a long and difficult legal battle in McNairy County as the Winkler case unfolded. (CREDIT: RUSSELL INGLE PHOTOGRAPHY)

McNairy County Circuit Court judge Weber McCraw listens to a sidebar discussion with the prosecutors. In a trial fraught with emotion, McCraw was a calming and authoritative presence. When he meted out Mary's sentence, many people were shocked. (CREDIT: RUSSELL INGLE PHOTOGRAPHY)

Corporal Stan Stabler of the Alabama Bureau of Investigation shows the Winkler jury the shotgun that was used to kill the Reverend Matthew Winkler. It was found in Mary's vehicle when she was arrested. The prosecution and defense differed on whether Mary understood guns. (CREDIT: RUSSELL INGLE PHOTOGRAPHY)

ABOVE LEFT: *Tabatha Freeman, Mary's adopted sister, testified for the defense, saying that Matthew had tried to cut off visits and communication between Mary and her family shortly after the Winklers' marriage.* (CREDIT: RUSSELL INGLE PHOTOGRAPHY)

ABOVE RIGHT: *Mary, the last witness for the defense, told the jurors that her husband insisted she wear shoes he'd seen on a porno site, and a wig when they made love. She seemed humiliated as Steven Farese questioned her about her intimate sex life with her preacher husband.* (CREDIT: RUSSELL INGLE PHOTOGRAPHY)

ABOVE LEFT: *Matthew's parents, the Reverend Dan and Dianne Winkler (Dianne shown here), did not believe the accusations Mary made against their deceased son. They are attempting to legally adopt the Winklers' three daughters.* (CREDIT: RUSSELL INGLE PHOTOGRAPHY)

ABOVE RIGHT: *Mary smiles for one of the few times during her trial as she realizes the verdict from the jury is not as terrible as she thought it was. Her sentence in June 2007 would be hotly debated for a long time to come.* (CREDIT: RUSSELL INGLE PHOTOGRAPHY)

■ ■ ■ ■

THE
PAINTER'S WIFE

■ ■ ■ ■

Every decade or so, Hollywood produces a movie with a story line that is all too familiar but whose theme is so chillingly intriguing that moviegoers flock to see it. When ordinary people become the victims of a home invasion, we all feel a sudden doubt: we may not be as safe as we thought we were. There are few thoughts more frightening than the possibility of someone hiding in our home — someone who really doesn't care if we live or die.

I always think of a particular movie when I read about actual cases of home invasion: *The Desperate Hours*. It first hit theaters in 1955. Humphrey Bogart starred as the villain who invaded Fredric March's home and threatened his family. In 1990, the same scenario starred Mickey Rourke and Anthony Hopkins in those roles. Both movies were based on a suspenseful novel by Joseph Hayes.

In the mid-fifties, Frank Sinatra played against type as a home invader in the movie *Suddenly*. His character was an insane fanatic who held a family captive as he waited in their home to shoot the president as he made a whistle-stop speech.

Perhaps the most frightening pair of same-titled movies about a criminal stalking and threatening a family are the two versions of *Cape Fear*. The 1962 version starred Gregory Peck as a prosecutor and a father trying to protect his family. Robert Mitchum was the alleged rapist who was out for revenge. In 1991, Martin Scorcese's production of *Cape Fear* starred Nick Nolte as the father and Robert De Niro as the heartless convict who insinuated himself into Nolte's home.

I happen to love these movies, probably because they scared me. I was suitably afraid and in suspense as I watched them.

However, what happened to a *real* family who lived in a quiet neighborhood in eastern Washington State is more compelling — simply because this is a factual story that seemed certain to end in horror.

Even though many years have passed, I have changed the names of the actual victims who survived to save them embarrassment and to avoid invading their privacy.

Tuesday, April 18, 1978, was a warm spring day in Pasco, Washington, but few residents in Pasco left their doors or windows open. They were all afraid, and the comfortable home of Martha and John Carelli* was closed up as tightly as their neighbors'. The Carellis were aware that four prisoners had escaped from the Franklin County Jail on Sunday, two days earlier. They kept close track of what was happening at the jail because they lived only six blocks away. Actually, everyone in the Tri-Cities area — which includes Richland, Pasco, and Kennewick — knew of the escape because it had been featured on the news as the headline story for days. The prisoners had managed to hide a razor blade, which one of them had held to the throat of a jailer. Once out of their cells, they waited while twenty-four-year-old Michael Anderson (AKA Johnny Hart, AKA Johnny Mimms) used the code he had memorized to operate the jail elevator. In a calm voice, he shouted, "Coming down," into the intercom, and unfortunately, an officer on duty pushed three door buzzers, not realizing it was four escapees and not corrections officers who were descending.

The newly free prisoners walked out and disappeared into the streets of Pasco.

The community had reason to be nervous. Anderson had been in jail awaiting trial for an armed robbery of a Safeway store, where he'd netted $21,000. He was also charged with sexual attacks on couples who had unwittingly opened their doors in local motels, and for credit card theft. He was on parole from prison in Joliet, Illinois, having completed a sentence for robbery and attempted murder in that state.

Although people in Franklin County were jittery, they had begun to relax a little. Two days had passed with no sightings of the tall, husky Anderson; the other fugitives' crimes hadn't been as serious, but they appeared to have gone underground too. Probably, people figured, all four of the men had left the Tri-Cities region, heading east toward Spokane, west to Seattle, or even south to cross into Oregon, across the Columbia River.

If they were smart, they wouldn't want to stay around Franklin County, where their mug shots had been flashed on television screens and printed on the front page of the *Tri-City Herald*.

On that Tuesday morning, April 18, Martha Carelli had seen her sons and husband off to school and work as usual, cleaned the house, and then gone off to join her bowling team. She had no inkling that someone who didn't belong there was in her house. Without knowing it, her family hadn't been alone there for the past thirty-six hours.

Michael Anderson had spent his first night out of captivity at a friend's home, and the friend had thoughtfully provided him with a gun and holster. But when a massive police door-to-door search got too close, Anderson left his friend's house and searched for another hiding place.

The Carellis' garage was the first spot he'd chosen. Martha had almost discovered him — although she wasn't aware of it — when she'd noticed the garage door wasn't quite closed. She'd tugged at the handle, straining to pull the door down, while Anderson waited only a few feet away, holding his breath, on the other side.

By Monday night, Anderson grew chilly as rain began to fall. He'd noticed that one of the boys who lived there had left the Carellis' back door ajar. When it was completely dark, he slipped in and crept downstairs to the basement.

The Carellis' home was quite large, with three bedrooms on the main floor and two unused bedrooms on the basement level. Anderson chose one of those, and he listened to the family's footsteps overhead. He wondered if anyone had heard him. Apparently not, because nobody came downstairs.

The basement bedroom was much more comfortable than the garage. Late that night, when he was sure the Carellis and their two sons were asleep, Anderson went upstairs to the kitchen and helped himself to some cake. He also made himself a strong drink with some rum he found in their bar. His hunger satisfied and his nerves eased by the alcohol, he returned to his hiding place in the basement.

With two sons in the house, Martha Carelli thought nothing about the missing cake. She had no reason to check the liquor cabinet.

While Martha Carelli was bowling the next day, Anderson leisurely prowled the house. He even used the phone to make some calls to facilitate his leaving town. When Martha returned around five, Anderson was almost caught upstairs, but he quickly fled back to the basement.

Martha didn't see him, and she didn't notice that more food was missing from the refrigerator and pantry. He'd been careful not to gobble down obvious things, and he'd thrown away empty cans that might raise her suspicions.

Still unaware that there was a stranger in her house, Martha hurried down the stairs. She wanted to get a load of laundry in before she started to fix dinner. As she emptied a hamper of soiled clothes into the washer, she heard a noise she couldn't identify. She thought it odd because she knew her sons were outside playing ball.

More curious than frightened, she noticed that the laundry room window was open, and decided the boys were probably planning to sneak in — or out — that way for one of their pranks. They were known for that.

Half smiling, she began a search of the basement rooms.

She had almost forgotten about the jailbreak.

As Martha walked into one of the unused bedrooms, she suddenly felt prickles of alarm, goose bumps dotting the flesh of her arms. The big man appeared in front of her, and he was holding a gun in his hand. For a moment, she froze with shock and disbelief, and then she screamed. She whirled and tried to run to the stairs, but Anderson snaked out a muscular arm and held her fast.

"Shut up!" he barked as he threw her to the floor. "You know I just got out of jail. You read the papers."

Martha Carelli continued to scream, hoping her sons might hear her and run for help, or that her husband might be coming home from work. But her cries only served to anger the stranger.

Mike Anderson kicked her viciously and repeatedly in the head until she saw waves of blackness, and then passed out. When she came to — she didn't know how long later — one of her eyes had begun to swell, and blood coursed down her face.

Fighting to stay conscious, she tried to think. Of course she had read about the escape. She knew that two of the escapees had just been captured and that two were still at large. She was most afraid for her family, and wondered frantically how she could warn them.

It was too late. Her eleven-year-old son and a neighbor boy came running down the stairs. They *had* heard her screams, and now they stopped short at the sight of her bleeding face and the man who stood over her. He held his gun on the boys and forced them into the bedroom, ordering them to lie on the bed next to Martha. Then he opened the cylinder of the pistol and showed them that it was fully loaded with six bullets.

They were sixth-graders, and they knew they couldn't fight him, or run for help before he caught them. Anderson tore sheets from the bed into strips, and he used them to gag and hogtie the youngsters.

"Don't look at me," he said to Martha. She wondered why he bothered to say that; he knew she had already seen him, and that she knew who he was. She wished mightily that she hadn't screamed. If she had just kept quiet, the boys wouldn't have come downstairs.

But now, things just kept getting worse. Her fourteen-year-old son walked into the bedroom, calling out her name. Anderson quickly overpowered him, too, tied him up as he had the others, and told him to lie on the floor.

Six bullets. Their captor had made a point of counting them out as he showed them his gun's cylinder. There were more than enough to kill all of them, Martha thought hopelessly.

"Who else is due home?" Anderson asked.

"Just my husband — but I don't know

when he'll be home."

That was true. John Carelli was a painting contractor, and his work meant irregular hours. His wife prayed that he would be late on this night. Perhaps if he tried to telephone and got no answer, he might be forewarned. He was the only one left who could save them, but she knew there were enough bullets for him, too, if he should be ambushed the way the rest of them had been.

Her heart sank as she heard the door upstairs open and her husband's voice calling for her. Moments later, John Carelli came bounding down the stairs. His eyes widened with shock as they grew accustomed to the dim light in the bedroom. The gunman loomed over him, aiming at his heart.

Carelli's eyes darted around the room, and he saw his injured wife, his two sons, and the neighbor boy — all of them bound and gagged. He realized instantly that if he tried to fight the man, there was a good chance that one of more of them might die. So Carelli stood helplessly as Anderson tied his hands behind him. Then, the huge convict picked Carelli up effortlessly, slung him over his shoulder, and started to carry him upstairs. Before he left the room, he turned back to Martha Carelli.

"Stay here. My friend is in the garage," he

warned. "If you move, everybody's going to get it."

She nodded her head. But then he changed his mind and ordered the bleeding woman to walk slowly ahead of him as he carried her husband upstairs. Once on the main floor, he dumped John Carelli in a bedroom.

Nudging Martha with his gun, he ordered, "Now we go to the kitchen. I want you to cook me that steak you've got thawing on the counter."

Trembling, she obeyed. She broiled the steak and fried some potatoes. Anderson wolfed the food down, but managed to eat with one hand while he held the gun in the other. When he'd finished, he instructed Martha to fix a plate of food for his "buddy." After she'd dished up more food, he told her to get the rum out and make two rum and Cokes. But she didn't have any Coca-Cola, and he was visibly annoyed. She grabbed some pineapple juice as a substitute. He swigged that down, and then headed out toward the garage with the second plate of food and a drink.

"And don't try anything while I'm gone," he warned gruffly. "My buddy has a police scanner and if you call for help, he'll know right away. If you want to see your family again, you'll keep your mouth shut."

Martha Carelli believed him. Why would he bother to ask for extra food and drinks if there wasn't another man hiding in the garage?

As Anderson walked back into her kitchen, they both jumped when a knock sounded at the front door. Her captor led Martha into a bedroom where she could look out and see who was there. It was a only a neighbor boy. They waited until the child stopped knocking and walked away.

A little later, someone else knocked at the door. Martha peeked out through a crack in the drapes and saw it was a man whose pickup truck was parked in the driveway. She didn't recognize him. Her sons had a paper route, and of course they hadn't delivered their papers. Maybe the stranger was a customer wondering where his evening paper was.

At length, he too got back in his truck and drove away.

"How about that other kid downstairs — the neighbor boy?"

Martha realized that Anderson must have been watching her family for some time. It was obvious he knew just who was supposed to be there and who didn't belong.

"Is anybody home at his place? Anybody who will miss him?"

She shook her head. "I don't know. His mother works nights," she said faintly. "His little brothers and sisters are over there alone."

"Good. When it gets dark, we're getting the hell out of here — and you're going to drive me. You just remember that my buddy's staying here with your family. You mess up or try to get away, and all it will take is one phone call back here and he'll take care of them."

Martha was sick and dizzy from the concussion she'd suffered. Her nose was broken and it throbbed with pain. One of her eyes was swollen shut, making her half blind. She had to do what he said.

Despite the strong drink, Anderson began to get jumpy, and he told her he'd decided they would leave before it got dark.

"We're going *now*."

Like a mother bird leading a predator away from her nest, Martha Carelli was almost relieved when they left her house. At least her captor wouldn't be able to shoot her family. She hoped his accomplice wasn't as jumpy as he was. She got behind the wheel of her car while the big man crouched down below the car windows.

He instructed her to head out over the old bridge to Kennewick. She had no idea where they were going.

Back in the house, John Carelli heard the back door shut. It was very quiet. Tied up and gagged in the bedroom, he had no way of knowing if his wife and children were still alive. He hadn't heard a gunshot or any outcries, but he had heard the stranger go down to the basement twice.

Carelli prayed the stranger hadn't harmed the boys tied and gagged down there. He struggled with his bonds, and eventually managed to get his feet partially free. Stumbling and falling, with his hands still bound fast behind him, he made his way to the front door and somehow managed to get it open. Painfully, he crawled across the street and kicked at his neighbors' door. They were shocked to find him crumpled there.

"Call the police," he gasped. "My wife — my children! There's a killer in my house!"

Carelli didn't know yet that the "killer" had left his house or that his wife was gone too, hurtling at eighty miles an hour on the freeway, putting as much distance as possible between their car and Pasco.

Acting Pasco police chief Lew Smathers and Franklin County sheriff Dick Boyles knew at once who the man in the Carellis' house was. Their street was soon alive with squad cars, and officers crept stealthily toward the house where Anderson had warned that his buddy was holding the youngsters at gunpoint.

But as the task force members prepared to storm the house, something happened. Thinking it was funny, teenagers drove by and threw out firecrackers. They sounded just like gunfire, and people hiding inside their houses thought that the jail escapees were shooting at the police. Fortunately the cops held their fire until they determined the source of the noise. But if the accomplice Anderson had warned Martha about had a gun, too, the pranksters' totally stupid and heedless act could have resulted in her family's deaths.

The Pasco officers checked the garage — and found no one. They entered the Carelli home and searched it room by room, including the closets.

They found no stranger there, either. The three boys were still in the basement, unable to call out because of their gags. Frightened but uninjured, they were found and led to safety.

Mike Anderson had pulled off a highly successful sham. It was clear now that he'd been alone, probably from the beginning. Still, his threats about leaving someone behind to kill Martha's family if she didn't do what he said had worked.

She had no way of knowing that her family was safe, and she still believed they were being held at gunpoint.

As she drove, Anderson regaled her with the details of the time he'd spent hiding in her house. He told her he had watched them as she and her family had gone about their usual routine, completely unaware of him.

"I watched you play with your dog. How come your husband didn't go shopping with you yesterday? I was watching you and listening all the time."

She realized with horror that Anderson had been in her home all during the previous evening and night. She had been all alone in the house with him. That gave her such a sick feeling — to know that someone had watched her when she had no idea he was there.

He gave her directions to a deserted fairgrounds, but when they got there, they found the gates were locked. Next he ordered her to drive to an area behind the Kennewick Hospital. Here he reminded her with a strange grin that she had promised to do anything to assure her family's safety.

She realized that he intended to rape her. She pleaded with him while he obviously enjoyed the thought that she was completely helpless. Finally, he let her alone, but she felt no sense of safety at all. He was as changeable as the wind that blew across the nearby desert.

"Now," he said. "you get in the trunk. You make a sound and you'll get it."

She crawled in and huddled in the trunk, her body aching as he gunned the motor and drove wildly, bumping over a rocky area. Then she felt the tires spin as if they were in mud. She held her breath as he drove a short distance and stopped.

She heard a woman scream, *"Get out of here! Don't kill my baby!"* My God, she thought, where were they and what was he doing? She heard a horn honking frantically. The screaming and honking continued until she heard his feet running back to the car and he started the engine again. He must have been trying to steal another vehicle and take another hostage.

They drove on over bumpy roads for a while, and then the car stopped again. This time he opened the trunk and she could see cars and lights, but again she had no idea where she was.

"You make any goddamn noise and you've had it," he growled. And then he slammed the trunk lid shut.

Martha tried to think. She knew she was in a fairly well-populated area. She could hear cars stopping, doors slamming, people moving about, but she didn't dare call out for help because she was afraid for her family. Anderson had told her one phone call would be their death sentence.

She waited, shivering from the cold and shock, for what she felt was about an hour. She listened to people coming and going so close to her car. But she was too afraid to scream for help.

They were in the parking lot of the Giant T department store in Kennewick, but Martha didn't know that. Nor did she know what was going on inside the store as she waited in the locked trunk.

Mike Anderson entered the store through a rear entrance and walked into an area marked "Employees Only." He knew he had to get another car as the Carelli car was probably on police hot sheets by now. They had spent three hours driving in circles around the Tri-Cities area, and he figured that the man back in the house had managed to untie himself and call the cops.

Mike Anderson needed another car, and he needed money, too — a lot of money — to help him get away. During the times when he'd stopped and parked along the way, he'd tried to figure out what he should do. He'd considered holding up a bowling alley, but there'd been too many people there. So he'd decided to rob the Giant T.

A stock boy walked into the storage area at the rear of the store and surprised Anderson before he'd fully formulated his plan. He held his gun on the kid and the two stood staring at each other as the voice of the store manager, twenty-eight-year-old Edward "Doug" Parry, sounded over the intercom. Three times Parry called for the stock boy, and three times Anderson shook his head.

The store was about to close and a customer was waiting. Exasperated, Parry walked into the storeroom, looking for the stock boy. He spotted Anderson holding the gun barrel to the frightened kid's ear. Parry knew at once who the gunman was. Not only had he seen the TV news with Anderson's picture, he had lived just around the corner from Anderson before the fugitive's arrest in February.

Parry was remarkably cool; before coming into management training for the Giant T stores he had been an ambulance driver, an EMT in San Francisco and Florida, trained to handle emergency situations. In fact, he'd been involved in so many bizarre incidents as an ambulance driver he had finally decided to get out of that field.

He saw the irony in his situation when he realized he was right back in danger — in the storeroom of the Giant T.

Parry was used to dealing with unstable individuals and he recognized that Anderson was on the ragged edge. He followed his orders carefully. Anderson slipped the gun into his pocket and walked Parry and the stock boy in front of him until they reached the only cash register that was still open. The female clerk at the counter was checking out the last customers of the night.

Anderson carried on a conversation with Parry, talking as if they were old friends. None of the few straggling customers realized what was going on. That was fine with Parry; he didn't want anyone to get shot.

As the last customer walked out the door, he locked it. Some regular customers appeared and knocked to be let in. They were surprised when the usually obliging Parry shrugged and shook his head.

They walked away, grumbling, unaware that he was trying to protect them.

"Have you called the police?" Anderson demanded.

"No," Parry said. "Why would I have done that? I didn't know you were back there."

Satisfied, Anderson said, "Okay, let's open the safe."

Doug Parry opened the large safe and Anderson was angry when there were only a few hundred dollars in it. Assuming that Parry was lying to him, he struck the assistant manager on the back of the head with the gun butt.

"I'll kill them," he said, pointing to the clerk and the stock boy, "if you don't come up with more money."

Ignoring his injuries, Parry put the cash in a brown paper bag. Anderson stuck his head in the safe and spotted an inner safe.

"What's inside that one?" he asked.

"More money," Parry replied. But he pointed out that the key to the inner safe was located in the pharmacy department. He said he wasn't sure if he could find it. Undeterred, Anderson marched his three hostages back to the drugstore portion of the store. Parry couldn't stall any longer, and he fished the key out of its hiding place.

Now, Anderson locked the clerk and stock boy in the pharmacy and returned with Parry to the safe. The inner safe held close to $6,000 and Anderson was finally satisfied that he had enough money.

"Okay. Now, you go with me," he told Parry.

He walked Doug Parry to the Carellis' car. Parry was shocked to see the injured woman who emerged when the trunk lid was opened. Blood had dried and coagulated on her face, which was swollen and bruised.

Anderson told them that they were going to change cars and the trio moved to Parry's new Volare station wagon.

"You drive," the escapee told Parry. "And she sits beside you. I'll be in the back with the gun cocked."

Martha Carelli, who had now been held hostage for five hours, began to cry softly. Anderson responded by hitting her in the head several times with the gun butt to shut her up.

Doug Parry felt great compassion for her, but he knew the only way he could hope to save her life — and his own — was to obey Anderson until he saw a chance for them to make a break. He looked at his gas gauge — less than half a tank left.

"You know the way to Seattle?" Anderson asked.

Parry nodded. "But I'll have to get gas. It's over two hundred miles to Seattle, and once we're on the pass, there won't be any stations open."

Anderson was angry, but he grudgingly allowed Parry to pull into a service station.

While they were getting gas, a carload of Parry's friends pulled in and tried to make conversation with him. He deliberately cut them off short and called to the attendant to keep the change from the $10 bill. He pulled out, leaving his friends perplexed at the usually congenial store manager's attitude.

It was 10 P.M.

Half an hour later, a Kennewick patrolman spotted the Carellis' car in the Giant T parking lot. He asked the Kennewick police dispatcher to send several backup cars. When the officers entered the store, they found the two badly frightened employees still locked in the pharmacy. They said they believed Parry had been taken hostage after their store was robbed, and gave the police a description of Parry's yellow Volare station wagon.

When it hadn't been sighted by midnight, the local area "want" on the car was widened to include an all-points bulletin to the seventeen Western states.

The Kennewick Police had found so much blood in the trunk of the Carelli car that they feared Martha Carelli might already be dead. No one in or around the Giant T could recall seeing her. She certainly hadn't been with Mike Anderson when he robbed the store.

■ ■ ■ ■

Many miles away, the yellow Volare headed west toward Seattle. Doug Parry drove, and Martha sat quietly beside him. His medical training told him that the woman was in deep shock, yet she was making a valiant effort to be alert. He didn't dare ask her any questions, and he had no idea who she was or where she had come from. He hoped that she could keep from crying, because this seemed to provoke their captor into violence.

Doug Parry had already made up his mind that he wouldn't leave her — even if he had a chance to escape himself. He was convinced that if he left her alone with Anderson, she would be killed.

Anderson was jumpy, apparently unsure of what to do next, and ready to kill anyone who got in his way.

Parry headed northwest toward Yakima, the first city of any size. From there they would go to Ellensburg, where they would merge onto Interstate 90, the freeway that climbed steadily to the summit of Snoqualmie Pass and then plunged down to Mercer Island and Seattle.

A white Washington State Patrol cruiser was gaining on them, and Parry's hopes rose as it pulled up alongside his station wagon. He looked for another cruiser in his rearview mirror, but there was only one.

But his optimism vanished when he felt the cold steel of the gun barrel against his head. Anderson had also spotted the state trooper, and he snarled, "If he tries to stop us, you're dead. And so is he, and so is the lady."

Parry didn't dare glance to the left as the trooper's car kept pace with his for a few hundred yards, and he hoped to hear a siren. But then it pulled ahead and disappeared around a curve. Apparently, the trooper hadn't been alerted yet about the robbery at the Giant T and their kidnapping. Parry wondered if he should have deliberately sped up, turned out his lights, honked his horn — anything to get the trooper's attention.

But the chance was gone. And Anderson was probably right; a lone trooper walking up to a car where a gunman waited probably wouldn't have had a chance. And if Anderson killed a cop in front of them, their own lives weren't worth much.

As Parry turned onto I-90 and headed up the grade to the summit of Snoqualmie Pass, the gunman alternately warned him not to attract attention by driving too fast or recklessly and urged him to speed it up.

Even in April, there were still snowbanks

this high in the Cascade Mountains, but the ski lifts weren't lit up, and it was so dark. Giant fir trees shrouded each side of the road, looming over them. Only rarely did Parry see another car on the freeway.

Martha Carelli was silent, but her fears for her family were growing. She could barely see now, and her nose was so swollen she had to breathe out of her mouth. Her head hurt fiercely and she trembled with shock.

The dashboard clock read midnight. Both Doug Parry and Martha Carelli were aware that their captor might decide at any moment to shoot them and dump them in the lonely forest.

They reached the summit a little after 1 A.M. Then they were heading down the western slope, passing the exit ramps to the foothill towns of North Bend and Issaquah. Bellevue and Mercer Island were densely populated and now there were more vehicles on the freeway.

They had been on the road more than three hours since leaving the Giant T store. Parry felt certain that the alarm must have been given by now. Surely police personnel in the Seattle area would be looking for them. He both sought and dreaded the confrontation that was to come. He had little hope that he and the injured woman beside him would survive if a shoot-out occurred. Anderson seemed to be under the influence of drugs, alcohol, or some mental disorder. At the very least, the realization that he faced a very long prison term if he was caught was enough to make their kidnapper reckless.

If he had nothing to lose, why should he care about what happened to his captives?

Doug Parry tried to talk calmly to Mike Anderson. The man was a powder keg ready to explode at any instant. He was panicky and not thinking clearly. Still, Parry was astounded when Anderson suddenly said, "Hey! I've never been to Seattle before. I want you to give me a tour of the city."

He had to be kidding. But he wasn't. Their abductor wanted to see the tourist spots in Seattle before he did whatever he planned to do to Doug Parry and Martha Carelli.

Parry complied, and exited I-90 on the west side of the floating bridge that connected Mercer Island to Seattle. Even though it was dark out, he drove slowly for a while along the scenic route that bordered Lake Washington, pointing out various spots of interest: the Stan Sayres hydroplane pit where the big boats raced every summer, the Arboretum, Husky Stadium, and the University of Washington.

The Giant T manager was worried about

Martha; he was certain she had a concussion and her wounds and bruises grew more obvious as time passed. Her head had swelled up to almost twice its normal size. But Anderson seemed to have no compassion at all for her.

After they had circled around the university campus, Anderson suddenly said, "Now, I want you to drive to a dark place — someplace like a parking lot or something."

"Why?" Parry asked, trying to keep fear out of his voice.

"Because I have to get rid of you," Anderson answered flatly.

Anderson obviously intended to kill them. Probably he always had, and he'd only been using them to assure that he got far away from Franklin County.

Doug Parry made his decision. Instead of heading meekly to a secluded spot where they would have no chance of rescue, he wrenched the wheel and drove rapidly toward University Way, the center of the University District, where even in the wee hours of the morning, lights blazed and the streets were alive with traffic. He turned left on Forty-fifth Street and headed west. Parry felt the loaded gun nudging his ear, but he tried not to think of it. Anderson must realize, he thought, that if he shot the driver, the car would crash. He could be hurt too, and a crash would attract attention.

Now, without asking permission, Parry turned his Volare into the parking lot of the Sherwood Inn. It was located on a busy corner next to I-5. He was relieved to see that people were walking around the parking lot and that vehicles were pulling in and out. Parry stopped and turned to Anderson. "Killing us would only cause you more problems, you know," he said with remarkable calm.

"What did you have in mind?" Anderson asked.

It was a bizarre situation. Parry was the captive, yet he was keeping his wits about him. He sensed that Anderson was near hysteria — unable to formulate a plan — and he intended to take full advantage of the gunman's panic and indecision, all the while knowing that he and Martha could be killed at any moment if he made a misstep.

"I've got a credit card," Parry offered. "I think we should get a room in the motel. You're exhausted, and so are we. Once we're in the room, you can tie us up. When you're ready, you can leave. We won't be able to get a phone — and we promise we won't cry out. Don't we, Martha?"

She nodded vigorously.

"You can have my car keys — all the money I have, my credit cards," Parry offered. "Think about it. You'll be home free, and you won't have a murder charge hanging over you."

Anderson pondered the offer. Then he nodded. "Okay, but if you tell the clerk anything when you register, I'll kill the lady first and then *you* before the police can ever get to me."

"That's fair," Parry said. "And I believe you."

Anderson told him to go check in, warning him not to say anything to anyone. "I'll be here with Martha, and I'll shoot her if I see you trying to get funny."

Doug Parry walked slowly into the lobby, where a single night clerk manned the desk. As he was about to subtly signal the clerk that he and Martha Carelli were in danger, he looked around and saw that Mike Anderson was standing near the door watching him. He felt they'd lost their last chance for freedom, but then their kidnapper whirled and ran back toward Parry's station wagon.

Martha Carelli was trying to get out of the car.

Parry looked at the clerk and said softly — but urgently — as he bent to sign the register, "Keep smiling. Don't give any indication that you are alarmed by what I'm about to tell you. There is a woman out in that yellow Volare who is very badly injured. She and I have been kidnapped and are being held hostage. I want you to give me the key to the room. *Keep smiling!* Give us time to go on up. Then call the police."

The clerk stared at him, a smile half frozen on his face. Parry could almost read his mind. He was wondering if Parry was crazy — maybe even a practical joker.

"Please keep smiling," Parry said again. "And hand me the key."

Despite what he had been through, Doug Parry was pretty sure that he looked like a solid citizen, but he wasn't sure if the clerk saw him that way.

Just then, the clerk glanced up and saw the tall black man leading a woman into the lobby. Even though her hooded jacket was pulled close around her head, he could see that her face was a mass of purpling bruises and her hair was matted with blood.

Now he believed Parry, and he responded with controlled casualness.

"Yes sir," he said easily. "Here's your key. That's room 303. The ice machine is down the hall. Have a pleasant stay."

Doug Parry's eyes met the clerk's, and he could tell that the man behind the counter was going to help them.

The oddly matched trio took the elevator up to the third floor, and they entered the nicely appointed room. It had two queen-size beds.

Martha Carelli asked their captor if she could get a washcloth to wipe the blood off her face.

"You go take a bath," he countered. "And you [to Parry] help me count the money."

Martha took a quick bath and wiped her face off the best she could. When she'd dressed again in her bloodstained clothing, she felt a little better — but she was still dizzy and nauseated. The gunman ordered both her and Parry into the bathroom so that they wouldn't overhear him as he spoke on the phone.

It was the first time Doug Parry and Martha Carelli had had a chance to talk. Now, she whispered to him that their captor had hidden in her home for at least twenty-four hours, and that he had kicked her into unconsciousness. She had had no choice but to leave her family tied up in their home, while the man who said his name was Mike had forced her to drive him.

"I don't know what's happened to them," she said tearfully.

Parry comforted her as best as he could

and told her he wouldn't leave her.

"I'll protect you," he promised. "Just don't get him riled up."

He didn't tell her that he had alerted the hotel clerk and that he thought the police were on the way. She was in deep shock, and he was afraid she might accidentally say something that would alert Anderson. They both had so much to lose. She had five children and a husband who needed her; Parry had a wife and four small children. And they were still at the mercy of a man with a fully loaded gun.

Mike Anderson came to the bathroom door and ordered them out.

"Now I'm going to tie you both up," he said, "because I have to make some calls and I'll be going back and forth. I want you where I can see you."

Anderson tore sheets from one of the beds into strips and then he hogtied and gagged Parry. That wasn't enough to satisfy him, so he tied the store manager's arms to the bed frame to make sure he couldn't get free.

Then he tied Martha Carelli's hands and feet to the bedposts. He gagged her too, but her broken nose kept her from breathing. When he saw that she was almost suffocating, he loosened the gag a little.

It was Anderson's first act of anything that

came close to kindness.

So much time had passed. Doug Parry began to wonder if the clerk had understood how desperate their situation was. He'd been listening for the sound of sirens, or the engines of a number of cars turning into the motel's parking lot. But it was quiet — too quiet.

He couldn't know that the Seattle Police Department's Emergency Response Team was at that very moment moving stealthily outside their room. All the rooms surrounding room 303 were being quietly evacuated.

Assistant Seattle police chief Richard Schoener and Captain "Smoky" Wesselius of the North Precinct directed ten members of the ERT, who were now deployed inside the Sherwood Inn.

Expert marksman Ken Starkweather was stationed across the I-5 with a rifle equipped with a scope and binoculars. He had a bead on the room where Anderson was holed up with his hostages.

Inside 303, Mike Anderson began to get antsy as he thought he heard rustling and movement in the corridor. Even though they were incapable of making much noise, he shushed his prisoners, and placed his ear against the door.

The evacuation of guests and the infiltration of the tactical squad had been accomplished with so little noise that most people wouldn't have noticed, but Anderson was jumpy.

It was near dawn now. Martha Carelli was able to talk a little through her loosened gag, and she assured her captor that he was hearing only the sounds of tourists leaving to get an early start on the road.

"It's 5 A.M.," she reminded him. "Remember, this is a motel, and a lot of people get up early."

Anderson accepted her reasoning. A short time later, he said he was hungry. He told them he was going down the hall to find a vending machine to get some candy bars and soft drinks.

"Remember," he warned, "if I come back and find that you've loosened those ties, I'll kill you."

And then he stepped out into the hallway.

He hadn't taken a second step before ERT members J. Guich, G. Reynolds, and their team leader, Gary Veatch, stopped him. They'd been poised in an alcove there, their guns drawn.

"Hold it! Freeze!" Guich shouted, and Anderson started to run down the hall, ducking into another alcove.

461

"Throw the gun out," the officers ordered. "You're covered on every side."

For moments they were all suspended in an agonizing pause as Anderson held on to his loaded gun. And then he tossed it out onto the rug of the motel corridor. Veatch and Guich approached him and ordered him to lie prone on the floor. They cuffed his hands behind him and checked his pockets, finding the key to room 303.

None of the tact-squad members had heard any sounds from the room, and they entered with some trepidation. They saw two silent figures bound fast to the beds and were vastly relieved when they moved.

The officers quickly released them from their bondage. Doug Parry was in good shape, but Martha Carelli was checked by waiting paramedics and then rushed to the Harborview Medical Center for treatment of her injuries. As serious as her condition was, she wasn't concerned about herself — she wanted to know if her family was okay.

She was assured that her family was safe. There had never been a second gunman in her home; it had all been a hoax, perpetrated by Mike Anderson.

Her family was just as worried about her fate, knowing that she was the hostage of a jail escapee with a record of violent crimes.

Calls were made immediately to the Tri-Cities area, letting their families know that both Doug Parry and Martha Carelli were safe. John Carelli and his grown daughter set out by private plane at once to be by Martha's side as she was given medical treatment. Her two grown sons headed for Seattle by car.

As the ERT members surrounded Anderson in the hallway of the Sherwood Inn, he'd dropped the brown paper bag he was carrying. It was stuffed to overflowing with currency — $5,862.50 worth of bills. He hadn't had a chance to spend even a single dollar of it. He'd netted himself nothing but big trouble when he escaped from the Franklin County Jail. Anderson was transported to the King County Jail.

Seattle Homicide detectives Bill Baughman and George Marberg were called at home in the predawn hours and asked to respond to the Sherwood Inn to gather evidence in the room where Doug Parry and Martha Carelli had been held hostage.

The double room in the luxury motel was littered with the torn sheet strips that had been used to bind the captives. The bathroom produced bloodstained tissues and towels, which Martha Carelli had used to try to clean the blood from her numerous head wounds. Money wrappers from the stolen currency covered the floor. Baughman and Marberg also found a matchbook with a Tri-Cities phone number written on the back and some mentholated cigarettes left behind by the kidnapper.

Checking at the desk, the two Homicide detectives learned that four calls had been made from room 303, all of them local Seattle numbers: they were all to the automated information numbers provided by airlines on flight schedules.

They determined that Mike Anderson had booked reservations on a United flight to Los Angeles that was due to leave at 7:45 A.M. And they realized that if Doug Parry hadn't alerted the desk clerk, there was every possibility that Anderson would have killed his hostages so that they could not identify him. He would have been long gone to California before their bodies were even discovered.

But now he was going to go back to eastern Washington.

"We want him," investigators from the Pasco Police Department, the Kennewick Police Department, and both Benton and Franklin County Sheriff's Offices said when Marberg and Baughman contacted them.

Joyce Johnson, of the Seattle Police Department's Sex Crimes Unit, a twenty-seven-year veteran of the Police Department, went to the Harborview Medical Center to take a statement from Martha Carelli. Despite the numerous high-profile cases Johnson had worked, she was shocked when she saw the terribly injured woman. She wondered how Martha Carelli had survived the ordeal.

ER physicians said that Martha had lacerations and contusions of the scalp and face, a severe concussion, and a broken nose. Her features were so swollen that she was unrecognizable. Even so, the courageous woman insisted on giving a statement.

Painfully, Martha related the events of her capture to Joyce Johnson. Her only concern was that her family was safe, that she had done nothing to endanger them. It was clear she still wouldn't believe they had all survived until she saw them for herself.

Physicians in the ER said that she would require hospitalization and further tests to determine the extent of her injuries.

Bill Baughman and Homicide detective Al Gerdes ran the .38 Colt taken from Anderson through the National Crime Information Center computers in Quantico, Virginia, and got a hit on it. The Richland, Washington, Police Department had entered it in the NCIC computers six weeks earlier.

The .38 had been stolen in the burglary of a sporting goods store in Richland. Someone had entered the store through a ceiling vent and taken fifteen guns and ammunition.

But Mike Anderson was already in jail by that time. He must have had friends outside who had provided him with the weapon after he escaped.

Detectives Marberg and Gerdes advised Anderson of his Miranda rights and he gave them a ten-page statement about the kidnappings and robbery of the Giant T. His version of the events correlated with those of Martha Carelli and Doug Parry — with the exception of Martha's report of attempted rape.

At length, Anderson admitted that he had attempted to molest his helpless captive. Now that he was the prisoner, Michael Anderson acted obliging and meek. He clearly wanted to come across as a good guy who sincerely wanted to cooperate with the police. He insisted he'd been *forced* to kick Martha Carelli in the head only to keep her quiet after she'd discovered him.

Kennewick detective Doug Fearing and Franklin County deputy sheriff Ralph Courson arrived in Seattle armed with a warrant from Judge Fred R. Staples charging Anderson with robbery, assault, conspiracy to commit escape, escape, and a second assault charge. His bail was set at $250,000. He was released to the eastern Washington authorities for prosecution in their jurisdiction.

Seattle Police and the Seattle news media had nothing but praise for the bravery of Doug Parry, and they credited his cool thinking with saving Martha Carelli's life. After a few hours' sleep, he returned to Kennewick to rejoin his wife and family.

For Martha, the ordeal was far from over. She had waves of flashbacks caused by post-traumatic stress disorder. Even her own home, which had always been a safe haven, reminded her what she had lived through. She couldn't go down to her basement alone, and the family garage frightened her. It didn't help that while he was awaiting trial, Anderson attempted two more jail escapes. Fortunately, they were unsuccessful. Still — when word of these aborted jailbreaks reached the Carelli family — Martha Carelli snapped back into the hours she had spent in abject fear.

Even so, she insisted that when she was well enough, she would testify against her kidnapper. She was frightened, but she was angry too.

"I'm not one of those citizens who refuse to

get involved and won't aid in prosecution," she told reporters. "I understand some of this man's other victims have been afraid to testify — but I swear I won't be."

Martha Carelli was saved from the witness chair when Michael Anderson agreed to plead guilty to the charges against him — but only on the condition that credit card fraud charges be dropped against a woman friend he apparently cared for.

He received multiple life sentences, to run consecutively. On July 5, 1978, Anderson was convicted in the earlier robbery of the Safeway store and received two five-year terms and a twenty-year term on those charges, all of which would not begin until he had served his consecutive life sentences.

The aftermath of a crime like Anderson's stays with the victims longer than anyone realizes. It would always be difficult for Martha Carelli to enter her own house when she was alone. The memory of the man who hid there never went away.

On one lovely spring day, Martha Carelli stood in her own yard and realized that she was afraid to go back into the house. Forcing herself, she entered and answered a ringing phone. Before she went outside again, she wedged a chair against the basement door.

While she was gardening, one of her sons

came home through the back door, but she didn't see him. When she went into her kitchen and saw that the chair blockade had been moved, she felt the grip of familiar terror. She backed out of her kitchen and bumped into her son and fainted.

How long would it be before the dread that someone was waiting, hiding in her house went away? No one could predict that. Her terror diminished with time, but it never completely disappeared.

The fear that Martha Carelli lived with is a sad commentary on the loss of trust felt by crime victims. Martha was lucky. She survived even though there were innumerable moments when she believed she was about to die. She lived through a dozen desperate hours at the mercy of a sadistic escapee.

She lived through almost three decades after her rescue, grateful to have a second chance at life.

■ ■ ■ ■

THE
MINISTER'S WIFE

■ ■ ■ ■

This book has explored a number of cases that look at different aspects of domestic violence. When most of us hear the term, our first reaction is to picture victims as vulnerable females, and statistically that is certainly true. Still, I remember a day when I received an angry phone call from a man who had attended one of my seminars and felt I hadn't been fair when I talked about strife between couples. He took issue with me because I had discussed only *female* victims who were physically or emotionally hurt by their male partners.

"Why don't you care about the men who get hurt?" he asked. "We're out here, and nobody cares what happens to us."

I had to admit that he had a point. Men sometimes *do* become the targets for punishment, although their abuse tends to be more emotional. And when they are injured by a woman, they hesitate to come forward because they are ashamed to admit it, thinking people will see them as "sissies."

And sometimes they don't come forward because they are dead. I have written books that focus on murder cases where, like a black widow spider, the female was, indeed, "deadlier than the male."

The case that follows was one of the most high-profile homicides in America in the past two years. By ordinary standards, the victim was the last person anyone would expect to end up murdered. The accused was just as unlikely to fill such a role. Anyone can be involved in a homicide investigation, of course, but I honestly don't recall a murder case like this in all of the thirty years I've been covering true crime.

And I'm still not absolutely sure which of the two people involved was the true victim. Perhaps they both were. I do know it's important to look closely at this case that began in a small town in Tennessee. Perhaps the answer is in those seemingly unimportant details that the nationwide media didn't focus on as they rushed to spread the news about a handsome young minister and his meek-appearing wife. There are several possible motives and possible catalysts that sparked murder, all of them bizarre.

Matthew Winkler was a minister in the

Church of Christ, as were his father, his grandfather, and many other male relatives. I happen to have grown up in the Church of Christ, attending services there until I was sixteen, mostly in Ann Arbor, Michigan. As a boy, my father always went to the Church of Christ in Ohio. It wasn't so different from other Protestant churches, although instrumental music — including the organ — wasn't allowed in the Ohio branch, and baptism was by full immersion in a hot-tub-sized pool behind the preacher's pulpit. The drinking of alcohol was a sin. I recall my elderly and extremely kind grandfather telling me solemnly, "Ann, I would rather see my daughter dead than married to a drunkard."

I would come to learn that there are many Church of Christ congregations, and their tenets and taboos can be vastly different from one another. Our Ann Arbor church was far less forbidding than the one we attended when visiting my grandparents in Ohio.

Divorce, however, is an abomination for a minister in the Church of Christ. That may have been why my grandfather preferred death to the dishonor of living with a drunk.

In the state of Tennessee, where the Reverend Matthew Winkler preached, divorce was not a viable option. How could a minister hold up his head if he couldn't keep his own marriage intact?

SELMER, TENNESSEE

Selmer, Tennessee, was reportedly named for Selma, Alabama; perhaps the *r* was added because of the way local dialect pronounced it. Located in West Tennessee, Selmer is the county seat of McNairy County, the kind of Southern town where people tend to know one another. Many residents belong to extended family clans. Few citizens are wealthy; the median income is $38,000 a year, and a sixth of Selmer's people live below the poverty level. There is a small hospital there, an elementary school, a middle school, and a high school. There are a few family-type restaurants and, of course, a Wal-Mart.

In many ways, it's a "Mayberry" kind of town, where most people smile and say hello to everyone and wave at drivers passing by. They eat "dinner" at noon, not "lunch." They eat "supper" in the evening.

McNairy County had its own almost-fictional sheriff in the 1960s and 1970s:

Sheriff Buford Pusser became famous as a crusader, a tremendously tall man carrying a big stick, who waged war against corruption in his county, whether it was suspect politicians or bootleg whiskey stills. In August 1964, he and his wife, Pauline, were ambushed and she was shot fatally. Buford lived almost exactly seven more years, his face scarred by the bullets that killed Pauline. Immortalized in the *Walking Tall* films by actor Joe Don Baker, Pusser died at thirty-seven as he lived, in a highly suspicious auto crash. His legend hasn't faded and his life is still honored.

Icons and folktales he left behind still attract tourists.

Long after Pusser's term in office, McNairy County has been tarnished by rumors of corruption, and Sheriff Tommy Riley was convicted in October 2005 of "facilitation of jail escape," but avoided a verdict of "official misconduct." One of the women in the county jail became pregnant after alleged intimate encounters with a jailer. Riley was charged with helping expedite her escape so that she could have an abortion. Through judicial diversion, Riley kept his job and avoided a three-to-six-year jail term. He was sentenced instead to three years of supervised probation.

District Attorney Elizabeth Rice demanded that he be ousted from office, however, citing "bad judgment" on the part of the presiding judge.

Most of Selmer and McNairy County is home to far more ordinary people who respect the law. Cotton, soybeans, corn, wheat, and hay grow in the fields that surround Selmer, and many farmers also raise horses, cows, and hogs. Loggers cut down trees and deliver them to sawmills. Scrap metal is the other main industry for the men of Selmer, and there are junkyards piled high with crushed cars and worn-out appliances awaiting transformation.

And then there are preachers and others at the two dozen churches in town. Located near the center of the Bible Belt, Selmer has needed its churches: the forty-five-hundred residents in Selmer might well wonder what kind of unlucky star has crossed over their town in the past decade and a half. Devastating tornadoes have touched down in Selmer, wreaking millions of dollars in damage and taking lives.

In 2007, dark shadows continued to hover over Selmer. NASCAR racing is a tremendously popular sport in the South, and, along with an estimated forty to sixty thousand other fans, Selmer residents were looking forward to the annual Cars for Kids Show, on the weekend of June 16 and 17. It was a huge draw in this small town, and usually raised at least $200,000 for charities that benefit children. The parade was a hit on Saturday, but a modified drag race at 6 P.M. on Mulberry Avenue, a city street without barriers to hold the crowd back or protect them, ended in disaster. It was intended to be a controlled burnout — the race car's rear tires spin until they blow out, while the brakes are on for the front wheels. The stunt generally produces clouds of dark smoke, thrilling crowds.

Something went horribly wrong, however, with this burnout. The car fishtailed into a light pole, and then plunged into the crowd, killing six young spectators, aged fifteen to twenty-two. Two of the dead were sisters. Twenty-three others were injured as the race car cut a swath through the crowd, trapping those who couldn't run fast enough.

All of Selmer wept, and on Sunday night a crowd gathered at the Sonic Drive-In on Mulberry Avenue to mourn the young victims. One of the teenage girls who was killed had been at work there just before the demonstration, leaving cheerfully to stand close to the road and watch the black smoke roil.

Many people wrote to the *Jackson Sun*,

placing blame on the sport, the fatal driver, the police, and even on the heedless spectators.

A few lumped this tragedy in with the Winkler case, wondering what in the world Selmer was coming to.

In actuality, there were no similarities between an ill-thought-out drag race and the shocking death of one of Selmer's most admired citizens. Still, people tended to ask why so much that was dark and deadly descended on a little town in Tennessee.

Both the dragster horror and the Winkler story made headlines all across America, causing complete strangers to ask the same thing.

It was the first day of spring 2006 when the marriage of the Reverend Matthew Winkler and his wife, Mary Carol, teetered on the edge of catastrophe. The day was clear and somewhat cool, and daffodils and tulips in bloom were buffeted by the wind. Trees were just budding out, but their branches were essentially bare. In another few weeks it would be full spring, and the azaleas, irises, lilies, and crape myrtles would brighten up Selmer.

The parsonage of Matthew's church was a neat small house that sat above Mollie Drive in Selmer. It wasn't lavish, but the one-story structure was cozy looking, built of brick, with four white columns in front and multi-paned windows with black shutters. The home had a good-sized lot, but the Winklers' lawn and shrubs showed signs of neglect; apparently neither of them had the interest or the time to worry about landscaping. The grass was raggedy, with raw patches of dirt, and there were no bulbs in bloom.

Matthew, thirty-one, was the youth minister at the Fourth Street Church of Christ, and Mary, thirty-two, appeared to be the perfect preacher's wife, supporting him in all of his church duties. In this denomination, the husband's role is far more important than the wife's. Matthew made all the decisions, while Mary, if not actually *obeying* him, deferred to him in all matters.

Quiet, sweet-voiced, Mary fit her role well. On Tuesday, March 21, she began her first day as a substitute teacher at the Selmer Elementary School. Although the pay wouldn't be much, it would help their budget. Unless they are television evangelists, preachers don't make large salaries, and Matthew and Mary had three little girls to raise: Patricia Dianne, eight, Mary Alice (called Allie), six, and Brianna, who had just had her first birthday.

It would have taken a very large salary, however, to solve the Winklers' financial woes. They were deeply in debt, both with their credit cards and because of an unfortunate business move.

Media reports would refer to the Winklers as the "perfect all-American family," but that is standard boilerplate journalism. People who live next door to serial killers *always* refer to them as "the nicest guy you could ever hope to meet," or they say knowingly, *after* the fact, "I always thought there was something creepy about him."

Reporters never describe a family hit by violent tragedy as "a rotten, dysfunctional, family" — even when it is. They thrive, instead, on positive descriptions so they can counterpoint that image more effectively with whatever disaster has struck the family down.

So couples viewed from the outside are invariably described as "loving, happy, and devoted." Nobody really knows what goes on behind closed doors, and it doesn't matter at all if those shut away by walls and drapes are factory workers, doctors, lawyers, or preachers. All of these occupations have been populated from time to time by men and women whose lives suddenly erupted in scandal.

Even so, a minister, his wife, and his children — a family moving in a world that is shaped by the church they serve — are expected to maintain a façade. That may be why any number of "PKs" — preachers' kids — turn out to be wild and rebellious. They are so often teased by peers that they act out to show they're just like anybody else.

The preachers themselves have an equally hard row to hoe. It's not easy for those who are supposed to teach by example to maintain a serenity that can often mask dissension and worries. And when they do have problems, ministers and their wives don't have the luxury of confiding in members of the congregation. The people Matthew Winkler preached to wanted to believe in him, and they wanted to see Mary as a loyal, devoted, and contented wife.

For a long time, the Winklers were able to be the couple that their families and their congregation wanted — even though they moved frequently (every time Matthew was called to a new church) . . . even though Mary suffered a miscarriage in 2003 — between Allie's birth and Brianna's . . . even though they sometimes worried about money . . . and even though they had serious disagreements about the sexual part of their union.

■ ■ ■ ■

Matthew Winkler was a handsome, dark-haired man, six feet one inch tall. He had been extremely good-looking in college, when he attended Freed-Hardeman University, in Henderson, Tennessee. Now he was thick around the middle at 235 pounds, and he had lost his clean chin line. But he was still attractive, and he hadn't lost his charisma. He was definitely the kind of preacher young people could identify with, and probably a few of the teenage girls in his congregation had a crush on him. His younger church members called him "Wink" — after his last name, and not because he was in any way a flirt. There was never even a whisper that he wasn't faithful to his wife . . . or that she wasn't faithful to him.

Mary was both pretty and plain, if such a thing is possible. At five feet one, she was a full foot shorter than Matthew, and she weighed 150 pounds, although no one would have guessed she was that heavy. She carried it well with good posture, despite her full bosom. She had dark brown hair, cut in a short bob that wasn't particularly flattering to her round face. Her high, rounded forehead gave her a resemblance to actresses Wynona Ryder and Christina Ricci. Her skin was lovely, she had even features, and she was very pretty when she smiled. She didn't wear much makeup, which was to be expected of a preacher's wife, and her preference in clothes was for something tailored rather than ruffled. Mary dressed in solid colors and often wore black and white.

Her place was always just behind Matthew. He was the one who stirred church members with his sermons, while she taught Sunday school to toddlers.

Matthew was usually smiling in his photographs, while Mary wasn't. But then, maybe it's easier to view her that way in retrospect, knowing what happened.

Staff members at the Selmer Elementary School noticed that Mary Carol Winkler seemed nervous — even upset — on March 21. Apparently, her distress wasn't due to her starting a new teaching job, but because of something else. Coworker Kacey Broadway noticed that Mary was talking a lot on her cell phone while she was at the grade school and that she paced nervously in the hallway as she did so. Some of the teachers complained about it. Once, Kacey thought that Mary was actually crying. She didn't ask her any questions; that would be invading Mary's privacy.

Later that Tuesday, around four, Matthew

was seen walking the Winklers' dog in the city park. He wasn't needed at the church that night.

A bank officer in Selmer would recall talking to Mary several times on the twenty-first, and attempting to get a commitment from Mary that she and Matthew would come into the bank to discuss a puzzling overdraft in their account. Lots of families get into minor trouble when they don't keep up with their checkbook entries.

Other than that, there were no ominous forebodings that signaled trouble in the Winkler home. That would change the next day — March 22. Mary didn't go to work, and their older daughters didn't go to school either. They were expected at softball practice at school later in the afternoon, but they didn't show up. When neither Matthew nor Mary was present at Wednesday-night services, church members began to worry. They were *always* at church on Sunday mornings and Wednesday evenings unless they called to say they were ill or had other pressing reasons not to attend. But they hadn't phoned in, and calls to the parsonage went unanswered.

Dr. William "Drew" Eason, who was both an elder in the congregation of the Fourth Street Church of Christ and a family friend, was concerned enough to drive to the Winklers' Mollie Drive home shortly after 7:30 P.M. No one answered his knock, and the front door was locked. At 9 P.M. Dr. Eason returned, accompanied by three other church elders. They found a key hidden in a fishing tackle box, unlocked the door, and walked into the silent house, calling out for Matthew and Mary.

None of their worries could have prepared them for the shock they experienced when they entered the master bedroom.

Matthew was there, lying on his back on the floor between the four-poster bed and the bathroom. He was entangled in sheets, blankets, and pillows from the bed. The bedside table and a lamp with an elephant base and a tiny flame-shaped bulb were wedged between his still form and the closed bathroom door. It looked at first glance as though he had gotten out of bed, tripped, and fallen, grabbing at the table and the bedclothes as he collapsed heavily.

Dr. Eason moved closer, however, and saw that there was pink-tinged white foam coming from Matthew's nose and mouth. His eyes were open, but he was dead.

What Drew Eason saw could not be real; it was as if the men had walked into a nightmare, one that didn't compute with what they knew about their pastor.

It was twenty minutes after nine when Eason called Selmer Police chief Neal Burks's office to report that Matthew Winkler was dead and that his wife and children were missing. Burks and his men responded and realized almost at once that they would need help. They alerted detectives from the Tennessee Bureau of Investigation.

Roger Rickman, an investigator with the Selmer Police Department with a quarter century of police experience, was one of the first to arrive at the parsonage. He saw that Matthew Winkler had apparently died where he lay. He wore a red undershirt, a green long-sleeved shirt, and what could be called either pajama or lounging pants. The minister's arms were flung out, with his right hand touching the bathroom door and the left extending under the bed. His right leg was straight and his left leg was bent at the knee so that his ankles were crossed.

At first glance, there wasn't much blood apparent, save for the froth from his mouth, which probably indicated some sort of injury to his lungs. But when the investigators turned the husky minister over, they found that he had lost almost all the blood in his body, bleeding out from a gunshot wound located to the left of his spinal column in the lower thoracic area, just above his waist. The bedding and the carpet beneath it were soaked with mostly dried blood. Whatever internal wounds Winkler had, his immediate cause of death would probably have been through exsanguination. He had bled to death.

He could not have survived such an injury, even if emergency medical care had been summoned immediately, but it was possible that he might have been alive and conscious for a very brief period after he'd been shot. Only an autopsy could discover the full extent of his injuries.

There was, of course, immediate concern for Mary Winkler and their three little girls. They weren't anywhere in the house, and the family's Toyota Sienna minivan was missing from the driveway. Had Matthew Winkler died trying to protect his family from someone who had broken into their home during the night before?

Were Mary and the girls now hostages of a maniac?

Every scenario that came to mind was terrifying.

While most members of church congregations revere their ministers and their families, there are always those whose mental balance is a bit off center. Was there someone in the Fourth Street Church of Christ who had snapped suddenly, or even harbored a long-held hatred for the preacher? Had he killed Matthew before abducting his family? Or had some stranger broken into their home the night before? Both were ominous possibilities.

If Matthew had been killed in a home-invasion robbery, something should be missing. And yet the detectives saw his money clip on the dresser with a good-sized wad of cash still in it. His driver's license was there, too.

A check of the other rooms in the house was a tiny bit reassuring; there were no signs of blood or struggle anyplace but in the master bedroom. Still, Winkler's family was gone, and Mary hadn't called to summon help for her husband. No one had heard from her — and that was frightening. One small woman and three little girls might be at the mercy of a killer, hurtling over highways hundreds of miles from home.

The parsonage was cordoned off with crime-scene tape; officers were stationed to protect the outside premises throughout the night; and investigators worked inside to gather any evidence they could find that might lead to the person or persons who had shot the young preacher in the back with a high-powered weapon.

The beginning of rigor mortis and the temperature of Matthew Winkler's body indicated that he had probably been dead for more than twelve hours.

In twelve hours, his family could be anywhere.

John Vinson, the medical examiner of McNairy County, ordered the removal of Winkler's body to Nashville, where a postmortem exam would be done as soon as possible.

Tennessee Bureau of Investigation agents Chris Carpenter and Mike Frizzell arrived near midnight. From the appearance of the single wound in Matthew Winkler's back, all the detectives felt the death weapon had been a shotgun, fired from some distance away. There was no gun in the house or yard, though, which meant his murderer must have taken it along with Winkler's family and vehicle.

Investigator Rickman gathered and labeled some physical evidence carefully so the chain of evidence could be tracked. Dr. Vinson gave him a single shotgun pellet that he'd found on Winkler's stomach when he lifted his shirt.

TBI criminalist Donna Nelson, along with Lauren James, Erica Catherine, and Francesca Sanders, would process every corner of the crime scene. Briefed by Chris Carpenter on what was known so far, the forensic technicians would not find much that would help the investigators. The latent prints, body fluids, hairs, and fibers in the parsonage were traced back to the Winkler family, which, of course, was to be expected. The bedding, sleeping pillows, and decorative pillows were also gathered up, bagged, and labeled.

The criminalists and the investigators processed the room where Matthew Winkler's body had lain undiscovered all day Wednesday. It was a nice enough room, with white crown moldings and bifold French doors against a fabric-covered wall. All light was shut out by the closed wooden blinds, and no one could have peered in and seen the minister's body lying there.

In contrast to the white woodwork, the Winklers' bedroom set was made of heavy dark wood. There was a sterile feel to the room, as if the occupants hadn't cared enough to do much more than make the bed. It was like the lawn outside — very basic. Three months after Christmas, a wooden box with snowmen on it remained on a round stand near the bathroom door.

The bulb on the lamp next to the bed wouldn't have given off enough light to read by; maybe it had been used as a night-light. A combination light and ceiling fan whirled slowly as the investigators worked. They took photos of every corner of the crime scene, and then measured the room. When they cut out a large chunk of the wall-to-wall carpet between the bed and the bathroom, they found the subfloor beneath was also deeply stained with blood.

Aside from the tangle of blankets Matthew Winkler had been wrapped in and the welter of blood beneath, there was no indication that there had been a struggle there. His autopsy would show that he had been shot just once — in the back — as he lay facedown, probably in the wide four-poster bed he shared with Mary. He might even have been sound asleep when he was shot. But he had been found lying on his back. Mary, even in desperation, could not possibly have lifted him and turned him over, so he had lived long enough to make that last, massive effort to heave himself out of bed.

Perhaps he had been trying to call for help? That would have been impossible. The white phone was on the floor several feet away from him, and its cord was unplugged — not from the wall, but from the phone itself, and the cord was coiled beneath his body.

At 3 A.M., a nationwide Amber Alert was

sent out by the Tennessee authorities. They used a smiling picture of the Winkler family they'd found in the house to help people recognize Mary and the three girls. These alerts are not issued lightly and are used only in cases where law enforcement agencies have reason to believe that the people missing are likely to be in extreme danger. Amber Alerts are usually employed to find missing or kidnapped children.

Every possible media outlet now repeated information and descriptions of Mary Winkler and her daughters, and the family's Sienna minivan. The picture of the perfect family flashed across TV screens and appeared on the front page of newspapers again and again. Illuminated signs along freeways also blazed with this information. If the minivan was on the main freeways, surely someone would spot it and call police.

But if Mary and her little girls had been abducted, whoever had them would probably know that and switch vehicles soon, or at least steal other license plates, so lawmen had to work fast.

Thursday dawned with no sightings of Mary Winkler and her three daughters. There were so many places where a minivan, perhaps holding the four bodies of the missing members of the family, could be hidden from view. Not knowing was somehow worse than knowing what had happened to them. The Reverend Dan Winkler, Matthew's father; his mother, Dianne; his brothers, Dan and Jacob; Mary's father, Clark Freeman; and Mary's four adopted brothers and sisters needed every scintilla of their Christian faith as they waited for word, even as they mourned the loss of Matthew.

Orange Beach, Alabama, is almost 350 miles from Selmer, Tennessee, a resort town with white sugar sand beaches on the Gulf of Mexico. Tourism brochures for the Alabama Gulf Coast cities and towns advertise the area as a place to "slow down, let loose, rediscover yourself," and let its attractions "cast a spell over you."

Beyond the beach itself, Orange Beach has a "Monster Theatre" with continuous film footage of sharks and other deadly sea creatures, a mall, a fifteen-screen theater, a Starbucks, and "the South's Tallest Ferris Wheel."

It hardly seemed like a place a killer would take a captive and grieving family, and yet, on the evening of March 23, that was where Officer Jason Whitlock of the Orange Beach Police Department spotted a Sienna minivan making an illegal U-turn on Perdido Beach

Boulevard. He pulled it over and with standard procedure used his radio to check for "wants and warrants" on the license plates. The report that came back galvanized him into action: he had stopped the vehicle that had an Amber Alert out for it.

Whitlock immediately called for backup, and three police units arrived to surround the Winklers' vehicle in the Wal-Mart parking lot.

Whitlock had no idea what they might find, and he used great caution as he walked toward the driver-side window. If Mary Winkler and her children — Patricia, Allie, and Brianna — were still alive and hopefully uninjured, he didn't want to do anything that might place them in danger. A kidnapper would probably try to hold them as shields to keep from being arrested.

But when Whitlock walked up to the window, he was shocked. A youngish woman who looked very much like the Amber Alert's description of Mary Winkler was at the wheel. Two little girls and a baby, all mercifully unhurt, were with her.

The Orange Beach officer scanned the inside of the minivan quickly, searching for someone who might be hiding there, perhaps covered with a blanket. But there was no one else in the vehicle.

And then he spotted a shotgun in its case. None of this made sense. Why wouldn't a kidnapper have taken the weapon with him?

The woman identified herself as Mary Carol Winkler. She didn't seem to be afraid, or upset; there was only a certain flatness in her affect. She was probably in shock, and she appeared to be exhausted, which could explain her lack of emotion.

She had not asked him a single question.

"It was almost like she was expecting it to happen," Whitlock would recall regarding Mary Winkler's calmness when she saw his police car and his uniform.

When he asked Mary if she would come to his department's headquarters, she agreed readily. Her chief concern was for her daughters, and he assured her that they would be well taken care of.

It would take so much time to sort out what had happened, but as what was left of the Matthew Winkler family arrived at the police station in Orange Beach, Alabama, one thing was clear. Their lives had changed forever. They had become public people, every detail of their lives sought out by the media. All over America, people who heard the news flash that the Amber Alert had been called off because the missing woman

498

and children had been found were relieved, but still curious about what on earth could have happened back in Selmer, and later, to Mary and the girls.

Mary was taken into custody; she didn't object. The girls went along to the police station with her. She was worried that they were hungry, saying she had been on the way to a Waffle House to buy supper for them. The Alabama officers were very concerned for them, too, and brought in food for Mary's daughters from McDonald's and then found a children's movie for them to watch.

Even the investigators were baffled when they realized that it was quite likely that the quiet little woman was *not* a victim — but a suspect in the shooting of her husband. Why else would she have had the shotgun in her vehicle?

What had caused Matthew Winkler's death was relatively easy to determine. Someone had blasted his life away with a shotgun. And Mary Winkler had that shotgun in her possession.

Why he became a homicide victim would be far more difficult to figure out. At 10 P.M., far away from home in Orange Beach, Alabama, on the night before the autopsy,

Mary Winkler explained what had happened, to Corporal Stan Stabler of the Alabama Bureau of Investigation and to Special Agent Steve Stuesher of the FBI.

At the police station, Stabler read Mary her Miranda rights, advising her that she did not have to talk to him and Steve Stuesher, that she could have an attorney present if she liked. And she nodded and said she understood, signing the form to show that.

She sat now at a long table in an interview room in the Orange Beach Police Department. A sensitive interview in a pending criminal matter doesn't start out with the questions that detectives are most anxious to ask. Rather, they begin with easier topics.

Mary gave her name, Mary Carol Winkler, and then added, "I'm a Freeman — maiden name."

She told them her address in Selmer, her phone number, and said she wasn't really employed. She was a student at Freed-Hardeman University in Henderson, Tennessee.

Mary seemed much more worried about Patricia, Allie, and Brianna than she was about the investigator's questions. Stan Stabler, a big man with reddish blond hair and a kind face, told her the girls were fine. They had their dinner and were now wrapped cozily in blankets in a nearby room, watching the children's movie.

"They're, you know, concerned about Mom," he said. "I told them you were fine, and we were fixing to come in here and talk with you, too, and your little girl wants to put my name on her list of names she's got of people she's talked to, so I'm gonna get back with her, too."

Finally, he now asked Mary when she had left Tennessee. She answered that they had left the day before — in the morning. "Wednesday," she added, "the 22nd."

She said she had driven as far as Jackson, Mississippi, where they stayed overnight at the Fairfield Inn. That would have been a very long drive — 287 miles. At legal speeds, it would have taken her four and a half hours.

When Stabler asked Mary why she had left Selmer, she said she wasn't ready to comment on that. She said she had never been to Orange Beach before, but "I wanted to take them to a beach, and I found a straight line."

She estimated that they had arrived in Orange Beach an hour or two after lunch on this day — Thursday.

"How long were you planning on staying?"

"Tonight."

She was planning to leave tomorrow, Friday, and drive back to west Tennessee. She had family in east Tennessee, in Knoxville, but she was planning to go to her in-laws' home near Selmer.

"How long have you been married?" Stabler asked.

"Nine years, eleven months."

It was so hard to dive in and ask the heavy questions that hung in the air. She clearly didn't want to talk about them.

"How was your marriage?"

"Good." She said nothing more than that.

Stabler could see that Mary was "getting cotton-mouthed" and he offered her something to drink. She asked for water, and as she sipped it, they talked about how beautiful the beach was and what roads she had driven south from Selmer. When she seemed calmer, he asked her again about her marriage.

She said they hadn't had any major problems.

"How were y'all financially?"

"Um . . . getting through."

Mary explained that Matthew was a full-time pastor and his church had a congregation of about two hundred. His only income was his church salary, and some from speaking engagements (income that was random and couldn't be counted on). Matthew was planning to start on getting his master's degree in the summer, or definitely by fall.

"When's the last time you talked to him?" Stabler asked.

"Yesterday morning . . . at home."

"What'd y'all discuss?"

"No real conversation . . . umm. Just no comment," she said. "I don't know."

She had come out from where her mind was hiding just a little bit, but now she scurried back. She didn't want to talk about Wednesday morning. Stabler talked quietly to her, asking her to tell him her side of what had happened — what problems she had faced. He asked her to tell him what was troubling her so much.

"I just can't right now."

"Okay."

"I appreciate — I feel like you have genuine concern and I do appreciate you, uh — I'm just not [up] to that right now."

And he did have concern for her, but he was also a detective who was trying to solve a bizarre mystery, and he pressed on.

Mary Winkler rambled quite a bit, telling him she had heard children's voices while she was handcuffed in an area of the police

503

station, and then realized it was her own children. "I about did a backflip," she said, "to get out of it because I was in line of sight."

She didn't want her children to see her in handcuffs. "Those three right there are my only concern right now."

She had sent word to Matthew's parents, "Nana and Poppa," to come and get Patricia, Allie, and Brianna, and they were on the way. She felt she could relax when they arrived because her mother-in-law would take good care of her girls.

Stabler asked her if she would tell him what happened.

"I haven't been told really . . . anything myself. I don't know."

"I've talked with the girls a little bit," he said. "Okay? And they've told me what they've seen and heard."

"Right," she said.

"I need you to fill in those gaps a little bit," Stabler said. "All three know — to an extent — what's taken place."

"What did you ask me?" Mary said vaguely.

"To tell me what happened."

Again, she said she wasn't ready to do that yet. As Stabler and Stuesher spoke about her children and what the events of the past twenty-four hours might mean to them, she listened quietly. And when she finally spoke, she talked not of her own complicity but of her concern for Matthew. And what newspapers might say about him.

"No matter what, in the end, I don't want it . . . umm, I don't want him smeared."

Mary Winkler talked in circles, saying that she didn't know what words to use to explain what had happened. "Sometimes I think something might have happened and then, there's *no way* . . ."

"Did he hurt you?"

"Not physically."

Stan Stabler asked Mary if she knew her husband's condition at the present time, and she said she didn't.

"Was he alive when you left the house, or do you know for sure?"

"I don't know."

"Mary," he asked quietly. "Why did you shoot him?"

She didn't answer.

"Had you planned ahead of time to shoot him — or did it happen, just on the spur of the moment?"

"Not planned."

Mary's answers came in one or two words, pulled with agonizing slowness out of a memory that she insisted was blurry. She was not sure of when it had happened. She knew that the shotgun was kept on top of their closet. Matthew had used it to hunt turkeys. She kept saying that she could "surely not" have shot her husband. She had never shot that gun. She kept denying that she had shot Matthew, but then she went back in her mind to the time when she was driving away from Selmer the day before.

"Driving down the road, something would go in my head, and I'd thought there is no way, what had just happened, and then I hadn't really seen anything or heard anything. I've used my name everywhere I went . . . And this was just my last time to be with them, and we were just going to have some fun. I just wanted to be with them before they had bad days — have a happy day."

Mary murmured that she wanted to have one last happy time with her little girls, and that was why she had driven them to the pristine beach on the Gulf of Mexico. Whatever else happened, she wanted them to remember this day they had spent together, having fun, making good memories that she hoped would one day obscure whatever bad memories they had.

As vague as she was, she seemed to know she was in a great deal of trouble, so much trouble that she might never be able to spend any happy days with her daughters again, perhaps not until they were grown women. She had planned to get them to Matthew's parents, who were on vacation, by Friday.

They were "good people," she said. "They're the family."

She spoke now about Matthew. She had been thinking about him and about how he had so many rules and schedules for her to follow, everything "in this certain order.

"I love him dearly," she said, "but gosh, he just nailed me to the ground. I was real good for quite some time. My problem was I got a job at the post office a couple of years ago — and the first of our marriage. I just took it like a mouse. Didn't think anything different. My mom just took it from my dad, and that stupid scenario. And I got a job where I had to have nerve and high self-esteem, and I have been battling this for years . . . For some time, at some point, it was really good. Then, I don't know. We moved over a year ago — February '05 — and it just came back out for some reason."

"He would knock your self-esteem down?"

"Uh — no. Uh, just chewing, whatever. And that's the problem. I have nerve now and I have self-esteem. So my ugly came out."

It was an unfortunate phrase for her to use, and Mary Winkler would hear it repeated over and over in the media in the months to come.

My ugly came out.

Mary tried to make excuses for Matthew, for what he did to push her over the edge. Even though he had controlled her, kept her on his schedule, undermined her self-confidence, she wanted the two investigators to know that Matthew was "so good — so good, too. It was just a weakness. I think a lot of times, he had high blood pressure, but he'd never go enough to the doctor to get medicine for it. He was a mighty fine person, and that's the thing. There's no sense, you know," she said. "Fox News saying some hick-town lady did this because he was a mean — you know. No sense in that. Just say the lady was a moron evil woman and let's go with it."

She had opened up to them, and she feared for her girls, although Mary was sure that "their nana," Matthew's mother, would get them through it. She worried for her father, and said she didn't want him devoting his life to her, coming to visit her wherever she was.

She didn't know what had set her off yesterday morning. There was no predicting how things would go. "I just never know what's coming next. I think we're having a good day, and then *bam!* I'm nervous about something and he's aloof about it. But it's just no excuse for anything. But you know, it wasn't just out of the blue either."

She hinted that Matthew had threatened her at some point in their marriage — had said something life-threatening. That had really scared her, but then, that was when he was at his absolute worst.

They talked for a long time, but Mary recalled few details. She admitted to them that she had shot Matthew, but everything was a "total blur" in her memory. She remembered being surprised that the shotgun hadn't had more of a hard kick when she fired it. She knew she had taken the girls with her and left, but she had only packed one thing: a pair of baby socks.

She didn't recall why she'd been angry the night before, except that Matthew had gone back on his promise to play Battleship with Patricia. They had started watching a movie, but she had fallen asleep, and that was one of her husband's pet peeves with her.

But now, she wanted to be fair. She wanted the news media to blame her. "There's no reason for him to have anything ugly [said about him] because I have obviously done something very bad, so let me just, you know, get the bad. That would be my request."

Steve Stuesher said, "Mary, that's very noble — but — very honorable of you to have that attitude —"

"I never spoke up," she said. "It's a two-way thing. I just kept it all inside. It's not healthy, you know, for him, not to have a clue what I thought. That's not fair to him."

Suddenly, she asked, "Has there been a funeral yet?"

She had clearly lost her sense of time. It had not been two days yet, and at this point, her husband's body was awaiting autopsy.

Steve Stuesher was about to turn off the tape recorder but he turned to Mary in an attempt to reassure her about her little girls.

"Your girls are going to be taken care of, okay? I'll tell you again; they had a great day today, yesterday."

"Beautiful," she said.

Neither Steve Stuesher nor Stan Stabler commented on the pain that the three girls would undoubtedly face for the rest of their lives. It seemed kinder to let Mary Winkler believe that she had been a good mother, perhaps for the last time.

The Reverend Dan Winkler and his wife, Dianne, had raced to Alabama to take charge of Patricia, Allie, and Brianna. Clearly, Mary liked and trusted them, and she was relieved to know that her girls were safe with them.

When her father-in-law first saw Mary in handcuffs in Orange Beach, he murmured, "I'm so sorry for all this."

Mary, still stoic and strangely flat emotionally, just stared at him.

"I wish we could take the handcuffs off," Dan Winkler said. "And I could give you a big bear hug."

At that point, Mary lifted her arms, her wrists still bound together by the cuffs, and reached toward Dan Winkler.

He told her he loved her, his instincts and training taking over as he comforted her. Even though their son was dead, the elder couple was not ready to condemn this little woman who had been a daughter to them for almost ten years. Forgiveness? Dan Winkler could not bring himself to do that — not yet. His belief, based on the Bible, was that a person had to have a broken and contrite spirit, be penitent, and confess his or her sin.

He knew that his daughter-in-law had shot his son. Ironically, it had happened on Dan Winkler's birthday, the day before, but he didn't yet know why it had happened.

The postmortem examination of the body

of Matthew Winkler took place at the State of Tennessee Center for Forensic Medicine in Nashville, Tennessee, under the direction of McNairy County medical examiner Andrew Eason, M.D. Forensic pathologist Staci A. Turner, M.D., an assistant medical examiner, performed the autopsy with Amy McMaster, M.D., observing.

It began on March 24, 2006, at 9:30 A.M., approximately thirty-six hours after the young minister's body was discovered. Rigor mortis had begun to stiffen his body, but was not yet complete; the red and purple markings on the portion of the body that had been the lowest — where blood had pooled when his heart stopped beating — were fixed and complete on his back and buttocks, with blanching along the parts that had touched the floor of the Winklers' bedroom.

There would be few surprises in this autopsy. Matthew Winkler had only one real wound, along with some scratches on the front of his right knee and lower leg, perhaps made as he crawled on the floor in a vain attempt to escape his killer. He had been shot in the back by a weapon far enough away that there was no soot around the wound.

"In the middle of the back is a three-quarter-inch-in-diameter shotgun wound of entrance with slight irregular margins, and an irregular one-sixteenth-to-one-eighth-inch circumferential marginal abrasion. The defect is located twenty-one and a half inches below the top of the head and at the posterior midline. Five evenly spaced half-inch-by-half-inch rectangular abrasions surround the defect."

As dictated by Dr. Turner, the "defect" left by the shotgun shell sounded clinical and had no emotion. But the fatal wound was horrific, of course, as all shotgun wounds are; pellets of birdshot and wadding from the contents of a shotgun shell had blasted into Matthew's back.

After it perforated his skin, fatty tissue, and the muscles in his back, the birdshot cut through four ribs in the middle of his back and tore through the lower lobe of his left lung, his diaphragm, stomach, spleen, pancreas, and left adrenal gland. There were contusions in the upper lobe of his left lung and the lower lobe of his right lung, and two of the vertebrae in his spinal column were broken. His trachea (windpipe) and lungs were awash in aspirated blood, and his stomach held a hundred milliliters of blood. White foam from his ruined lungs had bubbled from his nose and mouth.

Carefully, Dr. Turner collected scores of pellets of the birdshot and the plastic wadding from his internal organs.

Whoever had held the shotgun had stood above Matthew; the trajectory of the birdshot could be traced from his back to the front of his body and from right to left, and slightly downward.

Dr. Turner estimated that he might have lived a very short time before he lost a tremendous amount of blood from all these wounds.

Matthew Winkler had appeared to be a healthy young man, although he had fat around his belly. His heart valves and other aspects of his heart were normal, and on first look, his heart seemed okay. However, a silent killer had been at work, surely shortening his life span, even without the violence of a shotgun blast.

At the age of thirty-one, all of Matthew Winkler's major coronary arteries were 50 percent narrowed with calcified plaque. He probably had not yet suffered symptoms from this blockage of blood flow in his heart, but he would almost certainly have died young if he didn't change his eating and exercise habits. It didn't matter anymore.

In a thorough postmortem examination, all of the body's systems are checked. Some findings may seem unimportant at the time, but become vital later on. There was no food in Matthew's stomach, or any tablets or capsules. His bladder was extremely distended, holding a thousand milliliters of clear light yellow urine.

Blood samples from his heart and vitreous humor (from the eyes) were taken and labeled for tests to determine the presence of alcohol or drugs. Almost two months later, the results came back. Every single test — from alcohol to barbiturates, stimulants, amphetamines, sleeping pills, cocaine, marijuana, and even aspirin — came back negative. He hadn't ingested any of them in the period before he was killed; none of them were present in his blood and eye vitreous humor, not even in a half-life stage.

Dr. Turner's summary of the case of the death of the Reverend Matthew Winkler was succinct, and to be expected: "Autopsy reveals a penetrating shotgun wound of the back. A flower-shaped wad abrasion surrounds the entrance defect. . . . In my opinion, the cause of death is a shotgun wound of the torso. The manner of death is homicide."

MARY AND MATTHEW

Mary Carol Winkler's life imploded when she was thirty-two years old. With the news that she had been arrested for the shotgun slaying of her husband, virtually everyone who had ever known her was stunned. Those who knew her the best weren't surprised that she had, perhaps, lived a life of quiet desperation in her marriage. That she had chosen to escape from it by obliterating her husband was, nevertheless, unthinkable.

Sometimes it takes a stranger to catch a sudden glimpse of the relationship a man and woman share. They can see that instance with as much clarity as if an expensive camera's shutter opened briefly and then slid shut. A Selmer couple operated a small barbecue restaurant where Matthew and Mary had eaten a few times. They watched the interplay between the two with dismay.

"He always ordered the big barbecue plate,"

the female partner recalled, "while she had her our lowest-priced sandwich. Both times, they had their two older girls with them, and those children just begged for something to eat — but he wouldn't order anything at all for them. And it looked as if she wanted to — but didn't dare disagree with him."

Maybe that was simply Mary's personality; she had been a quiet person for all of her life. Like Matthew — whose father, grandfather, and great-grandfather had all been ministers — Mary grew up in a devout home and in the Church of Christ. She had seen her parents — Nell and Clark Freeman — practice Christian charity from the moment she understood the concept, and she had also seen more tragedy than most young girls have to endure.

Mary was born in Knox County in east Tennessee on December 10, 1973, five years after her parents married. She had a sister who was two years younger, but Patricia had contracted spinal meningitis when she was very young, and her mind would never mature beyond that of a five-year-old. Rather than being jealous because her parents had to focus so much of their time on their handicapped child, Mary Carol adored Patricia. She may have been told that her sister's health was fragile and that God could take her away at any time, or she may have only feared that.

She knew that Patricia was mentally slow, and she could see the braces she had to wear for her crippled hips. She was like a little mother, looking after Patricia and playing with her, albeit very carefully and tenderly.

Like many families with a child in precarious health, Mary's household bonded together tightly, gathering strength from one another. Because her sister needed so much attention, Mary asked for very little. She was reportedly a happy little girl — but quiet.

Patricia Freeman died suddenly when she was about eight years old. A neighbor recalled that her mother was giving her a bath when she passed away. "She was singing one minute," he said, "and dead the next." She had probably suffered a fatal heart attack.

Even though Patricia's life had been very difficult and her illness thought to be one that would shorten her life, no one in her family was prepared for her to slip away so rapidly, and the Freemans went through a very difficult time dealing with their loss — especially Mary. They had no grief counseling, but they prayed and shared their feelings with one another.

And they moved on. Nell Freeman taught school. She would later become a "Home-bound Teacher," the Tennessee school system's term for someone who tutored students whose illnesses prevented them from attending classes. She understood their special needs because of all the years she had cared for Patricia.

Clark Freeman remodeled houses long before "flipping houses" became the hugely popular endeavor that it is today. He bought them from the Department of Housing and Urban Development, fixed what was broken, refurbished and painted them, and sold them for a moderate profit. He was a man who worked very hard and seldom complained.

Freeman was also a lay minister in the Church of Christ, and the Freemans attended services at the Laurel Church of Christ in Knoxville. Like all men in this denomination, he was the head of the household, sometimes demanding and authoritative — but Mary and her mother accepted that was as it should be. They weren't always happy about it, though.

And then the Freemans did something that few couples would have the fortitude and unselfishness to do: they adopted five children, all of them siblings who needed a loving home. Mary Carol had lost her only sister, but now she was one of six children. Eric, Chase, Shannon, Tabatha, and Amanda joined her family. The six children in the Freeman household were all attractive kids. If Mary felt any diminishment in her role in her family, she didn't act out about it.

Some people who grew up with Mary and her adopted siblings in Knoxville remember her as vivacious and fun-loving, with a constant smile, but more recall that she was quiet, a little reserved, but always kind.

Mary Carol was very pretty then and excelled in anything musical, joining choral groups at Doyle High School, and she sang well enough to be selected for the Madrigals — which wasn't easy to achieve. She wasn't a member of the elitely popular cliques at her school, but she had many friends and she certainly seemed happy. When Mary graduated from high school in 1992, she had a long string of activities printed under her senior picture, including religious, musical, and sports clubs. She belonged to Future Teachers of America. She headed off to David Lipscomb University in Nashville, where she worked toward a teaching degree, and joined the University Singers.

And in 1993, Mary changed colleges. She moved to Henderson, Tennessee, and Freed-Hardeman University, where there was a program in special education, her ambition since she had helped care for her sister. Freed-Hardeman was established in 1869 and traces its heritage to the Church of Christ, which helped to build it. Indeed, even today, all members of the board of trustees for the university must be members of the Church of Christ, and the curriculum includes both an undergraduate and a master's degree in what is called simply "Bible."

The Freed-Hardeman motto is strangely non-religious-sounding: "Teaching How to Live, and How to Make a Living," but it may be only pragmatic for an area where surviving can be hardscrabble.

Matthew Winkler attended Freed-Hardeman after graduating from high school in Decatur, Alabama, thirty-five miles south of the Tennessee line. He was one of nineteen hundred students there, and he majored in "Bible." His father, the Reverend Dan Winkler, was a professor there so it was natural that Matthew would go to Freed-Hardeman. He apparently wasn't forced into a mold he resented; Matthew said he wanted to preach. But Mary always felt he would rather have been a teacher.

It was to be expected that Mary Freeman and Matthew Winkler would meet in a college as small as Freed-Hardeman. Although there were no fraternities or sororities there, at least half of the student body joined one of the college's seven Greek-named social clubs. Mary was a sophomore and Matthew a freshman when they both joined Phi Kappa Alpha. The social clubs gave them access to intramural sports, retreats, and the annual spring production of "Makin' Music."

With Matthew's plan to carry on his family heritage of ministry, he would, of course, need to marry a suitable wife. As he came to know and date Mary Freeman, she seemed to be a superlative candidate for the woman who would stand beside him, bear his children, sit in the pews of the churches where he would preach, teach Sunday school, deal with the ladies of the church, and maintain a neat and welcoming home.

Her own goal — to become a teacher — was completely acceptable for a minister's wife, and her lovely voice would be a bonus as future congregations sang "Throw Out the Lifeline," "In the Garden," and "We Will Gather at the River," three of the old-timey hymns popular in the Church of Christ.

And Mary was very pretty, slender, sweet, and fun. Their attraction to each other certainly wasn't just based on suitability. Matthew was popular and very good-looking. Even as a freshman in college, he had the charisma and confidence that drew people to him. He and Mary seemed to make a great couple, and they appeared to be in love. They had dated for only four months when Matthew asked Mary to marry him. Mary said yes immediately.

Both their families were pleased when they became engaged, the tall man majoring in Bible studies and the petite future teacher. On April 20, 1996, they were married in a ceremony with Mary's father officiating.

Matthew continued to work toward his degree, but Mary didn't graduate. She took a job in the deli department of the Piggly Wiggly supermarket to help support them. She was a little concerned when Matthew began to tell her what to do — and when, in the first months of their marriage, he turned out to be quite strict, much as her father was. And she worried a little that he was trying to isolate her from her family. But she wasn't really unhappy. The Bible, which Matthew knew like the back of his hand, said that when couples marry, they move on from their families and "cleave" to each other. But somehow Matthew went beyond that, reportedly urging Mary to sever her connections to old friends, and to limit her visits with her parents and adopted siblings.

A woman who lived next door to Mary's

parents felt that Matthew was "domineering. He was never nice when he was around here," she told reporters a long time later. "He was always very controlling with her and the kids."

Mary's sister Tabatha would recall a conversation with Matthew where he called the Freeman family together and explained that they had to accept that Mary would not be a part of their family the way she had been before. He and their marriage had to come first. Tabatha was stunned. She didn't see why being a wife would preclude Mary from being a sister.

Mary and Matthew lived in Henderson until July 1998, when Matthew graduated. During that time, Mary gave birth to Patricia Dianne, named for her long-dead sister and Matthew's mother. She was an exceptionally devoted mother and delighted in her baby girl. Matthew seemed happy to be a father, and their family album had many photos of him smiling with Patricia.

In July 1998, Matthew accepted his first call to a church. The family moved to Baton Rouge, Louisiana, where he became the youth minister at the Goodwood Boulevard Church of Christ.

Mary rarely visited her family in Knoxville,

and Matthew preferred not to spend holidays there. She must have been torn; her mother, Nell Freeman, was very ill with colon cancer that had spread to her lymph system. When she died on April 10, 1999, Mary was six months pregnant with her second daughter, Allie. One can only imagine how difficult it must have been for her to lose her mother, be pregnant, have a toddler, *and* be a good minister's wife.

Seven months later, the Winklers lived in Pegram, Tennessee, a town of two thousand residents, and a suburb of Nashville. Matthew had a new job as youth minister with the Bellevue Church of Christ. They were settling down for a while, and bought their first house in a neighborhood of young families. Outwardly, Mary and Matthew seemed happy, although this was the time when Mary told Detective Stan Stabler that Matthew had been "at his worst" and had actually threatened her life. Perhaps.

She and Matthew were much admired by the congregation in Bellevue and considered "a real benefit and blessing. He was a good daddy. She was a good mommy," a church elder recalled. "And he was an excellent youth minister."

Mary was twenty-six; Matthew was twenty-five. And both of them were trying very hard to present the best face they could to the world. What they showed to each other, no one knew.

Matthew was doing well; he received a call to be the youth minister of the Central Church of Christ in McMinnville, and they moved in April 2002. McMinnville had a population of almost thirteen thousand and was southeast of Nashville. They bought a house in McMinnville in September 2002 but weren't able to sell their Pegram home until May 2003.

And Mary was pregnant again. She lost the baby at nine weeks in 2003. Matthew had wanted a son. He once mentioned their loss in a church sermon as an example of how people can suffer losses and manage to go on.

The Winklers' having to carry mortgages on two houses for eight months on a minister's salary may have been the beginning of their financial difficulties. With two small girls and her church duties, it would have been hard for Mary to take a teaching job — even substitute teaching. She found a job at the post office, and that helped some. In the fall of 2004, Matthew started teaching Bible classes to boys at the Boyd Christian School in McMinnville.

Mary was soon pregnant for the fourth

time, due in the spring of 2005. As she told the detectives in Orange Beach, she had begun to have difficulty keeping up with Matthew's many schedules and doing things the way he wanted them done. Her neighbors and church members in Mc-Minnville remember Mary as being full of energy, always scurrying from one commitment to another. Most of them admired her for the way she handled her latest job — at the Super-D drugstore — and her duties at Matthew's church so well, while, at the same time, she managed to have birthday parties for Patricia and Allie and keep up with her housework.

When Brianna was born prematurely on March 5, 2005, she had such serious breathing problems that Mary had to leave her behind when she left the hospital. When her third baby was allowed to come home, Mary tiptoed to her crib several times a night to be sure she was breathing.

As far as their neighbors knew, the Winkler marriage was sound. Some thought Mary was more friendly than Matthew was, while one man described her as "odd. She wasn't too friendly — she didn't mix well."

Sometimes Matthew and Mary engaged in what is known today as "public demonstrations of affection" (PDAs), and they were glimpsed hugging each other or even exchanging a discreet kiss during church parties or trips.

According to Mary, they *did* have problems in their marriage, but they involved things that she would never have told anyone else — things too embarrassing to tell, things too disturbing to contemplate.

As the investigation continued, no one knew about those secret, shameful things. And the detectives wondered what might possibly have been the catalyst that triggered such bloodshed in this seemingly impossible puzzle, this incomprehensible set of circumstances.

Was it possible that Matthew Winkler had been all façade and charisma, a man who gloried in standing in the pulpit preaching or being the center of a group of young people who viewed him with adulation, while at home he ruled with an iron fist and demanded too much of a wife who was run ragged with his edicts? Was his Christian love all for his congregation and his fans? Or was he the sincere and caring Christian that most of Selmer saw?

Was Mary Winkler a bitter woman who schemed to shoot her husband in a cold, premeditated act of violence — so that she could be free of him? In the Church of Christ, divorce wasn't really a choice. Had Mary Winkler decided to "divorce" Matthew with a single shot from a shotgun?

Or was Mary a victim herself, caught in a loveless marriage where she finally turned off her emotions, after holding them inside for years? She had lost her little sister, her mother, her third baby, and apparently her hopes for the future.

Up until March 22, 2006, Mary had managed to deal with her disappointments and anxieties by burying them so deeply that she didn't have to face them. Surely, something had to have happened to change her coping mechanism, and she had awakened that morning to a crisis she could not avoid.

It had.

Mary Winkler had fallen victim to a con game. Con games are as old as mankind, but the one that tricked her bloomed with the millennium and the Internet: "Nigerian fraud."

Anyone with a computer and an e-mail address linked to the Internet receives dozens, scores, hundreds, even *thousands* of spam messages from con artists who promise huge rewards to those who are naïve enough — or greedy enough — to take the bait.

It's not unusual for e-mail boxes to be clogged with more than three hundred offers of access to fortunes every day, most originally from Nigeria; but they come from all over the world.

The spammers usually claim to be bank officers representing wealthy deceased clients with no heirs. Sometimes they say they are the widows or the orphaned children of high-ranking officials in foreign countries (who always tend to be "dying" of "esophageal cancer"). Working from boiler rooms with banks of computers and Internet coffee shops, the crooks send e-mails to every screen name they can get their hands on.

Some of their offers are quite sophisticated, while others are transparently phony — full of misspellings and grammatical errors.

It would seem that no one would actually believe there are perfect strangers anxious to share huge fortunes by transferring millions of dollars into United States bank accounts. But people do believe these lies, even though common sense should tell them that no American could deposit so much money in a bank account without the Internal Revenue Service being notified.

More pragmatically, there is no "free lunch," but there *is*, as P. T. Barnum once said, "a sucker born every minute."

And Mary Winkler was one of them. She wasn't stupid; she had completed several years of college, and she was still taking classes at Freed-Hardeman.

But she was desperate.

Matthew often criticized her bookkeeping abilities, even though he assigned her to pay their bills and balance their bank accounts. In the fall of 2005, Mary had fallen behind, and she was ripe for a phony come-on that offered her more money than she had ever imagined. The offer that arrived in the Winklers' e-mail didn't come from Nigeria; it came from Canada.

All Mary had to do was to serve as a middleman to collect payment for oil deals. She quickly sent her name, address, bank account numbers, and then checks for several thousand dollars in transfer fees.

Beginning in October 2005, Mary Winkler received checks totaling over $17,000, and she deposited them at once. Of course, the Canadian checks bounced. However, her own checks for "transfer expenses," which would eventually overdraw the Winklers' bank account by more than $5,000, had already been mailed.

If Mary thought she was in trouble over finances before, she was probably worried sick on Tuesday evening, March 21, 2006.

Up to that point she had managed to cover her losses by running from bank to bank, but now it was all tumbling down on her.

It's likely that Mary and Matthew had an argument over their finances that night. Whether she told him that their bank had issued an ultimatum saying they must *both* come in for a meeting the next day, no one really knows. It's doubtful that Mary confessed the enormity of the problem that arose when the foreign checks bounced.

She would have had no resources to make up the $5,000 overdraft. Check kiting was a felony, and Mary might even face arrest, a trial, and jail time.

Such a scandal would, of course, damage Matthew's reputation, too, and a minister's reputation is paramount to his success.

But on March 22, 2006, Mary Winkler was expected in her banker's office, along with her husband, to explain why she was overdrawn. This would account for her behavior at the Selmer Elementary School on March 21, when she was on her cell phone so often, appearing distraught and close to tears.

Mary Winkler was backed into a corner. Writing a fraudulent check was certainly not what was to be expected of a Southern preacher's wife. Already, according to Mary,

Matthew had come to disapprove of almost everything she did. He didn't like the way she talked, or the way she walked, or ate, or fell asleep when they were watching movies on television. He told her she was too fat, she said, and insisted that she diet, sometimes even telling her she should skip a meal while he took extra portions.

What on earth would he do when he found out that she was overdrawn at the bank?

Five thousand dollars overdrawn.

When Mary was arrested in Orange Beach, Alabama, she didn't tell anyone about her financial crisis; that paled beside her current situation. She was in far more trouble than she had been a day and a half earlier. Matthew would never worry about his public image again, and Mary was headed for jail back in McNairy County.

A lot of wives struggling to keep up with what their husbands and community expect of them might empathize with Mary's predicament over money. Very, very few of them would shoot their husbands in the back.

There had to be more to the story. Mary had insisted to Stan Stabler and Steve Stuesher that she loved her husband. Indeed, she had gone even further and insisted that she didn't want his image smeared by the newspapers and television. She seemed more anxious to protect him than to save herself.

Still, in order for Mary Winkler to avoid spending life in prison, cut off from her three precious daughters, she would almost certainly have to have had more reason to shoot Matthew than the revelation that she had written NSF checks.

Mary had told authorities that she had only wanted a few precious days with her children, and that she'd planned to return to Tennessee and give Patricia, Allie, and Brianna to her in-laws. If she hadn't been arrested in Orange Beach, she may well have done that. She didn't have enough money to start a new life somewhere far away, and she certainly didn't have any in the bank. When she fled to Alabama, she had had her wits about her enough to take cash with her. Although she packed only baby socks, she had a few hundred dollars with her. She still had $123 left when she was arrested. She could have taken more, but she'd left behind Matthew's money clip on the bedroom dresser, and it was full of bills.

On Saturday morning, March 25, Baldwin County, Alabama, authorities released Mary Winkler to the custody of McNairy County sheriff Ricky Roten when he and officers from the West Tennessee Drug Task Force (Selmer Division) traveled to Alabama to transport her back to Selmer. She signed a form waiving extradition, agreeing to go to Tennessee. The fact that the drug task force officers went with Roten wasn't significant; they often doubled as backup for the sheriff's office in non-drug cases. Feelings were running high in the Winkler murder case, and it was a safety precaution.

Mary gave a statement to TBI agent Chris Carpenter. She was now more forthcoming about what had happened in the little house on Mollie Drive on the morning of March 22. She admitted shooting Matthew, but insisted that she hadn't done it deliberately. She'd had the gun in her hands, not intending to shoot, but she'd slipped on some decorative pillows that had fallen on the floor.

Mary had lengthy fuzzy gaps in her memory, however, about the details of what had happened.

She told Carpenter she remembered wiping blood from her husband's mouth and that he had looked at her and gasped, *"Why?"*

Lodged in the McNairy County Justice Complex, Mary had no money for bail or for attorneys. Although her family and many friends rallied around her, offering to put up their homes as security for bail, she remained in jail. To say that the citizens of west Tennessee were scandalized would be an understatement. For the moment, she was probably better off behind bars than out in the community.

But Mary was to get a break in terms of attorneys: she would have her own "dream team." Prominent criminal defense attorneys Steven Farese Sr. and Leslie Ballin stepped forward to represent her pro bono. They would not charge her for the hours and hours of investigation and courtroom time they would spend trying to save her from the death penalty — at worst — or from fifty-one years in prison. Their pro bono offer probably wasn't entirely altruistic. If the defense should prevail at trial, both Farese and Ballin would be even more sought after by potential clients than they already were. Farese's peers had recently named him one of the top ten defense attorneys in America. The Mary Winkler case would focus media spotlights all over America on her attorneys.

When Mary was arraigned at the Justice Complex on March 27, 2005, she walked into the courtroom clad in orange jail scrubs, holding hands with her attorneys. Her hair was freshly cut in a bob reminiscent of children of the 1930s, and she herself looked childlike, given her tiny size and the fact that she stared at the floor rather than meeting anyone's eyes. She actually had to reach up to grasp Farese's and Ballin's hands. She looked to be no more than twelve or fourteen. She clung to her attorneys as if they were a lifeline. And indeed they were.

Mary spoke only once, saying, "No sir," to Judge Bob Gray when he asked her if she had any questions. He entered a not-guilty plea for her.

Farese wouldn't tell reporters what his defense tactics might be. He said he hadn't seen Mary's "alleged confession," and that his defense so far was "every defense known to man." He would take a wait-and-see attitude before he decided what his approach was.

Later that day, more than three hundred mourners filed through the Shackleford Funeral Home for a viewing to pay their last respects to the body of Matthew Winkler. And at 5 A.M. the next morning, Mary herself was escorted quietly to the funeral home for a final private moment with her husband. She stayed for more than an hour.

On that Tuesday, March 28, funeral services were held for Matthew at the Fourth Street Church of Christ. The media was not invited to Matthew Winkler's funeral, but it seemed that at least a third of the people in Selmer and McNairy County attended. The sanctuary was filled to its five-hundred-person capacity, and the overflow crowd, relegated to the church basement, watched the services on closed-circuit television.

Later, Matthew was buried in the Carroll County Memorial Gardens in Huntingdon, Tennessee. His two older daughters were allowed to pick flowers from the many arrangements sent to the Fourth Street Church of Christ, mementos they could press in a Bible to remind them of their father.

In less than a week, their entire world had changed: their father was dead, their mother was in jail, and they were now living with their paternal grandparents.

The investigation into Matthew Winkler's violent death continued, and so did the gossip. Mary received jail visits from her family, a number of loyal friends, and even some members of the Fourth Street Church congregation. Locals appeared to view her either as a Jezebel or as a pathetic woman who'd been driven to kill.

TBI agents obtained a search warrant that permitted them to remove the Winklers' computers — both from their home and from Matthew's church office. Neighbors peeking out of their windows watched the investigators carry the towers and monitors away, but they had no idea what the agents might be looking for.

TBI agent Chris Carpenter worked along with Selmer Police criminal investigator Roger Rickman and the Drug Task Force agents in an attempt to discern what had really happened inside the Winkler marriage. They knew who the victim was and who the shooter was. They just didn't know why it had happened.

Steve Farese and Leslie Ballin arranged to have Dr. Lynne Zager, a psychologist from Jackson, Tennessee, spend many hours with Mary. Indeed, Zager and Mary would log forty-one sessions together. Farese hinted to the media that he feared Mary's detachment might suggest that she was suicidal, perhaps still suffering from postpartum depression after Brianna's birth. He also speculated that the shooting might well have been accidental.

On March 30, Mary appeared in court again. Again she spoke only once, saying, "Yes sir." She waived her right to a preliminary hearing. Her attorneys explained that she didn't want her children to hear "gruesome things" about their father's death. She did not ask for bail, and would now wait in jail for the next meeting of the McNairy County Grand Jury — which wouldn't convene until June.

Although Steve Farese told reporters that every big name in television had called — from Oprah to Dr. Phil to Diane Sawyer, and even beyond — the defense team didn't want Mary to do interviews. She was seeing her psychologist regularly while she was in jail. Even visits from her children were delayed; she didn't want to say or do anything that might make their lives more difficult.

Mary Winkler's first trial date was set for October 2006. In August, after 144 days in jail, she was released while she waited for trial. Her father posted her $750,000 bond, and she had a job waiting for her. She would live and work in McMinnville, the little town near Nashville where she and Matthew had once lived. Cleaner's Express, a dry-cleaning business, held a job open for her, and a couple who were close friends had invited her into their home.

Court watchers thought they saw a defense plan emerging: the Battered Woman's syndrome. Although Mary refused all offers to appear on television, her father gave an interview on *Good Morning America*.

"I saw bad bruises," he told Diane Sawyer. "The heaviest of makeup covering facial bruises. So one day, I confronted her. I said, 'Mary Carol, you are coming off as a very abused wife, very battered.' She would hang her head and say, 'No, Daddy — everything's all right. Everything's all right.'"

If Mary Winkler had been an abused wife, would a jury find that a justifiable reason to shoot her husband in the back?

That question would not be answered in October. Her trial, which had been set to begin the day before Halloween, was delayed because of scheduling conflicts. Steve Farese and Leslie Ballin had filed far too many motions to be addressed before the autumn trial, and Mary's next hearing was set for February 22, 2007.

Mary remained free on bail, and her three daughters continued to live with their grandparents — Reverend Dan Winkler and Dianne Winkler. Mary saw her daughters for a brief visit on October 16 but spent the holidays without them.

Mary seemed to be living a circumspect life, working at the dry cleaner's and staying in the home of the couple who stood so firmly behind her. She had been happy once in McMinnville, and she was cosseted there now by many friends.

But Mary Winkler had almost a talent for

saying and doing the wrong thing. Her comment to Stan Stabler on the night she was arrested in Alabama had never really vanished from news coverage: "My ugly came out."

It may have been Southern slang, but it had a brutal ring to it, and she could not separate herself from it.

Her public image got worse on New Year's Eve. She had every reason to want to leave 2006 behind, although her choice to celebrate the end of the year wasn't a good idea at all. Mary went out that night — to the same bar she had visited three or four times since her release from jail. It could have been worse. It wasn't *only* a bar; it was the New York Grill Restaurant. But it happened to have a cocktail lounge. Mary had gone there on her birthday on December 10, too, and no one had paid much attention to her.

But on New Year's Eve, things took a negative turn. Mary, not looking at all like a little girl, sat at the bar with a beer in front of her and a cigarette in her hand. Her haircut was short and sleek, and she held her head up proudly, scarcely resembling the meek Mary of the courtroom who almost always kept her eyes downcast.

Another patron was at the bar with his wife, who nudged him when she recognized Mary. He had his cell phone with him, and it had a camera in it. Apparently without Mary's knowledge, he took several pictures of her as she sat at the bar, smoking.

A short time later, he went over to her and asked her if she was the "preacher killer," or the "husband killer."

He was laughing when he asked what to almost anyone with tact would seem to be a rude and thoughtless question. He claimed later that Mary laughed when she said, "Yeah," and then reportedly added, "You want to be next?"

Others at the bar joined in the hilarity. Apparently, Mary wasn't upset by the incident, and she and her friends remained at the bar until after 2 A.M.

Armed with his blurry phone photographs, the bar patron went to WMC-TV-5 and sold the images of another side of Mary Winkler. When they appeared on the nightly news, there was a huge negative backlash in Tennessee. And the photos of Mary soon hit the Internet as one of the most viewed videos on YouTube.com.

The manager of the dry cleaner's where Mary worked gave an indignant interview to WKRN-TV in Nashville. "It was New Year's Eve. We went to the New York Grill. What were we supposed to do — sit home and cry? She's not a preacher's wife. She used to be a preacher's wife, but he's dead now. She's not married. She's nobody's wife."

None of this helped to paint Mary Winkler as a vulnerable little woman, cowed by her abusive husband and desperate enough to snap and shoot him. It would have taken a top political spin doctor to erase public reaction to the image of Mary sitting at a bar.

Maybe if the Winkler case were taking place outside the Bible Belt, there wouldn't have been so many cries of outrage. But this was small-town Tennessee, where people believed that women about to go on trial for husband killing shouldn't be sitting in bars smoking and drinking.

There were man-on-the-street interviews where perfect strangers commented on Mary Winkler's morals. Predictably there were those who thought she had betrayed her Christian faith by even being *in* a bar, those who saw no harm in it, and those whose opinions fell somewhere in between.

Mary's attorneys said they would not dignify the coverage by commenting on it, beyond saying that they hoped it would not become open season on Mary as a target for camera stalkers who hoped to get pictures they could sell.

Steve Farese said that the beer in the photos wasn't even Mary's drink. The cigarette in her hand, of course, was her own.

Mary's pretrial supervision order did not forbid her to drink, but only stipulated she must not imbibe alcohol "to excess." No one had even suggested that she was intoxicated on New Year's Eve. At least she didn't have to go back to jail for violating her probation.

Staff writer Russell Ingle of the *Independent Appeal* in Selmer had his fingers firmly on the pulse of anyone concerned with Matthew Winkler's murder, and he regularly wrote thoughtful pieces on the progression toward trial. He quoted a beauty shop customer who doubted Mary's faith, saying, "Because she confesses [*sic;* she probably meant "professes"] to be a Christian, she ain't got no business being in there [the bar] whether she killed her husband or not."

A local man was more forgiving: "I wouldn't condemn her if she stayed drunk all the time, going through a psychological thing like shooting your husband."

And still, no one outside the case knew what had happened to provoke Mary to shoot Matthew. The State had charged her with premeditated first-degree murder, and a conviction might bring her the death penalty. On the other hand, her defense team felt that under Tennessee law, she should be allowed to walk free. The rumors that circulated only brought more questions with no answers.

But west Tennessee and the rest of America would soon hear the fine points of both sides. McNairy County Circuit Court judge Weber McCraw set Mary Winkler's murder trial for April 9, 2007.

As Mary Winkler's trial approached, even spring in McNairy County turned bleak. Crape myrtles and azaleas bloomed right on time, and farmers watched the first green sprouts of their early wheat plantings burst from the soil, only to lose their crops to a killing frost. Flowering shrubs froze, too, and the whole area seemed blighted.

But by the next week, the weather had turned warm and sunny. The Winkler trial was to be held at the McNairy County Justice Complex in a courtroom that can hold about a hundred spectators, and interest ran high, of course. A few local restaurants showed their entrepreneurial spirit by offering hot lunches and sandwiches, delivered to the Justice Complex so that the media army and trial attendees wouldn't have to leave to eat.

The complex was built in 1994, and Judge McCraw's courtroom was far more modern than many of Tennessee's county justice hubs. Although the wood was the ubiquitous oak of most courtrooms, the room was carpeted in blue, the walls were a light mauve, and the jury sat in comfortably padded rose-covered chairs that swiveled when they turned to look at the defense table, on the right, or the prosecution, closer to where they sat. Unfortunately, the acoustics were poor, and those in the gallery had to strain to hear testimony.

No one would want to miss a single word in this trial.

District Attorney General Michael Dunavant and Assistant District Attorney General Walt Freeland were representing the State, and Mary's dream team of Steve Farese and Leslie Ballin was there to fight for her freedom. Before the trial began, Dunavant announced that the State would not seek the death penalty. This seemed to set well with everyone; during man-on-the-street interviews in McNairy County, not even her detractors said they wanted to see Mary die for what she had done.

Jurors had several choices. They could find her guilty of first-degree murder, which meant fifty-one years in prison, and that Mary Winkler would be eighty-four years old before she was eligible for parole. But there were lesser included offenses that would mean far shorter prison terms: second-degree murder, carrying at least a twenty-year sentence; voluntary manslaughter with three to six years in prison; reckless homicide, with two to four years; or criminally negligent homicide, for which the sentence would be only one to three years behind bars.

It took three days for a jury to be winnowed out from a pool of 160 possibles — not so long considering the massive amount of pretrial publicity. Of the twelve jurors and two alternates, a dozen were women. Some people think that women jurors will go easier on a female defendant, but that isn't necessarily true. Women tend to think, "What would I have done if it happened to me?" And the vast majority of women — albeit not all — don't turn to violence in domestic disputes. Male jurors are not as likely to see themselves as victims, but may often view a tiny, vulnerable defendant as pitiable.

Only time would tell. The jurors ranged in age from twenty to sixty-two, and eleven of them were churchgoers, although none stipulated the Church of Christ. Most were Baptists, two were Catholics. The majority were Caucasian; two were African American.

The jurors chosen were a fair representation of the citizens of McNairy County. They would be sequestered, although after so much publicity it seemed a little like locking the barn door after the horse has run away.

One potential juror was excused quickly when she said that the Winklers had been her neighbors and that Matthew had once threatened to kill her dog if it came in his yard again.

Steve Farese and Leslie Ballin submitted a list of forty-four potential witnesses, while DA Walt Freeland listed only thirteen.

The woman on trial scarcely resembled the image of Mary Winkler at her arraignment thirteen months earlier. Then, she had seemed a timid child; now she held her head up, carried a briefcase, and often strode into court ahead of Farese and Ballin. She had had dozens of hours of therapy, received many, many letters of support from around the country, and was bolstered by her attorneys.

In opening statements on April 12, Walt Freeland characterized Mary as a cold-blooded woman who had intentionally shot her husband in the back as he lay in bed early in the morning of March 22, 2006. He said she had deliberately unplugged the cord from their phone so that Matthew could not call for help after she left. He noted the financial catastrophe that was about to descend on the Winklers because Mary had been carrying out a check-kiting scheme since November 2005, depositing phony checks in several bank accounts.

"The house of cards she set up was falling down," Freeland said. "The defense will not produce any evidence of any good reason Matthew Winkler was murdered by Mary Winkler — because there *is* no good reason."

Steve Farese described the Winklers' marriage as "a living hell behind closed doors." He told the jurors that Matthew's demands made Mary tiptoe on eggshells, and even then everything she did seemed to displease him. "He would destroy objects that she loved," Farese said dramatically. "He would isolate her from her family, and he would abuse her. He would tell her she couldn't eat lunch because she was too fat. Not only did she have to be perfect, her children had to be perfect."

The battle lines were drawn, and they were almost diametrically opposed. Local residents who were polled were fifty-fifty in support of Mary or in their allegiance to Matthew.

Mary's attorneys said that she had done everything for her children in a desperate effort to protect them from their punitive and unbendable father. They clearly intended to show her as a woman beaten down by domestic abuse, almost a heroine who stepped forward to save her three little girls.

Mary had seen her daughters only twice since her arrest, and she had explained that she didn't want to upset them. That may have been true, but it also had become a difficult process for her to have visitation with them. Her in-laws were no longer supportive as they had been in the beginning, and they weren't anxious to expose Patricia, Allie, and Brianna to the woman who had shot their son.

The usual parade of patrolmen and investigators took the witness stand, told of the bloody crime scene, the frantic search for Mary and her daughters, her arrest, her statement in Alabama, and her second statement to TBI agent Chris Carpenter. Photographs of Matthew's wound were introduced as his autopsy was explained.

Mary glanced away; she didn't look when photos of the shotgun wadding and the seventy-seven pellets of birdshot that had penetrated her husband's body were introduced into evidence.

Walt Freeland questioned Stan Stabler about Mary's statements in Orange Beach, and the taped interview was played for the jurors. Mary's voice was very soft and vulnerable as she came almost to the point of admitting that she had shot Matthew.

Asked if the Winklers' shotgun could have gone off accidentally, Stabler said, "I don't know."

TBI ballistics expert Steve Scott testified that it would have taken 3 to 3 3/4 pounds of pressure to pull the trigger on the shotgun. The defense clearly wanted to show that it might well have gone off accidentally. There were discussions and testimony about how easy it might have been for the barrel to be "racked," and the suggestion that it might have been stored high on the master bedroom closet shelf already racked and that it would have taken only a light touch on the trigger to fire the gun.

On the third day of trial, courthouse security was mysteriously beefed up. An anonymous man had phoned Ronnie Brooks, the court clerk, three times, complaining that the district attorneys weren't doing their job "properly."

Extra court guards appeared and they used handheld metal detectors to check any potential spectator trying to gain entry to the courtroom, something that is done routinely from the start of trials in most courtrooms today.

Mary Winkler no longer rode in her lawyer's sports car but arrived in a heavy-paneled SUV. She clearly hated the media attention, but she no longer seemed terrified of either reporters or curious crowds.

Some of the witness testimony disturbed her, and she sometimes appeared to be crying. On closer observation, it was more that she blew her nose vigorously when difficult issues came up.

One aspect of her demeanor troubled some of those in the gallery: Mary didn't seem to make eye contact with anyone — not even her own attorneys. She no longer gazed at the ground the way she had when she was first arraigned, but she focused her eyes obliquely as if she existed in some other dimension far away from her trial.

Her clothing was probably decreed by her attorneys; defense attorneys are experts in "staging" the look of their clients. Mary's clothes were matronly and plain. She often wore the same white cotton cardigan over rather drab dresses.

Clark Freeman, Mary's father, barred from the courtroom until he testified, sat behind her thereafter, as did close friends from Mc-

Minnville. She had her supporters in the rows behind the defense table.

Spectators knew there had been many rumors about a bank scandal involving the Winklers. Now, finally, Jana Hawkins, representing Regions Bank, took the stand to explain what had happened. She said she had called Mary on March 21 to tell her that the Winklers' account was $5,000 overdrawn. Mary said she was aware of that, and asked if she could remove Matthew's name from the account. Told that wasn't possible, Mary asked to meet with Hawkins, saying, "I know I've made a bad situation worse and I can't fit $5,000 into my budget."

Leslie Ballin cross-examined Hawkins.

Amy Hollingsworth, a drive-in teller at the bank, had also spoken to Mary by phone that day, suggesting she come in and talk to the branch manager, and told her that things weren't "impossible" to fix.

Hollingsworth testified that she hadn't questioned Mary when she'd earlier deposited a check from Canada for $6,445 because she knew her so well.

Mary Paulette Guest, a Fourth Street Church of Christ member who worked at the Regions Bank, testified that she had informed Mary that she was guilty of check kiting and could face criminal charges.

When Guest was cross-examined by Leslie Ballin, she said that Mary didn't seem to understand what she tried to explain, not even when she was told that her accounts had been frozen. That frustrating conversation had occurred at 4:15 on Tuesday afternoon.

Mary and Matthew were supposed to come into the Regions Bank at 8:30 on Wednesday morning.

Mary had talked to her letter carrier about changing her address, and Walt Freeland suggested that she planned to do this to hide her financial predicament from Matthew.

But Mary Winkler had been in way too deep, and it was little wonder she had spent her day at Selmer Elementary School on March 21 pacing the school halls as she spoke on her cell phone.

April Brown, a fraud investigator for Regions Bank, took the witness stand next. She said that Mary had deposited certain checks at an ATM. Brown explained that these funds went into the Winklers' Regions account. However, the bank had had no way of knowing there were insufficient funds until the check was returned from the bank it was written on.

Mary had written four checks totaling $17,000 on a new account she opened at the

First State Bank in the neighboring town of Henderson. Then she deposited them in a personal account in only her name — one she had set up at Regions Bank. They were deposited in an ATM between February 17 and March 20, 2006. All of the checks bounced. Regions Bank had lost almost $4,000 in the shady transactions.

Apparently, Mary had deposited two fraudulent checks sent by the Canadian con artist into the First State Bank. Those — for $4,880 and $4,900 — went into an account she had opened with only $100. The Henderson bank returned the fake checks and lost no money.

Running frantically between two banks and their ATMs, Mary Winkler had to have known that it would all fall apart within days. That happened on March 21 when she and Matthew had been summoned to the bank the next morning.

Only, Matthew couldn't go because he was dead by then.

The prosecution had made the difficult decision to bring nine-year-old Patricia Winkler into the courtroom. There would be no cameras, no audiotaping, but Patricia would see her mother for only the third time in more than a year. With the first few questions from Walt Freeland, Patricia began to sob. Judge McCraw comforted her, and she was finally able to continue.

Patricia testified that she had been awakened on March 22 by the sound of a big boom, and she also heard someone falling. When she hurried to her parents' bedroom, she saw her father lying facedown on the floor, and her mother walking around. She heard her father groaning. Her little sister Allie had followed her to the doorway. When her mother saw them, she had closed the door.

"We were scared," she testified. Frightened, she and Allie had sat on the floor right outside the master bedroom. Her mother came out and told them that an ambulance was on the way to take their father to the hospital.

But they didn't wait for that.

Patricia said their mother had gathered them all up and taken them to their van, telling them that they were going "someplace special."

When Freeland asked her if she had ever seen her father being mean or bad to her mother, she said, "No."

Rather than stand to question the witness as he usually did, Steve Farese sat at the table next to Mary Winkler as he cross-examined Patricia. That forced her to look at her mother as she answered his questions.

She said she was happy to see her mother when Mary got out of jail, and that they had hugged and kissed. They hadn't talked about the bad time when her father died.

"Did you want to see your mother again?" Farese asked her.

". . . I don't know."

"Why didn't you see her again after that?"

It was too much for a little girl. Patricia broke into tears again. "Because I didn't want to see her. Well, I mean, I still love her."

It was one of the saddest moments of the trial.

Prosecutor Walt Freeland summoned Dr. Staci Turner to the witness stand. She had performed the postmortem examination of Matthew's body. The most horrifying findings from the autopsy had already been covered. Now Dr. Turner discussed something that, on the surface, didn't seem so important. But it was.

A layman would probably not even notice the significance of the contents of Winkler's bladder at the time of autopsy. Freeland set out to explain what it meant.

"You have indicated that you weighed the kidneys and indicated that the bladder contained approximately a thousand milliliters of urine," Freeland began. "Is that correct?"

"That is correct."

"Now, not knowing much about the metric system, obviously, a thousand milliliters is the same as one liter?"

"Yes."

"That would be the same way to describe the amount of urine you found in the bladder?"

"Yes."

Freeland held up a large liter bottle filled with water. "Now, for demonstrative purposes, do you have any problem — if this is a liter — with this being the amount of fluid or urine that was found in the bladder?"

Dr. Turner indicated that it was.

"Are you familiar with any studies that determine when the urgency to urinate first comes about — and when it becomes intense? Or when it becomes urgent?"

Dr. Turner said she had read several such studies. "Generally," she testified, "a person can feel the urine between a hundred and two hundred milliliters, with an urge to urinate around four hundred. And a pretty severe urge around five to six hundred."

"And this was a thousand?"

"Yes."

Even a lay jury could understand that Matthew Winkler must have gone all night long without getting up to go to the bathroom. He would have felt a tremendous need to urinate by the time he had a full liter of fluid in his bladder.

Why it mattered so much wasn't immediately obvious — except that it certainly seemed to indicate that he had been shot while he lay in bed asleep.

Freeland would come back to this testimony.

The prosecution had presented a woman who was about to be exposed for writing bad checks, a woman who had admitted to shooting her husband in the back before she ran away to another state. Steve Farese and Leslie Ballin faced a formidable challenge as they would now try to rebuild Mary's side of the case.

They presented a number of witnesses who vouched for Mary Winkler's positive image in the community and in her church community.

And they set about demonizing Matthew.

Dr. Lynne Zager, the forensic psychologist who spent forty-one sessions with Mary

Winkler, testified for over two hours. If Mary herself should not take the stand — which was likely — Zager had clearly committed her patient's life to memory, almost from birth to the morning Matthew died. The psychologist said she had diagnosed Mary with mild depression and post-traumatic stress syndrome. She traced the PTS disorder back to the time that Mary's sister died suddenly of a heart attack. The Freeman family had no counseling at the time, and Dr. Zager felt Mary had carried the emotional burden ever after.

Although Matthew had controlled Mary, she tried to excuse his actions to Dr. Zager. "She often said that Matthew helped her to be better. He helped her to improve herself. He was concerned about her improving herself."

Dr. Zager presented Mary Winkler as most vulnerable for domestic violence, a woman already psychologically damaged who had been subjected to a decade of emotionally abusive treatment by her minister husband.

The defense had come up with their scenario of Matthew's murder, and now they padded out that skeletal structure with more and more witnesses.

A Tennessee highway patrolman testified to his contact with Matthew when the Winklers lived in McMinnville. When he had visited his terminally ill grandmother, who was a neighbor of the Winklers, the trooper said Matthew had walked across the street and shouted about a small dog that was keeping him awake. The patrolman said he'd heard about the minister's reputation as a bully, and that he had nicknamed him "the Tasmanian Devil."

Matthew's parents and siblings watched the proceedings. His brother Dan looked startlingly like Matthew, so much so that it was almost as if the victim himself was in the courtroom. All three of the Winkler sons — Jacob, Matthew, and Daniel — were large men who had once been athletes. Dianne Winkler, Mary's mother-in-law, was extremely poised, attractive, and beautifully dressed. She must have been a daunting example for Mary to emulate during her ten-year marriage. While the Winklers had been somewhat supportive of Mary right after she was arrested, they no longer were.

Asked about a time in McMinnville when Matthew had allegedly locked Mary out of their home, his father testified that on two occasions, Matthew had had a bad reaction to medications he'd taken for a toothache and an upset stomach and become disoriented. That might explain such an occasion

— if it had really happened.

Dianne Winkler remembered one of his bizarre reactions to medication. He had a hallucination. "He saw a woman with black hair at the end of a hall — coming at him with a knife," she testified.

That caused a gasp in the courtroom. And later, outside the justice center, townspeople wondered about the possibility of illegal drugs being involved.

Mary had suffered a black eye in McMinnville, but she had explained it away at the time, saying that she'd been playing with the girls and her eye had been hit accidentally, probably by an elbow.

TBI criminal investigator Howard Patterson and Phillip Hampton, a forensic computer expert, both testified about "certain images" retrieved from the Winklers' computers; 263 images had been printed out. Although they didn't spell out what the images were, the truth was that they were pornographic downloads, some stills, some videos — material not to be expected on a minister's computer.

Back and forth the testimony and exhibits went. A church secretary at the Central Church of Christ in McMinnville, who had worked there for thirty-five years, testified that Matthew had been "nice" when he first

563

came to her church but that he had begun to "treat others as lower than himself." She said he soon began to give orders, stepping over bounds "considerably."

She told the jurors that she had heard him speak to Mary angrily, and that he sometimes locked his wife and children in his office for twenty to thirty minutes. When she asked him why, he said it was "to keep them safe."

She also testified that he had made frivolous purchases on church accounts.

Timothy Parish, the pulpit minister at the McMinnville church, took the stand to say that he felt the Winklers' marriage was not as happy as his own. Sometimes Mary seemed happy, but there were many times when she didn't.

Tabatha, Mary's sister, recalled that Mary had been very happy during the early years of her marriage, but that that had changed. "[My] very bubbly, outgoing sister became subdued."

Tabatha recalled the time when Matthew had summoned Mary's adopted siblings to explain to them that she wasn't really their sister any longer, and that they shouldn't expect her to be there for them the way she had been before her marriage. Matthew had struck Tabatha as very controlling, and he only rarely attended his in-laws' family functions and celebrations.

Criminal defense attorneys agree that it is almost always a bad idea for a murder defendant to testify in his or her own defense, even though many of them want to take the stand. Once they testify, they open themselves up to cross-examination by the prosecution.

In this trial, however, it seemed important for the jurors to hear Mary Winkler speak. In many ways, she was a mystery woman, and the rumor that she was going to testify flashed around Selmer on April 18.

And she did.

On April 19, 2007, Mary took the witness stand. As Steve Farese led her through what was virtually the story of her life, her whole mien was meek and respectful. She answered, "Yes sir," and, "No sir," as if she were a schoolgirl being questioned by her principal.

It was difficult to discern who Mary Carol Freeman Winkler really was.

It was even harder to figure out who Matthew Winkler had really been. He could not take the stand to tell his side of their marriage and the last morning of his life. A lay jury would decide which of them had been at fault — or, perhaps, if both of them had acted in ways that had led inexorably to a deadly shotgun blast.

On the witness stand for this extremely important day in her life, Mary wore her black and white dress and the white cardigan. Steve Farese pointed out that, for Mary — as in T. S. Eliot's poem — April was the cruelest month, a month of sad anniversaries. Her sister had died on April 15, and her mother on April 10, and tomorrow she would mark the eleventh anniversary of her wedding to Matthew, an event that had promised so much and ended in blood and ashes.

And now, it was April again, and she could go to prison for half a century if the jury didn't believe her story.

Farese began with Mary's childhood and gradually asked questions that led to her meeting with Matthew and their early married life. The material he covered was essentially what psychologist Dr. Lynne Zager had already presented, but it had more impact coming from Mary's own mouth. Many of the questions hinted at behavior by Matthew that verged on bullying.

"Can you tell the jury about any of the bad times you had," Farese asked, "anything that you think was unusual now?"

"There were many times I just got hollered at, and got onto. At one time Matthew thought that I had done something with the shirts wrong, and I felt like it was my fault. But when I look back in pictures now, Matthew had just gained weight."

She mentioned a time when Patricia was about a year old and had suffered a dislocated elbow. It happened when Matthew was taking care of her. Mary said she didn't know how it happened.

Mary testified that her husband had yelled and screamed at her often. Urged to tell the jurors about an incident when they lived in Pegram (near Nashville), she said that "he just flailed [at me] — he's a big guy and he was just all over."

"Did you ever ask him what you had done wrong?"

"No."

"Did he ever point at you?"

"Yes sir. He was very — just inches away from my nose."

"And what would he say to you?"

"Whatever he was upset about, it was my fault. Don't do it again."

"If he thought you had done something wrong or talked back to him, did he have a word?"

"Yes sir. 'Ugly.'"

"Tell the jury how he would use that word."

"On occasions if I felt like I could talk to him about something and he didn't agree with that, he would tell me that would just be 'ugly' coming out, and it needed to be put away."

"Whose ugly coming out?"

"Mine."

Farese had succeeded in defusing that one early statement Mary had made that threatened to devastate her case.

Mary had hinted from the beginning that her life had been difficult when they lived in Pegram. Her in-laws had testified that Matthew had suffered bad reactions to medications during that time. Now Farese focused more closely on that period.

"Matthew's temperament escalated," Mary testified when questioned about Pegram. "He would just be furious about certain things. He went from certain threats to more serious threats."

"Can you be specific to the jury about any threats?"

"He told me one time he was going to cut the brake lines of my van."

"Why?"

"I don't know."

To further questions, she recalled a time

when her husband had been "out of control," so enraged that he had grabbed his recliner chair and turned it upside down. Mary said she then "snuck" out of the house to call one of Matthew's brothers, Jacob. But he lived forty-five minutes away, so she went to their neighbors Glenn and Brandy Jones. Glenn was Matthew's college roommate and best friend. When Glenn went back to the Winklers' house, Matthew shrugged off his friend's concern, saying that he had only mixed up his medicine and had a strange reaction.

"Who gave that explanation?" Farese prodded.

"Matthew did — but I may have said it as well."

"Was he taking medicine at the time?"

"I don't know."

It was an odd story. Mary testified that Matthew had staggered around and pretended to be "high" or "medicated" when his friend was there, while he had been acting like a "tyrant" when they were alone. She added that she had been very frightened.

Mary said that Matthew hadn't really wanted to be a minister at all; he really wanted to be a history teacher. Everything had come to a head in Pegram, and she was glad to leave there.

Even so, her life had continued to be very hard. Allie, her second daughter, was born five weeks prematurely only four days after they moved to McMinnville. Mary liked their new town, but she worried a lot about Allie. Her lungs weren't fully developed and she had to be on a "breathing machine" for about a week.

It was in McMinnville, Mary testified, that she'd gotten up the nerve to ask Matthew for a divorce. "It was just very bad. I [had] asked Matthew to have a divorce, and he absolutely denied it. That would not be allowed."

"Why did you want a divorce?" Farese asked.

"It was just so bad and I just wanted out."

"Why was it so bad?"

"He just can be so mean. I was 'fat.' My hair wasn't right. With the girls — if something went wrong with them, it was my fault. If it rained, it was my fault. I didn't know when it was coming. I didn't know what mood he was going to be in. I didn't know [whether] to relax and have a good day or to be watching every move if he was coming out after something. I just didn't know."

Matthew hadn't been pleased at the way his career in McMinnville was going, she said. He'd expected to be moved up to the main preaching position after the current minister resigned — but that didn't happen. Mary testified that Matthew had told her to send an anonymous note to the head minister that suggested he needed medicine for "diarrhea of the mouth."

She had done as he said.

Mary told the jurors that her husband hadn't hurt her physically until they moved to Selmer in 2005. But that changed in February. "We were arguing about something and he knocked something over and I bent down to pick it up and he kicked me."

"Where did he kick you?"

"In my face."

She had been hit on that side of the face a few days earlier by a softball. That didn't hurt her so much, she said, but being kicked in the face was "excruciating pain."

Mary was seven months pregnant with Brianna at the time, and she started to have severe pain in one of her teeth. Her mother-in-law had driven her all the way to her dentist back in Nashville.

She testified that she hadn't told anyone about being kicked in the face.

Steve Farese was adept at bringing out a series of negative events in the Winklers' marriage. When Mary failed to give details, he pursued that line of questioning until she revealed more.

Now the defense attorney asked her how she and Matthew had corrected their children. Mary said they got spankings.

"Did any of the spankings ever get out of hand?"

"Yes sir."

"Tell the jury."

"Patricia and Allie had got in trouble at some point, and [if] he was having a bad day, then they would just get some of it, too. And then they stayed home from school. Matthew didn't want anybody to see their legs."

"Why?"

"They were bruised."

"Girls love their daddy?"

"Yes sir."

Mary said the girls hadn't changed how they acted around Matthew, and they weren't worried when he came home.

"And how were you acting around him when he came in?"

"I'd just do anything to help him stay happy."

Farese was building up to something, and the gallery leaned forward expectantly when he asked the judge if he might approach his witness. He had a paper bag in his hand, and he asked Mary to open the sack and describe what she saw inside.

"A shoe and a wig," she said reluctantly.

"Show me the shoe that's in there."

She pulled it from the bag, and set it up on a stand near the witness chair. It was a white strappy shoe with a very high heel — at least six inches high — and a four-inch platform sole. Mary ducked her head in shame as she showed it to the curious jury.

Next, she removed a wig. She answered her attorney's questions, admitting that Matthew had bought both the shoes and the wig for her. He wanted her to wear them.

"What do you mean he wanted you to wear it, Mary?"

"To dress up . . ."

"Dress up, for what purpose, Mary?"

"For sex."

Those listening gasped — almost as one.

"*Sex*." Farese let that answer sink in. "Besides the wig and the shoes, how else did he make you dress?"

"Just skirts — very, very, short."

The gallery was hushed; this was a shocking and fascinating turn of events no one had really expected — not right out in front of everyone.

"During the course of this," Farese persisted, "did you ever have occasion to be asked to look at his computer?"

"Yes sir."

"What were you asked to look at?"

"Pornography."

"What kind of pornography? Still photographs or movies — or what?"

"I think they were moving movies."

"Were any of them still?"

"There might have been."

"Well — why did you look at them? Did you enjoy that sort of thing?"

"No — he told me to."

"What would occur after he would ask you to look at the photographs?"

"We had sex."

"Did he ever ask you to engage in any type of sex that you felt was unnatural?"

No one in the courtroom dared to take a breath for fear they might miss the answer.

"Yes sir."

"Tell the jury what that was, Mary."

"Ummm . . . he just wanted to have sex with my bottom."

"Did that concern you and worry you?"

"Yes sir."

"Did it hurt you?"

"Yes sir."

"What were you told when you expressed your concern?"

"He said okay, but then he would do it again."

"What was his answer for if it did hurt you?"

"[He said] sometimes that does happen — that they have surgery that can fix it."

Mary's father, Clark Freeman, sitting just behind the defense table, covered his eyes with his hand and bent his head in shock and grief as he listened to her explicit testimony about her sex life with her late husband.

The expressions on Dianne's and Dan Winkler's faces were frozen, and then Dan seemed to glare at the daughter-in-law he had once loved. It was obvious he didn't believe what she said. Whatever had happened, these three parents clearly agonized over what had become of their children's "perfect" marriage.

Steve Farese continued with this line of questioning.

"When he had you dress up, did he ever engage in any other kind of sex that you felt was unnatural?"

"Umm, not unnatural, but stuff I didn't always want to do."

"Could you give just one example?"

"Just, uh, oral sex."

Now Farese showed Mary Winkler a stack of photographs — Exhibit #72 — the pornographic images that TBI investigators had downloaded from the Winklers' computer.

She said these had been on the computer they kept in their living room. Asked about when Matthew used the computer, Mary testified that she had found him there at "all hours — up until two to three in the morning."

Mary said she would check on her husband when he hadn't come to bed at night, and find him at the computer. "He would click the screen blank," she testified. She didn't explain why he sometimes hid what he was watching online, and at other times forced her to watch it with him.

Steve Farese showed her one of the still photos. "Do those shoes look familiar in any way?"

"They're the same as my shoes, but they're black."

Almost shuddering, Mary looked through Exhibit #72, following her lawyer's suggestion that she save herself by glancing only at every fifth photo. She acknowledged that she recognized them as those her husband had downloaded and that he had urged her to look at so that she would "become aroused."

The images were passed on for the jury to look at. In some other town, some other place, the recent testimony and the proliferation of "dirty pictures" might not have had the shocking impact they did in McNairy County. But this wasn't some other town. This was the Bible Belt, and these had come, reportedly, from a minister's computer.

Suddenly, Mary Winkler's future didn't seem so forbidding, given what she had suffered in the past.

And Matthew Winkler still could not speak about his side of the marital battles. Nor could he ever.

Mary was holding up fairly well as her hours on the witness stand progressed. Matthew's reputation was trailing in tatters. She recalled that he had threatened her with the shotgun many times, pointing it at her face or heaving it toward her. "He told me if I ever talked back to him he would cut me into a million pieces."

She said she had been "scared."

Asked about her own knowledge in operating a shotgun, Mary said she had none at all. She had never loaded one or shot one. She had no idea how a shotgun worked. Indeed, she didn't believe that she had *ever* pulled the trigger — Matthew's gun had simply gone off by itself.

Now she answered Farese's questions about how Matthew had treated Allie when she was small.

"If she was crying when she was told to go to bed, he would suffocate her to get her quiet and go to sleep."

"What do you mean, he *suffocated* her?"

"He'd pinch her nose and hold her nose."

"Would you *let* him do that to your child?" Farese asked, incredulous.

"I just couldn't stop him. I physically couldn't do anything."

The questioning moved on to the financial problems that had ensued with the fake checks that came to Mary from Canada. Mary insisted that these, too, had been Matthew's idea. He had asked her to fill out every contest form, every lottery — Publishers Clearing House, anything like that — that came in their mail. Her husband had urged her, she said, to pursue any avenue that might help their shaky finances.

She testified that she didn't really understand about the problem with the banks, and that they wouldn't tell her what was wrong unless she and Matthew came in. Matthew hadn't understood it either, she said. It had all been very confusing to both of them.

Farese hurried quickly over this line of questioning.

But now they had moved up to the night before Matthew died. Mary said they had ordered takeout from Pizza Hut, watched

Chicken Little with the girls, and then put them to bed. When Matthew put on a movie, Mary had tried to watch with him, but, exhausted, she had fallen asleep. When they went to bed together later, they had "relations."

"Were they ordinary — normal?" Farese asked.

"Ordinary for us," she said, not explaining what she meant.

The girls were sound asleep, even Brianna. Brianna was named after her father — his middle name was Brian — even though he had been very disappointed when the ultrasound showed that they were having another girl. Matthew came from a family of three boys, and he wanted sons, Mary told the jurors.

Matthew's alleged displeasure over the sex of his unborn baby seemed to be one more nail in the coffin of his reputation.

Mary Winkler's testimony had progressed to the morning of the murder, and the courtroom was hushed as she responded to Steve Farese's questions.

After they had marital relations on Tuesday night, the next thing Mary remembered was it was early Wednesday morning. She heard Brianna crying, and she said that Matthew had placed his foot on her lower back and literally kicked her out of bed so that she would go and quiet the baby.

But then he had changed his mind — and suddenly gotten out of bed and walked into the living room, heading for Brianna's room. When Mary caught up to him, she said he was already "suffocating Brianna — pinching her nose."

"I said, 'Could I please have her?'"

"Did you get her?"

"Yeah. He just threw up his arms and walked out — walked away from the crib . . . . He just said he was tired of hearing it and when he walked through the door, he slammed the door frame with his open hand. I picked Brianna up and calmed her down and then I changed her diaper and [found her] pacifier somewhere and just put her back down and put music on."

Mary testified that Brianna had gone back down easily, and she had gone to the kitchen to make coffee. She wanted to talk to Matthew. "I just wanted him to stop being so mean."

He had gone back to the bedroom by then, back to bed. "He liked to sleep as long as possible," she added.

"Did you go back in the bedroom to talk to Matthew?"

"Yes sir."

"Did you talk to him?"

"No. I couldn't. I was just so scared."

"Scared of what?"

"Scared of Matthew."

That dark Wednesday dawn had been the start of a day she already dreaded: whether Mary Winkler understood the fine points or not, she and Matthew were due at the bank. Did he know she was $5,000 overdrawn?

She had testified that he did, but if he didn't, she had good reason to be frightened. Almost any husband would be angry and embarrassed to have such news sprung on him. If, as Mary had said repeatedly, he blamed her for everything, she was going to be in really big trouble.

"Do you remember getting a gun?" Farese asked her.

"No sir."

"Do you remember having a gun — holding a gun?"

"Yes sir."

"Do you remember pulling a trigger?"

"No sir."

"Did you pull the trigger?"

"No sir."

"How do we know that, Mary?"

"Because I'm telling you."

Mary Winkler said she recalled that "something went off," but she didn't know what it was. She had heard a "boom!" and smelled an awful smell she could not identify. All she could think of was getting her children out of the house.

She knew that Matthew would be mad at her for shooting him, she said. "'Cause he would think I wanted to do that."

And she *hadn't* wanted to shoot him. Mary recalled running out to the carport, and then returning to waken her daughters. She looked in the living room, but nobody was there. She thought she remembered that Patricia might have come out of her room and asked what was happening.

"I went back to the bedroom . . . Matthew was laying there on his back."

"How did he look? Did you see blood or anything?" Farese asked quietly.

"Yes sir. In his nose and the back of his ears."

"Did you do anything or say anything to him?"

"I wiped his mouth. I don't remember saying anything. I don't know."

"What were you thinking then, Mary?"

"Something terrible had happened. That it was just an accident and that I'd lose my girls —"

"Did you know what had happened?"

"Not for a fact, but —"

"What did you do?"

"I just ran away. I just put the girls in the van and I just drove."

As direct examination of Mary Winkler came to an end, she denied that she had intentionally or purposely killed her husband. She had loved him.

"Do you still love him?" Steve Farese asked.

"Yes sir."

"Even through all that?"

"Yes sir."

Mary testified that she had tried to protect Matthew's good name when she was first questioned by police in Alabama. She hadn't cared about herself. All she cared about was "Patricia, Allie, and Brianna."

Judge McCraw called for a break in the proceedings. And everyone in the courtroom needed that. It was as if those who had listened so intensely were suddenly able to breathe again. As they walked outside into the April spring air, they found their voices.

Was Mary Winkler telling the truth, or was she only playing the part of an abused wife who had suddenly snapped and shot her husband in a kind of fugue state in which she had no awareness of what she was doing?

Prosecutor Walt Freeland rose to cross-examine Mary Winkler. He would now bear down on those areas that Steve Farese had skimmed over. Mary denied having been coached prior to her testimony, even though there is no rule against defense attorneys preparing their clients for trial. It was obvious that Farese and Leslie Ballin had told her what to expect, and that she had probably undergone a test run. Any good defense attorney would have done that.

Mary grudgingly agreed with Freeland that she had praised Matthew in the Orange Beach police station.

"You stated that he was so good — or something to that nature. What did Matthew Winkler do to deserve the death penalty?"

"Nothing. Nobody made that decision," she answered, warily.

"Matthew Winkler, in fact, did not deserve to die — did he?"

"No."

Freeland switched to the tangled money transfers and checks from the swindlers in Canada. Mary repeated that it was Matthew who had urged her to enter all the lotteries and sweepstakes that came in the mail. "Any dollar amounts, vehicles, TVs . . ."

"And it would have been a big thing for you and Matthew financially if you had, in fact, won a sweepstakes?"

"Yes sir."

And yet, Freeland pointed out, the Winklers hadn't told their families about the big checks coming in from Canada — for $6,900, $4,900, $6,455. Mary said that she didn't understand just how the transactions were to be handled — she had left that all up to Matthew. They hadn't celebrated.

"Matthew said it wasn't a million — but it was something."

Mary said they had simply put the checks in the bank, and hadn't told the elder Winklers because nobody knew of the overwhelming credit card debt they had.

Her answers were very vague about all of the bank problems — she maintained that she just didn't understand them.

Freeland moved on, questioning Mary about almost everything she had testified to on direct examination. In Pegram — on the night Matthew had flipped over his recliner — she admitted that she had laughed when Brandy and Glenn Jones had come over to see to Matthew.

"Were you laughing on the inside or just on the outside?"

"Just on the outside."

"You were able to convince your friends of something that was not true?"

"Yes."

She acknowledged that Matthew had scared her so much that night that both his brother Jacob and Glenn Jones had spent the night at her house because of that.

But still, she had laughed. Later, she and Brandy Jones had ended their friendship. So, apparently, no one had been witness to her desire for a divorce from Matthew.

Freeland pointed out that Mary had lied again when she denied having a bruise from being hit in the face by a softball. She shook her head. "The reason I went to the doctor was because I had been kicked in the face."

Yes, she had sent an antidiarrheal prescription to Reverend Tim Parish, the pulpit minister, at the McMinnville Church of Christ, telling him it was for his mouth — but that, too, had been on Matthew's instructions.

Walt Freeland suggested that Mary hadn't always been seen as meek and loving. In fact, hadn't she been advised that she was too stern when she took her little girls out of church services?

"*You* were the one being counseled for being rough to the kids, weren't you?"

"It was brought to my attention that my body language was looking stern when I took the children out, and so Tommy [Tommy Hodge, a church elder], as a friend, came to me and said not to frown and to loosen up my body language."

Mary blamed the way Matthew treated her for her "body language."

"So Matthew is the reason . . . that caused concern with the church elders?"

"Yes sir."

To Freeland's questions about her accusations against Matthew, Mary insisted that he *had* threatened to cut her van's brake lines and shoot her with his shotgun.

When the district attorney reminded her that her children were in danger of being shot as they slept in their bedrooms because of the way their house was designed, she said that had never occurred to her.

Brandy Jones had confided to investigators that Mary told her Matthew had taken her to the gun range to practice using his shotgun if she ever needed it to protect herself. But Mary now said that wasn't true.

"Brandy Jones — in earlier testimony — has characterized herself as being your best friend?"

"Was . . ."

"What changed that?"

"She was affected by all this and she chose not to believe in me and not support me through this."

"Did you tell Brandy Jones . . . sometime

in February 2006, that that was the happiest time you have had in your life?"

"I very well may have said that. That may have been my public statement."

"So you said things that weren't true to fool people?"

"To cover up [for] our family. And to cover up the problems we had."

She wanted to explain further, but Freeland stopped her.

"Now, this is a yes-or-no question. You told stories to people to fool them?"

"Yes sir."

"Now you can explain," Freeland offered.

"I was ashamed. I was ashamed about Matthew and I didn't want anyone to know about it."

"Well, how would being ashamed lead you to tell your friend that this was a happy time?"

"That's picking out one comment," she argued, "where if anyone ever talked to me over ten years, all I would have to say is how happy we were and how great life was."

Freeland returned to the complicated problems Mary had had with banks. She seemed to remember that in mid-March the Regions Bank's security officer had told her her overdraft might go to collections.

"Do you recall her telling you that thirty

days after a check — an earlier check — you had to do something?

"I think that I had asked her when did it absolutely have to be taken care of? I couldn't get Matthew in the bank with me."

Mary recalled her day of substitute teaching, and that she might have received one call from the bank. The only person she herself had called was Matthew — who was sleeping at home — because she was trying to get him up. She had also seen the number of a credit card company flash on her phone.

She denied worrying about her bank problems. "Matthew could have gone in, and I told Jana Hawkins that Matthew had perfect credit because nothing was in his name. And we [she and Matthew] decided that day that getting a loan would be an option because Matthew had perfect credit."

Mary denied ever hearing the term "check kiting," and it appeared that she had blocked the memory of anyone telling her that, or that she wanted to give that impression. She insisted her church friend who worked at the bank had told her, "Don't worry about it. Y'all can come in."

Now she testified that while they were eating pizza on Tuesday night, she had mentioned going into the bank to Matthew, that they were supposed to go in the next day, and he hadn't been at all concerned.

"What did you say?" Freeland asked. "'Oh, by the way, the bank called and says I'm doing illegal stuff'?"

"No sir. I said he's got to go in there, but I probably spelled it out — or whispered it to him, because Patricia and Allie were around us."

"What was his reaction when you said, 'The bank says what I am doing is illegal'?"

"He said I was misunderstanding them."

"Was he upset?"

"No. He just thought it was stupid . . . He just said, what in the world are they talking about? We shared the same opinion, I believe."

Mary recalled that Matthew had been "ranting and raving" over something that night, but she couldn't remember what. Maybe it was some church business.

Mary Winkler's memory came and went. Asked about the statement she had given to the TBI investigator Chris Carpenter in which she had given a much more favorable view of her marriage, she remembered that she hadn't wanted anyone to think badly about Matthew. Now she couldn't recall what she had said; she did remember that she had talked to the TBI men.

Asked about the morning Matthew died,

Mary said she wasn't sure what time it was; she only knew that the alarm hadn't gone off yet.

"Do you remember telling Agent Carpenter that when you got up Matthew was still in bed?"

"I don't remember those exact words."

She couldn't recall going to the closet and getting the gun. Obviously, she had been able to reach it, but she didn't know how she got it off a high shelf there.

"Do you recall telling Agent Carpenter you heard 'a loud boom' and you [said you] remembered thinking that it wasn't as loud as you thought it would be? *Had* you thought about how loud a boom from a shotgun would be?"

"I guess just — I never thought of it before. That's just in reference to movies and TV."

"You remember saying you heard the boom?"

"Yes sir."

"And that he rolled out of bed?"

"I just remember that I don't actually remember saying any of this, but I do remember being there and him [Carpenter] writing this."

Mary's direct testimony, led by Steve Farese, had been relatively incisive, but now she was floundering. She wasn't sure if she had told Chris Carpenter about seeing blood on the floor, or that her husband was bleeding from the mouth. She did recall wiping his mouth with a sheet.

"Do you remember today that you told Matthew that you were sorry and that you loved him?"

"No sir."

"You don't recall Matthew asking you, *'Why?'*"

Freeland's voice was full of doubt.

"No sir."

Even when she looked at her initials on the statement to Chris Carpenter, Mary denied that Matthew had asked her why she had shot him.

"Do you recall that Patricia came to the hallway, and you told her Daddy was hurt?"

Mary did not remember that, or that she had said Matthew was groaning.

She did not agree with her own daughter's testimony.

Either Mary Winkler had blanked out her own memory or she was conveniently recalling only those things that served her defense best. She felt that she had been "beaten down" by her life by the time she got to Orange Beach, even though she had managed to drive there without having an accident and had been aware enough to register in hotels — even looking until she found one where there was a swimming pool.

Freeland suggested that her foggy spots came and went.

"When you're so beaten down," Mary testified, "you just don't understand and you don't think you've got a way up. At that time, I was led to feel like I didn't have a family. I never would have imagined I would have been able to have any kind of attorney. I just — if I got into talking about anything — why did I even want to talk to him [Carpenter] that morning? I was going to have to talk about how he [Matthew] was — and I didn't want to get into that."

"Well, why in the world would it have smeared Matthew if you said it was an accident? Why would you have to talk about the way he was? What would that have to do with anything if the gun just accidentally went off?"

"Because what led me to get in that position."

Why had *that* led to an accident? Mary insisted she had only wanted to talk to Matthew.

"It wasn't an accident, was it?" Freeland asked quietly.

"Yes sir."

"You just wanted to talk to him and he wouldn't listen. So you shot him in the middle of the back while he was asleep. Now has that memory come back to you, Ms. Winkler?"

She denied any such memory.

Walt Freeland returned to the testimony of the woman who said she had once been Mary's best friend: Brandy Jones. Brandy was far from being a layperson; she worked at the Carl Perkins Center in Jackson, an agency dedicated to protecting abused children and working with dysfunctional families.

At any time, Mary could have gone to Brandy with her anxieties about her marriage — but she hadn't done that. Nor, Freeland pointed out, had she ever gone to Department of Health Services (DHS) and their child protective services or to her church for counsel or help. If, as her attorneys had pointed out, her life was a "living hell," there had been many counselors who could have helped her and kept her problems private.

Mary Winkler had once told investigators that she slid on decorative pillows on the master bedroom floor just before the shotgun boomed. But now that awful morning had faded into smoky, blurred places in her mind with only bits and pieces of memory floating there.

And finally her testimony was over and she stepped down.

It had become a battle of titans; both the prosecution and the defense teams had raised serious questions in a case where Mary Winkler's motivation — if any — would certainly be the deciding factor for the jury.

And the jurors had an awesome task ahead of them.

Steve Farese and Leslie Ballin had presented Mary as an abused wife, frightened, desperate, and trying to protect her children.

There were some physical evidence problems, however, that drew the attention of experts and made portions of her testimony unbelievable.

- Why had Mary unplugged the phone line before she left her critically injured husband lying on the floor? The shotgun blast with its seventy-seven pellets ripping through his body had done horrible damage to a large percentage of Matthew Winkler's internal organs and it would have taken a miracle for him to survive. Even so, there was something disturbing about her removing the last possible avenue he would have had to call for help.

- Patricia had testified that the phone was not unplugged when she first looked into her parents' bedroom, but later it was — and the phone had been moved far out of her father's reach. He had been alive and groaning as he lay on his stomach when Patricia first saw him. He was, of course, on his back when his worried church friends found him.

- There was a second, more complicated finding that had surfaced during Matthew Winkler's autopsy. His bladder still held an entire liter of urine. Dr. Turner had testified about how humans reacted to varying amounts of urine. With a whole liter in his bladder, Matthew wouldn't have gotten up, "suffocated" his baby daughter, smacked the doorjamb in frustration, and *then gone back to bed, without going to the bathroom!* He would have had a tremendous urge to void and been almost in pain with a bladder stretched to its capacity. More than likely, he would have ducked into the bathroom five feet from their bed even before he walked to Brianna's room.

596

All of these discrepancies made Mary's story about the morning Matthew was killed either a partial lie or the result of a buried memory.

The jurors in Mary Winkler's trial listened attentively to the final remarks made by Walt Freeland and Steve Farese, and then retired to deliberate on Thursday, April 19, 2007. They deliberated for only eight hours. When they returned, their foreman, Bill Berry, announced their verdict.

Guilty.

But it was a gentle guilty. They had gone over Judge McCraw's instructions, weighed the evidence and testimony, and found Mary guilty only of voluntary manslaughter.

Mary still clutched her attorneys' hands. She didn't understand what that meant. They spoke to her, explaining, until she broke into a half smile of relief. She had escaped spending fifty-one years in prison. In fact, she might be locked up for only three to six years. But that wasn't clear-cut at this moment.

Circuit Court judge Weber McCraw could, at his discretion, consider alternatives to incarceration. It was possible that she might only get probation. But Mary wouldn't know what her future held until her sentencing date: May 18. Until then, she would return to McMinnville and her life there, back to working at the dry cleaner's.

Public opinion hadn't changed a great deal during the trial. Now, a little over half of those polled felt the verdict was fair. Others said they thought Mary Winkler had gotten away with murder.

Whatever her sentence would be on May 18, she would have a long series of obstacles. The Reverend Dan and Dianne Winkler filed a $2 million wrongful death suit against Mary on behalf of Patricia, Allie, and Brianna. They also petitioned to adopt their three granddaughters.

There could be no happy ending to the Winkler murder case, almost always referred to as "the Preacher's Wife Murder." Mary's sentencing was delayed to June 8, 2007.

Both Mary herself and Matthew's family were given the opportunity to speak before Judge McCraw handed down his sentence.

Matthew's mother, Diane, had not found forgiveness in her heart, she said. She chastised Mary because she had never apologized to Patricia, Allie, and Brianna for robbing them of their father, saying, "You've never told your girls you're sorry. Don't you think you at least owe them that?"

Dianne Winkler said that the girls had

nightmares, and that Patricia often sat next to her father's grave and wept.

Matthew's brother Daniel spoke of the pain to his family and to Mary's family.

Mary told those in the courtroom that she thought of Matthew every day and would always miss him and love him. She turned to his family and said she was "so sorry this has happened."

She said she knew that they were angry with her and assured them that she prayed each night for them that they would find peace.

Somehow, none of it seemed real.

Now Judge Weber McCraw spoke. The standard sentencing range for voluntary manslaughter in Tennessee is three to six years in prison, but Judge McCraw had some discretion over the time he deduced Mary should serve.

He sentenced Mary Winkler to only seven months' incarceration — *310 days*. Ironically, that penciled out to ten days for every year Matthew Winkler had lived. Since Mary had already served five months while she waited for a bail agreement to be worked out, she owed the state of Tennessee just sixty-seven days.

She was taken into custody after the sentencing on Friday, June 8, and served twelve days in the McNairy County Jail.

Judge McCraw ordered that she spend the remaining fifty-five days in a mental health facility, and that location was to be kept secret.

On August 16, 2007, Mary walked out of the still-unnamed mental facility a free woman.

Mary Winkler will be on probation for three years. For the rest of her life, people will remember her and wonder about her. Seven months in jail is a remarkably short sentence for shooting a man, perhaps a sleeping man, in the back.

Angry comments vied with sympathetic responses as people wrote to the *Tennessean,* discussing her release, and there is no indication that the heated debate will soon end.

It may be true that Mary suffered from post-traumatic stress disorder. However, it seems unlikely that she still suffered acutely twenty years after the death of her handicapped sister. The most obvious explanation for the final violent act in her marriage is that she had given up little pieces of herself to Matthew's more powerful personality, bit by bit, over ten years of an increasingly confining marriage. Each time she capitulated, she probably felt frustrated, weak, and a little angry, but as she had learned from the time she was a child, her church said that the husband is the unchallenged person in charge in a marriage. The wife is to be a helpmate and a subordinate.

It was that way in her parents' marriage, and it was even more true in her own. Matthew Winkler was not only her husband; he was a minister. Although he never had a chance to defend his reputation, he probably wasn't nearly as abusive as he was portrayed to be in Mary's trial. Had she found her self-esteem early in their marriage, he probably would have backed down on his demands about her weight and the small things she did that annoyed him. Had they realized how skewed the power was in their marriage, they should have sought counseling.

Marriage counseling, even within the church, could have defused the danger emerging. Their differing sexual preferences didn't mark them as such an unusual couple; that was something that might have been dealt with in counseling. Did Matthew demand that Mary wear shoes like those in the pornographic images found in his computer? No one really knows where the white platform heels that Steve Farese showed to Mary came from. They apparently weren't listed in the evidence removed from the

Winklers' home. Mary identified them, and the jurors believed that.

For most mothers, if there was a deal breaker in the Winklers' marriage, it would have been Matthew's alleged practice of "suffocating" their baby daughters to make them stop crying. Did he really do that? If Allie and Brianna already had breathing problems and their father pinched their noses closed, most mothers would understand that Mary Winkler would do anything to stop him. There are very few things more powerful than maternal instinct in both animal and human mothers. They will literally die to save their young.

Mary Winkler probably repressed her emotions many times over the length of her marriage. And perhaps she could do nothing right in her husband's eyes. That, we will never know, because Matthew Winkler isn't alive to tell his side of the story. He may have been an unpleasant and demanding husband — but that is no just cause for murder. It is only cause for divorce, and church or not, Mary could have found a way to leave.

But she didn't leave, and I think she became involved in the Internet con game without Matthew's knowledge. She became more and more entangled in an illegal operation, and on Tuesday night, March 21,

2006, she probably confessed that to Matthew. Although she claimed to be confused about check kiting and NSF checks, I think she knew what she had done. Maybe she had only been trying to please Matthew by coming up with a lot of money — if she was truly naïve enough to believe that she could collect oil profits due to a Canadian firm.

But I'm sure he was very angry when she had to confess they were due at the Regions Bank early the next morning. *That* surely was what they had fought about, even though she claimed not to remember. During that raging argument, Brianna may have cried, and Matthew may have silenced her by pinching her nose closed.

Not in the early morning, but sometime on Tuesday night. I don't think Mary had planned to kill him over a long period of time. She hadn't set up a prepared scenario for weeks or months beforehand, telling friends and family that he was abusing her and the children. Nor did she attempt to blame anyone else for Matthew's murder. There were no stories of bushy-haired strangers or burglars who forced their way into her home. This was not, in my mind, a premeditated act.

But Mary Winkler had backed herself into a corner where she had no hope for the future, where she feared what was going to happen at the bank, feared being separated from her children, and, most of all, where she could no longer stand by and let Matthew "suffocate" her baby.

And so she shot him in the back as he lay sleeping — without thinking of the future or punishment. Or even that she was taking another human being's life.

As Mary told the court and those at her sentencing, she has lost almost everything that mattered to her and she cannot really be punished further. She has no husband. She has no children.

Since the verdict, she has filed many motions to have her children returned to her. But her in-laws are also moving through tedious court processes, seeking to have Mary's maternal rights terminated so that they can adopt her three daughters. Their opposing goals seem only to make a tragic situation more tragic.

Whatever the outcome, it seems likely that Mary Winkler will spend the rest of her life going over and over what she did in a moment that even she cannot explain.

In a sense, she did get a life sentence.

AFTERWORD

MARY AND OPRAH
September 12, 2007

Mary Winkler hadn't been out of the mental health facility even four weeks when a startling announcement came from *The Oprah Winfrey Show.* As Oprah's new fall season began, Mary was slated to be one of the first week's guests. Whether Reverend Daniel Winkler and his wife, Dianne, would join the show was a question, but in the end, they declined.

It was only Mary who met with Oprah, and she was not a live guest on camera but an image on film as she met privately with Oprah sometime before September 12, the date the show aired. This was probably one of the oddest interviews Oprah Winfrey has ever conducted, even though she has questioned thousands of people, from movie stars to criminals. Having been on the set with

Oprah when she talked with Diane Downs, who was with us by satellite in 1985, I believe that was the last time I've seen Oprah so bemused by her subject. Mary was in her own world and she didn't let Oprah in.

Diane Downs, convicted of shooting her three young children two years earlier, denied that she had done so, and her affect was animated and inappropriately cheerful. She actually enjoyed her moment in the spotlight on Oprah.

Mary Winkler, having admitted shooting her husband, was certainly not animated and seemed hesitant to speak at all. Although it could not be more different, her affect was just as peculiar as Diane's. Many times during their conversation, Oprah did a subdued double take as if she could not believe what she had just heard, and she did her best to coax *some* kind of response from Mary. *Any* kind of response.

Mary dressed very much like she had during her trial — a white cardigan jacket cut like the sweater she wore when she testified. Her haircut was the same, and her shy expression and head-ducking pose were almost identical to those shown on news clips during her murder trial. On Oprah's show, however, Mary rarely — if ever — met Oprah's eyes, gazing off to the left. It was almost as if she existed in another dimension, and the questions, however gently probing, never quite penetrated an invisible wall she had built around her.

From time to time, her response was only a quiet "hmmm" that was almost cheerful in an absentminded way. For instance, when she had just mentioned how Matthew had "suffocated" their baby — "to put her to sleep" — Oprah followed up with something like, "*What* did he do?" her tone reflecting her shock. Mary only "hmmmed." Yes, Matthew had often "suffocated" their children, and she'd been powerless to stop him.

Never looking into Oprah's eyes, Mary explained that she had been terrified of Matthew that morning, but at the same time she'd just wanted to talk to him. "I wanted him to be happy, to stop being so mean. Just to enjoy life and [tell him] he didn't have to be so miserable."

"Had you ever said that to him before?" Oprah asked.

"He never would have allowed me to say that."

Some of Mary's recitation of the facts of the morning of the shooting tracked with the version presented by the defense during her trial, but others were slightly changed. Now, she recalled that Matthew had been sitting on the bed. Months ago, she said he had gone back to bed.

"I just wanted to talk to Matthew," she explained to Oprah. "And then there was that *awful sound* . . ."

She hurried on to a safer subject, but Oprah tugged her back, asking her to explain what that meant.

Mary clearly could not bring herself to say the words "gunshot" or "shotgun shells."

She explained that she never in a million years would have thought that there was "something" in there. "He always took it out." She meant the shotgun shells, but she could not say the words.

She showed no emotion at all as she explained that she thought something had hit the ceiling or one of the windows. Instinctively, she had run away, and then realized that Matthew wasn't chasing her.

Asked where the girls were at that time, she answered Oprah in a peculiar way: "I want to say they were watching TV."

But it was early in the morning, and the little girls were either in bed or sitting out in the hall, as Patricia had testified, frightened about what was happening in their parents' bedroom.

Mary said, "I still ask myself, What in the world happened?" She had a vague memory of Matthew "laying there," but he didn't say anything. She had wiped his mouth because there was blood coming from it, and it just kept "coming and coming."

But she couldn't see anything wrong with him and couldn't understand why he was bleeding. And now, it was akin to a shade coming down over Mary's eyes, although they were still open. Almost to herself, she spoke of how people's appearances can change in a matter of seconds. She meant as they died, but she could not say that either. "It's just terrible," Mary said, describing how dead faces change.

"I just took off," she said. "We ran away. We didn't go to his parents because they were on vacation. I was going to Memphis." But then she had become aware that she was headed toward Mississippi instead.

In the same breath that she described her fear of her husband, Mary said with as much feeling as she had mustered so far, "I *do* love him. I do love Matthew." She told Oprah she could not imagine life without him.

Just before "something very bad happened," Mary said she felt her life was in danger. But now she was better. She said she was only beginning to find out who she really was, describing how frightened she once was because she had broken the sun visor on her car and had been afraid to tell Matthew. Now, she told Oprah, she saw that it had been her car, and that she shouldn't have been afraid over a broken visor.

When Oprah asked about the financial crisis that came about after she bounced some checks in the computer scam aftermath, Mary said she wasn't upset about that. She had had nothing to do with that — it had all been Matthew's idea. Yes, she paid the bills and balanced the checkbook — but it was Matthew who participated in the "Nigerian bank scam." No, she told Oprah, he wasn't angry with her because it was his doing.

She knew virtually nothing about the bank problem. That jarred with almost everything in the courtroom testimony about Mary's frantic efforts to hide the check kiting.

And still she seemed unable to explain what she was afraid of on the morning Matthew died.

Possibly the most painful parts of Oprah's interview with Mary Winkler were the questions about the couple's sex life. During her testimony, Mary had been terribly embarrassed about Matthew's insistence on anal sex but hadn't been disturbed by references to oral sex. Now, she included both in her litany of sexual abuse at Matthew's hands. She waffled about whether he had struck her physically.

A doubter might say that Mary's excruciatingly long pauses after Oprah asked her a question came about because she was trying to remember what she had said earlier.

As Mary-on-film spoke, her attorneys, Leslie Ballin and Steve Farese, were live in Oprah's audience. Farese's sister was handling Mary's legal struggle to win back the custody of her three daughters.

Will that happen? Should it happen? This is a question almost as difficult to answer as one about Mary Winkler's possible motivation for shooting her husband.

When Oprah asked her why she should have her girls back, Mary's answer was simple, and she gave no concrete reasons.

"I'm their mother."

They have not seen her for a year. She lives in McMinnville, Tennessee, in a house provided by a supporter. Can Mary answer the questions that her three little girls will surely ask her? Can she look them in the eye, tell them as much of the truth as they can handle, and make them feel safe? Can she feel safe enough herself to deal with reality and not try to relegate it to the cloudy past where facts keep changing?

Certainly, both Mary and her daughters should continue to receive mental health counseling and therapy. The very bad thing that happened will be a dark ghost hovering over all of them until they can learn to deal with it.

Even Oprah Winfrey, who can get almost anyone to talk about almost anything, had an extremely difficult time trying to get Mary Winkler to tell her what had happened to her and why her children should be returned to her.

I'm sure Oprah was still shaking her head in puzzlement when the studio lights went down, and that her hours spent with Mary Winkler will remain a sharp memory for a very long time.

It soon became clear that the saga of Mary Winkler would spark continual headlines. In Huntingdon, Tennessee, on September 19, Carroll County chancellor Ron Harmon listened to eight hours of often-conflicting testimony from Mary, her former father-in-law, Dan Winkler, and four psychologists regarding her suitability to visit with her three daughters, now age nine, eight, and two.

Dr. Lynne Zager repeated her opinion that on the morning Matthew was shot Mary had been suffering from mild depression and post-traumatic stress disorder, which resulted in a "dissociative episode," or a break with reality. Zager was not concerned that Mary would be "a significant risk of hurting herself or others, including the children." She felt that Mary's main stressor had been her marriage to Matthew Winkler, but that was no longer an issue, and Mary had received treatment, had a good support system in friends and family, and now knew how to recognize what events could trigger dissociative episodes. In short, she felt that Mary was no longer dangerous.

Dr. Robert Kennon, however, representing the elder Winklers, testified that he had interviewed Mary's daughters only five days before this hearing. Patricia, nine, had expressed fear of her mother. "She killed my father," Patricia allegedly said. "I don't know if she will kill me . . ."

Dr. Kennon offered his opinion, saying that he was concerned with the longevity of Mary's dissociative disorder, extending, possibly, from the time her sister died many years before to the period of Matthew's murder and to her flight afterward. In his experience, only 30 percent of patients with dissociative episodes actually got better with treatment and medication. The rest of these patients demonstrated mild to severe symptoms, Kennon said, and some grew markedly worse.

Reverend Dan Winkler acknowledged that although he still loved Mary, warnings from psychologists made him afraid for his grandchildren. He said he had noted drastic changes in the children's behavior after they visited with their mother.

That, of course, had been approximately a year earlier. Mary had neither seen nor talked to them for many months.

Another psychologist, Dr. John Ciocca, spoke for Mary's side and said that it was quite possible that separating the girls from their mother could be hurting them.

The sun had set by the time Chancellor Harmon handed down his decision. He granted Mary Winkler supervised visitation with her daughters but said it must be for "a limited time under limited conditions." He also said she could speak to them by phone every other day.

It seemed a huge coup for Mary. She was elated and, showing far more emotion than onlookers had come to expect from her, hugged her family and friends when she heard the news.

Next, the Winklers' attorney, Bill Neese, and Kay Farese Turner (Steve Farese's sister, who represented Mary), would meet to work out a schedule for times, dates, and places of visitation.

It was only the first battle. Dan and Dianne Winkler's suit to terminate Mary Winkler's parental rights was still pending, as was their petition to adopt her children.

A first visit was to take place on Saturday, September 28, but it didn't happen. Mary was devastated when a final-hour motion to block visitation was filed by Matthew's parents' attorneys. The court of appeals granted the motion.

Mary's legal team would have ten days to respond.

On that same last weekend in September 2007, the national tabloids reported that Mary Winkler had had a close relationship with a man for months. Darrell Pillow, forty-one, a truck driver for a grocery company and the brother of Paul Pillow, who owns the dry cleaning shop where Mary works, verified that they were very close friends.

Still, despite the tabloid reporters' efforts to slant the friendship toward an affair, it seemed more a casual thing than a blazing romance. Mary didn't comment on Darrell Pillow at all, and he spoke mostly of casual meetings: visiting her in the mental health facility where she spent the summer of 2007, or of eating lunch or dinner together. He seemed far more taken with Mary than she with him.

Before her surprisingly short sentence was handed down in April, Pillow said that Mary had been reluctant to make plans for the future. During her trial, she told him that she might not have any future but "years and years" behind bars.

Pillow, a short man with bright blue eyes and dark hair, spoke with Tonya Smith-King of the *Jackson Sun.* He said that when Mary was released from the treatment center, she had told him she "needed to be single," and he felt her pulling away from him.

"I was hurt," Pillow said. "The times that me and Mary spent together, I thought there was more there. I asked her, 'Mary, am I going to be history when you get out of here? Am I going to be done? Are we going to be over?'

"And she said, 'No. Absolutely not!' I just kind of had the feeling that as time was getting close for her to be a free woman, I was kind of getting a little feeling that she was fixing to go her separate ways when she gets out of here, and I don't know if that's still gonna happen."

Pillow said they had spoken of marriage, and that he liked Mary because she reminded him of his mother, who had died when he was fourteen. "We looked good together. She was my height. We just seemed to make a good couple — I thought we did, anyway. I don't really know what she was thinking . . ."

Her boss's brother carried pictures that he said Mary had given him of her and her girls and one that included Matthew. Still, it seemed obvious that her main concerns were all about her daughters and that more than anything else she wanted them back in her custody. Her attorneys had told her it was best if she remained single without any complicating factors like a boyfriend or lover.

Darrell Pillow evinced no concern at all about his own safety should he and Mary eventually hook up. He found her a sweet and considerate woman, and he clearly cared a great deal for her. He refused to say if they had been intimate.

Whether they will ever be together is an unanswerable question. Mary faces one legal hurdle after another as she fights to be reunited with her children.

And marriage, as she has known it, hasn't left Mary Winkler with positive feelings about the institution. Only time will tell.

ABOUT THE AUTHOR

Ann Rule is the author of more than two dozen *New York Times* bestsellers, all of them still in print. A former Seattle police officer, she knows the crime scene first-hand. She is a certified instructor for police training seminars and lectures frequently to law enforcement officers, prosecutors, and forensic science organizations, including the FBI. For more than two decades, she has been a powerful advocate for victims of violent crime. She has testified before U.S. Senate Judiciary subcommittees on serial murder and victims' rights, and was a civilian adviser to the VI-CAP (Violent Criminal Apprehension Program). A graduate of the University of Washington, she holds a Ph.D. in Humane Letters from Willamette University. She lives near Seattle and can be contacted through her Web page at www .annrules.com <http://www.annrules.com>.